An astonishing achievement. I relished the crackle of ⟨...⟩ *music of unfamiliar words. The whole thing [is] magnificent.* ⟨...⟩
Richard Mabey, author of 30 books [*Food for Free, Flora Brit...*, ⟨...⟩ *Home*]

Extraordinary long-form prose-poems, a reminder of Benjamin Britten's operas… There is real rhythm and sound and bite.
Roma Tearne, author of *Mosquito, Brixton Beach, The White City*

Wonderful! We speak the sagas out loud while silently reading. Such a bold and wide-sweeping work.
Julia Blackburn, author of *Time Song: Searching for Doggerland*

Stunning, an exceptional text; a deep sense of place and myth.
Rachel Lichtenstein, author of *Estuary, On Brick Lane, Diamond Street*

Mesmeric writing, spellbinding magic of descriptions, the flow of time and sea and the magic of the naming of people and things. A rich cultural treat.
Robert Golden, photographer and film-maker

The drama, emotion and practices of the sea-faring world brought into contemporary relevance. Marvellous, all sorts of new colours and emotional depth.
Patricia Gillies, *Longman Anthology of Old English, Old Icelandic and Anglo-Norman Literatures*

A beautiful, profound work.
Douglas Christie, author of *The Blue Sapphire of the Mind*

Rare and audacious, genuinely brave. The natural and the human are presented as inextricably linked, each creating the other over long stretches of time. A book of sounds and rhythms that points to a new genre, a wonderful achievement and a joy to read.
Geoff Wells, Director, Rural Communities Australia

Engaging all the essence of the epic: high, ennobling, central theme, extensive physical environment, and some kind of journey. A fine and imaginative piece of work, a flow and continuity like the sea itself.
David Butcher, author of *The Driftermen, The Trawlermen, Following the Fishing*

Wonderfully well researched and beautifully written, an antidote to the frustrations of lockdown.
Mike Mitchell, President, Shellfish Association of Great Britain, board member of Seafish (Defra), author of *Hope Street*

Intense, ambitious, flowing rhythms and language, evocative of my times spent afloat around the Thames Estuary, and life remembered here on the Colne and Blackwater in memory and myth.
Fabian Bush, boat-builder, Rowhedge, Essex

SEA
SAGAS
of the North

Hawthorn Press

SEA
SAGAS
of the North

Travels & Tales
at Warming
Waters

Jules Pretty

Hawthorn Press

Hawthorn Press
Published by Hawthorn Press, Hawthorn House,
1 Lansdown Lane, Stroud, Gloucestershire, GL5 1BJ, UK
Tel: 01453 757040 Email: info@hawthornpress.com
Website: www.hawthornpress.com

Cover design and typesetting by Lucy Guenot
Illustrations and photographs by Chris Pretty and Jules Pretty
Typeset in Myriad and Albertus fonts
Printed by Short Run Press Ltd, Exeter
Printed on environmentally friendly chlorine-free paper sourced from renewable forest stock

Published in association with the Stefansson Arctic Institute, Akureyri, Iceland.
http://www.svs.is/en

British Library Cataloguing in Publication Data applied for

ISBN 978-1-912480-74-6

For Gill,
Freya and Theo

CONTENTS

Sea Sagas of the North is illustrated with monochrome images by the author, and maps by Chris Pretty to depict the territories of tales and stories. There is one map of the whole region, and regional maps for each chapter and its related sagas.

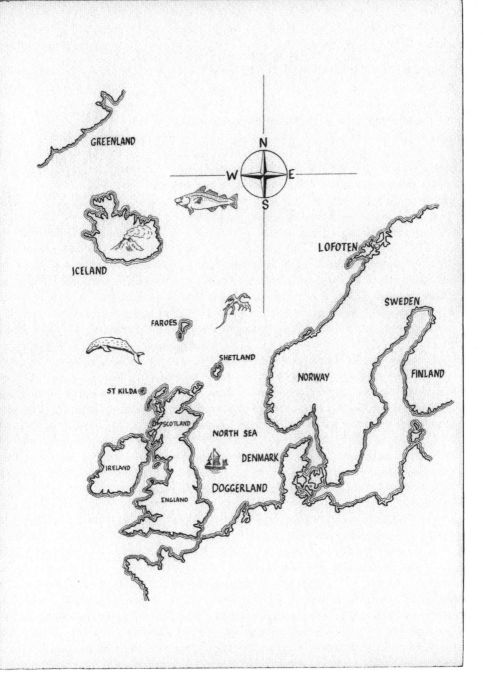

PREFACE

The Territory of the North

This was the way.

The sound of lapping wave, a whispered splash of oar, the mast that creaks.

By day there was the taste of tarred plank blistered by the sun, by briny dusk the fragrance of the oak-smoked fish. At this circled sea, families and friends stared long at the blue horizon, their sailors far beyond. All seas were ponds, hooped they said. There was land and danger, on this side, and on that.

No sea is ever flat, it curves to fit the planet. Each is heaped by wind and wave, contains dip and bulge, long swell and growler. The sea gods gather wreck and tomb, treasure trove, clutch long the famed and poor alike. There was nothing worse, drowning full in sight of shore. The graveyards of each fishing village filled up slowly, the drowned held fast. Now would come another crushing silence, three sheets on every sail, the blue marine quite undone.

There was an endless argument of weather and the swell of climate change, the decay of empires, and yet solace was found in nature. At every place, there was the kindness of shore people who rescued sailors and welcomed migrants. There was also the race for profit over care, the hopelessness of fish and whale, the open slavery of children. Women waited at the shores for news, yet were also fighters and scalds, rescuers and protestors.

Dragons and wyrms were protectors of the people, for gold was a metal of strife. And people did find an inner peace. They sought comfort from the gods, yet also felt the sadness of abandonment. It was remarkable how flood narratives survived for many thousand years.

It once was cold, a fire flickering in the hearth. Outside, snow flurries dashed, a storm was looming. It was a time for tales.

Each story is a living heritage, a sarsen set in soil.

A story is a common, it expands with telling, with the song. We hear there is glamour in those mythic pasts, even when the ends are known to all. At summit of this scroll, it may not finish well. The gods will feel betrayed, begin to wreak revenge. Docks will have crumbled, moss grown over stone, glaciers melted. Wooden hulks will be rotting in the mud, and breakers wash the rusted ship remains on the pearls of pebbled basalt. Ancient cities of fish will have shrunk to hamlet-size. They feel betrayed by the air-gods up above their worlds of water, who cast line and net with ever-smaller meshes.

On the saltings will be a bird, a snowy heron with a crest of tropic feathers, standing still in mirrored water, and trolls will slouch on slope and under cliff, casting sombre shadows on the future.

It might not happen. We wish it could be so.

It is said a serpent might take revenge, the waters surging cross the land again. There will be only plastic left in oceans, the seabirds long since dead. Forests will flame and oceans steam, black ash fall. At the close, it could be that ancient prophecies come true, of further flood and burning of the forests. Climate change drowned Doggerland, the sea rose, and the steppe became an isle. It was a shock, for one day the sun rose from the water, set too in waves.

Yet there is hope. A white whale swims on, beckoning people to find a way to tell a different story. Some cities have become greener and happier. There is renewed pride. Others have rewilded farms and forests, created new commons, and birds have returned to emptied isles. When economies cease to seek growth at any cost, then stability brings the space for stories as a new currency. Listen to birdsong, and at the end the birds will still be there. Watch the moonway on the night sea, and the moon will come again. Listen to a story, and the words and guidance can carry you across the ages.

A story grows with the telling. Gary Snyder wrote, 'Stories keep us going,' and the great Navajo storyteller Yellowman said, 'If children hear stories, they will grow up to be good people.'

These sea sagas weave tales of the North Sea and North Atlantic, stories of the rise and fall of gods, of people and the fish, the ebb and flow of mariners, the fish grounds that were common meeting places. Crossings carry danger, the seas are mighty, many monsters lurk in the dark beyond. But there is silence too. The scald sees from near and far, speaks of days gone by and eras still to come.

Pull up a chair by the blazing fire, come listen to those voices, from the distance fading in and out, come listen, before the wind winnows all. There are hints of bright halls, the synchrony of oars pulled together, the earth still rising green and fertilie.

The Saga Tradition

These *Sea Sagas of the North* have roots in many literary cultures, all of which we can assume had prior oral traditions. People made sense of the world by telling stories, indeed created the world itself through their actions and choices. Stories linked together individual components of nature and people's lives, giving coherence and a way of encoding collective memory. We can learn from stories, and become more humble. We come to know, and then we can do the right thing.

For many of the ancient sagas, little is known of the originators. There were long spoken traditions, evolving as centuries passed, then at some point stories were committed to the written word.

These *Sea Sagas* find echoes in texts from Mesopotamia and Greece, China and Japan, in Tuva and India, from Arab travellers and North American cultures, trickster tales and ancient koan texts. The most famed and relevant to the lands and seas of these sagas are the Norse sagas of Iceland and Scandinavia, and the Anglo-Saxon poems and tales of the British Isles.

Many authors are long unknown, including those of *Beowulf, The Seafarer, The Wanderer, The Battle of Maldon (Mældune), The Lay of Wayland, The Lay of Skirmir* and *The Lay of Eirikr Bloodaxe. Beowulf* has 3,200 lines, composed between the seventh and tenth centuries in Anglo-Saxon. Heroic poems include *Deor, The Dream of the Rood* and the famed short old English poem, *Cædmon's Hymn.* Later came Geoffrey of Monmouth's *The History of the Kings of Britain*, completed in the early 1100s, containing an account of the prophecies of Merlin, and tales of Vortigern, Arthur and Gawain. The author of *Sir Gawain and the Green Knight* is also not known, as is the Icelandic composer of the *Saga of Volsungs*, the Norse epic of a dragon-slayer in Continental Europe. At the same time, there are ancient oral tales in all indigenous groups and communities. Robert Bringhurst recorded in *A Story as Sharp as a Knife* the Haida oral sagas: *Raven Travelling* has 1,400 lines, the *Qquuna Cycle* is 5,000 lines long.

Many of the major characters of Icelandic sagas were poets themselves. Famed authors include Snorri Sturluson, Egil Skallagrimson, Bragi Boðdasson, þódólfor, Eilífr Godrúnarson, Ulfr Uggason. The scaldic poetry of Snorri Sturluson includes *Heimskringla* (The Orb of the World), *The Prose Edda*, and *King Harald's Saga*. He in turn drew upon the written work by Ari Thorgilson the Learned and Eirik Oddson. The scalds Kormak, Hallfred and Gunnlaug, authors of the *The Sagas of the Warrior Poets*, were known as great creators as well as awkward characters. Some tales are known for their appearance in uniquely illustrated manuscripts: the manuscript of the Flateyjarbók found on the isle of Flatey in western Iceland, and the Gospels of Lindisfarne.

The technical feats of scalds could be extraordinary. Some used a fixed number of syllables per line, they rhymed with alliteration, half-rhyme and full-rhyme, both within and across lines, and used many kenning metaphors, where two words are used to form a new expression. Saga and tale passages were sometimes set out as prose, sometimes verse. Verse suggests song; and it is likely that Homer and fellow poets sang, accompanied by string instruments. The *Tale of the Heike* from the 1100s in Japan was accompanied by biwa lute music, and sung by blind Buddhist monks. They travelled widely to perform, some said to hold in memory more than 24,000 lines of tales.

Sometimes lead characters become themselves storytellers within sagas, reciting their own adventures. Characters reveal themselves by what they say and do. Saga styles tend not to contain internal monologues or paraphrasing of a character's thoughts. Events serve as windows into their mind and soul.

Poets celebrated objects well and truly made, the skills of craftspeople, the surrounds of nature, the active agency of plants and trees, animals and fish. Fates turn on small moments and misjudgements, on changes across deep time too. Some qualities of people in these tales appear inalienable, permanent attributes in a changing world. They indicate heroic pasts, but suggest too that the people of today and tomorrow could be equally heroic in the face of their contemporary worlds of change and threat.

One thing binds the sagas of the epic poets: amongst the harsh natural settings and often violent events, there is understatement, grim humour and wit; there is also a distinctive ethos, people and all types of god bound by moral significance. Whether these heroes live well seems defined by actions and behaviour choices. Sagas often represent a search for identity and wholeness. The hero begins in their ordinary world, and travels out to a special world. They return changed.

Saga tales are thus inner journeys as much as external, shaped by outer events that readers or listeners will recognise. Something is at stake, and we learn from it. In the days of Anglo-Saxon and Viking courts, scalds and poets were often hired commentators, accompanying king and earls. They composed the stories, helped boost the reputations of their employers. In the modern era, such stories come to be told by writer and journalist, by jester and also scientist and poet.

Some sagas follow tradition and form, others were deliberately experimental with language. Many made use of word play and alliteration, and built tension through repetition and slight variations. In the sagas of the Icelanders, the dominant style unfolded events in chronological order, rather than beginning in the middle of things. And though they were written up to a thousand years ago, the places remain recognisable today, as illustrated by W G Collingwood and Jón Stafánsson in their handsome *Pilgrimage of the Saga-Steads*, and then too a century later by Richard Fidler and Kári Gíslason in *Saga Land*.

At the end of a journey, you have a story. You carry some form of potion, perhaps the tale alone, and might have returned sadder though wiser. These *Sea Sagas of the North* are about the women and the men, the gods who flew and fixed, the animals and plants, the changes to the climate and so much plastic in the sea. Fish and whale were harvested so fast that they one day disappeared.

Fish communities had been nurtured at coasts, then clear-felled and became deserted. The waters warmed, yet despite it all, people of the seas and shores still were mostly kind.

GLOSSARY

The Pantheon of Gods and Places

There are more than eight hundred named god, giant, dwarf, elf, animal, tree and other characters listed across the sagas of the Norse.

Ægir	The god of the sea. Ran is his wife, and their hall is under the waves. Fishermen in the twentieth century still threw back the first herring or cod from the net for Ægir.
Æsir	The gods who live in Asgard, led by Oðinn.
Alfheim	Realm of the Light Elves.
Asgard	Realm of the gods.
Baldr	The Beautiful, son of Oðinn, his horse burns with him, and he will come from Hel after Ragnarök.
Bifrost	The flaming rainbow bridge between Asgard and Midgard, the trembling way between earth and heaven.
Cædmon	Anglo-Saxon monk, composer and poet, died 680 CE.
Earth	Mother of Thor, wife of Oðinn.
Elli	Old Age, the old woman who outdid Thor in a wrestling match.
Erce	Goddess of the sea; also Earth goddess.
Fafnir	The shape-shifting dragon killed by Sigurd in the *Saga of the Volsungs*.
Fenrir	He is a fierce wolf, son of Loki, eventually bound by the gods until Ragnarök.
Fimbulvetr	The terrible three-year winter that comes before Ragnarök.
Freyja	Daughter of Njord, the most splendid of the goddesses.
Freyr	Son of Njord, given the fastest ship *Skiðblaðnir* by dwarves.
Grendel	Monster, ogre, troll, slain by Beowulf.

Hel	The goddess of the underworld.
Hel	Realm of the dead.
Heorot	Great Hall of the King Hrothgar in the Beowulf saga, located at modern Lejre.
Herne the Hunter	Ghost of the deep woodlands, wearing antlers.
High	The High One, one of the Æsir.
Huginn and Munnin	Thought and Memory, the pair of Oðinn's wise ravens who fly across the realms each day and bring the news back to Oðinn.
Hymir	The giant who fought Thor.
Jörmungandr	The serpent or dragon who encircles Midgard and holds in the sea, also called the Midgard Serpent.
Lejre	On Sjælland, seat of Danish kings, location of Heorot in Beowulf.
Loki	The attractive and ambivalent god, son of two giants, called the Sly One, the Trickster, the Sky Traveller, the Shape Shifter. He is bound until the coming of Ragnarök.
Mjollnir	Thor's hammer made by dwarfs, symbol of fertility, resurrection and destruction.
Muspell	Realm of fire in the south.
Niðhogg	Dragon who gnaws at the roots of Yggdrasil and chews corpses.
Niflheim	Realm of freezing mist and darkness under one root of Yggdrasil. Hel is in Niflheim.
Njord	God of wind and sea, father of Freyja and Freyr, married to Skaði.
Oðinn	Foremost of the Æsir gods. God of poetry, god of death. Called the Allfather, the One-Eyed, the Terrible One. He has one eye, and relies on his two ravens to see the world in all its dimensions.
Ragnarök	Final battle between the gods and giants, when all life is destroyed and the nine worlds are submerged by the warming, rising seas.
Ran	Wife of Ægir, she drags drowning sailors and fishers down with her net. She has nine daughters who are each a wave.

Ratatosk	The squirrel (swift-teeth) who runs up and down the World Tree, Yggdrasil, carrying insults between the eagle Vedrfolnir in the topmost branches and dragon Niðhogg in the roots.
Sif	Thor's wife with the golden hair, cut off by Loki.
Skaði	Daughter of Thjazi the giant, married to Njord, left him to go to the mountains.
Skoll and Hati	The two wolves who chase across the sky the sun, and then the moon.
Sleipnir	Oðinn's eight-legged fast horse.
Surt	The giant who has guarded Muspell, the realm of fire, since creation, and will set fire to the world at Ragnarök.
Thing	Public meeting places for passing of laws and hearing of law cases, held regularly as places of public assembly.
Thor	The big god, son of Oðinn, god of sky and thunder, he maintains law and order in Midgard. Thor is the Thunder God and Charioteer. In the twentieth century, fishermen from England still wore Thor hammer amulets at their necks.
Utgard	Realm of giants.
Valhalla	Hall of the Slain, the immense hall presided over by Oðinn, where the dead warriors fight and feast and await Ragnarök.
Valkyries	Choosers of the slain. They are the women who choose those at battle doomed to die, bringing them to Valhalla.
Weyland	Supernatural blacksmith, called Völundr in Norse.
Woden	God of battle and death, worshipped by Anglo-Saxons in England (variant on Oðinn).
Yggdrasil	The World Tree, the ash that connects all the worlds.
Ymir	The first giant, formed from fire and ice.

TIMELINE

Key Events in the Sea Sagas

7500–6200 BCE	The dry plains of Doggerland are drowned by the rising waters, and the shallow North Sea is formed.
5000 BCE	The 300 km by 100 km Dogger Isle remains in the new North Sea, with a host of smaller islands. It soon will sink.
2600 BCE	*The Epic of Gilgamesh* is written on mud tablets, the oldest surviving written story. A flood plays a key role.
450 CE	Vortigern is king, and comes to meet the lad Merlin, who releases two dragons and makes a number of telling prophecies.
634	Oswald becomes King of Northumberland, based at Bamburgh Castle.
635	Lindisfarne monastery is formed by Aidan (later a saint).
650s–662	St Peter-on-the-Wall stone chapel is built on the Saxon shore of the Dengie peninsula, by Cedd (later Saint) of Lindisfarne.
664	Synod of Whitby hosted by Abbess Hildr.
676	Cuthbert moves to Inner Farne to live as a hermit.
699–714	Guthlac lives as a hermit on the Isle of Croyland (now Crowland), providing refuge for a future king.
c700–1000	The epic poem in Anglo-Saxon (Old English), *Beowulf*, is written.
793	The first Viking longship happens to arrive at Lindisfarne, and England's most famed monastery is raided.
803	The cross of Easby is carved.
835	The first overwintering of Viking longships in England, at the Isles of Thanet and/or Sheppey.
855	The boy Edmund is crowned King of East Anglia on Christmas Day, at the site of the stone chapel on the hill above Bures.
870	First Norse settlers arrive in Iceland.
886	Alfred becomes King of England.
mid-900s	Ingimund sails from Norway to settle in northern Iceland.
930	Icelandic chiefs establish the national Althing assembly.
c970	The Exeter Book is written in Anglo-Saxon (Old English), containing the famed poems, *The Seafarer* and *The Wanderer*.
978–1013, 14–16	Æthelred is King of England for 37 years.
991	A fleet of 100 longships led by Olaf Tryggvason sails up the Pant/Blackwater estuary to raid the mint at Maldon. The epic poem, the *Battle of Maldon* (Mældune), is written about this episode. Byrhtnoð is Earl (Jarl) of Essex, and leads the defending force.
1002	The grim genocide of Danes living in England is ordered by Æthelred the King and Archbishop Wulfstan.
1016	Knut (or Canute) becomes King of England and Denmark, uniting the two countries.

1066	Battle of Stamford Bridge, where King Harald Hardrada of Norway is killed. Battle of Hastings, where King Harold of England is killed.
1179–1214	Snorri Sturluson lives and writes in Iceland.
1190–1320	The main period of Icelandic sagas.
1197–1206	*Orkneyinga Saga* written.
1200s	Landnámabók (The Book of Settlements) written in Iceland.
1380	Denmark, Norway and much of modern Sweden form into a single North Atlantic empire that includes Greenland, Iceland, the Faroes, and isles of Shetland and Orkney.
1472	Shetland and Orkney transferred to Scotland after 500 years closely linked to Norway.
1530s	Henry VIII of England orders destruction of abbeys and monasteries to obtain their land and riches; also bans pilgrimages.
1600	The play *Hamlet* is set by Shakespeare in Kronberg Castle in modern Helsingor.
1611–13	The Kalmar War between Sweden and Denmark.
1620s to 1720s	Dutch engineers led by Vermuyden are commissioned to drain the common Fens and convert them to private farmland.
1723	The Waltham Black Act is passed in England.
1783	Eruption of Lakígigar (known as Laki) in southern Iceland, beginning the break of the trade stranglehold of Denmark on Iceland. The Fire Sermon is delivered.
1880s early	First lifeboat service established at the Grit fishing village, Lowestoft.
1828	Elias Lönrott sits with Juhana Kainulainen to receive the oral tales and sagas that became Finland's epic of national identity, *The Kalevala*.
1838	The steamship *Forfarshire* is wrecked on the Farne Islands, and father and daughter William and Grace Darling row to the rescue.
1862	Sabine Baring Gould travels around Iceland, stays on farms, travels past the Okjökull glacier and visits Akureyri.
1864	Flatey public library opens, the first in Iceland.
1868	The territory of Schleswig-Holstein is lost in war by Denmark to Germany.
1872	The Merchant Seaman Act permits use of orphan boys as bonded apprentices on sailing smacks, and launches forty years of slave labour from Grimsby.
1879–1933	Greenland-Danish explorer Knud Rasmussen completes five expeditions in the Far North.
1880s	Eiði church holds in secret the first sermon in Faroese.
1913	Kunoy disaster in northern Faroes, three boats sink drowning all but one adult men in three whole villages.
1914–18	The First World War, called by many coastal and rural people the Fourteen War.
1922	Shackleton is buried in the graveyard on South Georgia, South Atlantic.
1930	St Kilda is abandoned and evacuated, against the wishes of some of the 120 residents. Some are given work in forestry, even though they have never seen a tree in their lives.
1940s	The evacuated Grit fishers' village on Lowestoft beach is used for army training.
1943	8,000 Jewish Danes are carried to safety across the Øresund from Gillileje by a flotilla of small boats.
1944	Independence for Iceland is celebrated at the Althing held at Thingvellir. The rain is heavy this June day, and all the crowd is smiling.

1947	The Grimsby trawler *Epine* is wrecked at Djúpalónssandur beach, Iceland.
1947	Wrecking of Fleetwood trawler *Dhoon* at Látrabjarg cliffs, rescuers led by þórður Jonsson.
1948	Wrecking of Hull trawler *Sargon* in Patreksfjördur, rescued again by þórður Jonsson and farmer colleagues.
1940s–1950s	The last barges sail the trade roads and routes of the North Sea.
1950s	The villages on Hornstrandir are abandoned.
1955	Icelandic author Halldór Laxness is awarded the Nobel Prize for Literature at the age of 53.
1953	The night of January 31st: the North Sea floods coastlines of East Anglia and the Netherlands, drowing several thousand people.
1958–76	The three cod wars between Iceland and mainly the UK.
1960	The first trawler with freezing machine is launched from Grimsby.
1960s early	Herring have disappeared from the North Sea.
1962	Shetland delegation visits the Faroes to observe how they have protected and valued local culture.
1963	Surtsey Island appears in North Atlantic off southern Iceland.
1968	The Triple Trawler Disaster (February): in the worst storm ever experienced at Ísafjörður, three Hull trawlers and all but one crew are drowned. The gang of four Hull women organise, meet ministers in London and succeed in introducing safety measures for ships at sea. The leader of the women loses her job, and is prevented from further local employment.
1969	First oil flows from the commercial oilfield Ekofisk in Norwegian waters.
1971	The Flateyjarbók is returned from Copenhagen to awaiting crowds at Reykjavik
1973	Eruption of Eldfell on Westmann Islands of Iceland.
1974	Texan oil families set up an American football team, the Roughnecks, at Lowestoft-Great Yarmouth to play US air force teams.
1978	First oil arrives at Sullom Voe on Shetland.
1977–2015	Austin Mitchell is MP for Great Grimsby.
1983–89	Archaeological excavation finds the largest Viking longhouse in Europe in western Lofotens.
1984	Iceland adopts a quota system for its own fisheries and fish grounds.
1986	The commercial hunting of whales is banned worldwide by the International Whaling Commission.
1990	Atmospheric carbon dioxide passes 350 ppm, the last safe place for humanity. By 2022, it will have risen to 417 ppm, rising by 2 ppm per year.
1991	The first offshore (in the sea) wind farm built by Denmark
1991	The cargo ship *Finnpolaris* sinks in the waters west of Greenland.
1991	Iceland makes its fish quota system transferable, resulting in rapid increases in the size of a few large businesses, and the loss of small, village-based fisheries.
1992	First estate in Scotland bought by community at Assynt, beginning a repeopling of the Highlands and Islands.
1997–2017	Alan Johnson is MP for Hull West and Hessle.
1997–98	Archaeologist Bryony Coles coins the term 'Doggerland' to describe the dry plains beneath the current North Sea.
2000	The first offshore (in the sea) wind farm built by the UK (off the

Northumberland coast).

2003   Two inshore fishers, Erlingur and Örn, protest off Patreksfjördur at the removal of common rights to fish for Icelandic fishers.

2008   Global financial collapse, prompted by unregulated lending and borrowing, particularly sub-prime mortgage markets in the USA, and against secured promises of returns on cod quota by three private Icelandic banks.

2010   Eruption of Eyjafjallajökull in southern Iceland, leading to the closure of skies across north-west Europe.

2011   Reykjavik becomes UNESCO City of Literature, and Harpa concert hall is opened.

2014   Mary Glew is elected as the first female mayor of Hull.

The isle of Wallasea in the Essex archipelago is converted back from crop land to wetland and marsh. The seawalls are breached, and the sea permitted in.

2018   The final (perhaps) Hull trawler, *Kirkella*, is launched and registered. The skipper is Charlie Waddy of Hull.

2019   Beavers are reintroduced to a farm in the east of England, the first to live and breed there for 1,000 years.

2019   Ravens repopulate the east of England, following the arrivals of buzzard and red kite from the west.

2019   39 migrants from Vietnam are killed in a lorry container on the Essex coast.

2050   There are different versions of the near future:

Ragnarök has begun, carbon dioxide has reached 475 ppm in the atmosphere, world temperature is over 2.5°C above pre-industrial, glaciers worldwide have melted.

Countries worldwide have delivered on net-zero carbon promises, fossil fuels are a thing of the past, and the seas have stopped warming and rising. The planet has begun to heal.

ON SPELLING AND PRONUNCIATION

There are many old and current languages situated in communities around the North Sea and North Atlantic. Some have similar historic roots, such as Old Norse, Anglo-Saxon, Old English and Norn, Gaelic and Irish. Throughout the chapters and sagas, I have favoured local spellings and norms. In accordance with the custom in English, I have simplified names where it seems desirable. The overarching aim is to ensure the reader in English does not find names and terms confusing or disruptive to the flow.

The characters 'eth' (ð, Ð) and 'thorn' (þ, Þ) have mostly been rendered as 'th' and 'd'. In the original, ð and Ð are voiced as th, as in *then*; while þ and Þ are voiceless as th, as in *thin*. But I have not sought consistency, especially when a name is familiar to English speakers. Thus you will find Thor not Þor, and also Þórður Jonsson (the famed farmer and rescuer of wrecked seamen) and not Thordur. I also prefer Oðinn to Odin. The diagraph Æ/æ is also preferred, thus you will find Æthelred and Ægir rather than Ethelred and Aegir, and Sjælland rather than Zealand. The final 'r' of names is mostly omitted, but not always. It is not a separate sound, thus Audr sounds like Aud. In Icelandic, the accent falls on the first syllable. There may also be different names for the same term, such as Jarl and Eorl/Earl.

It became familiar in recent spoken English reports to stumble over the name of the volcano that erupted in 2010, closing the airspace across Europe. Yet Eyjafjallajökull is simple if split into three parts: Eyja (eye-ya), fjalla (fyalla), jökull (yokel). The full name means, of course, the Eyjafjalla glacier.

Sometimes I have allowed the name of a place to contain a geographic tautology, where it helps in English to identify the geographic feature. Thus 'ey' is an island in Icelandic, so Flatey is clearly an isle. But here I favour the English norm of calling it Flatey Isle. Jökull means glacier, so it is already clear that Vatnajökull and Okjökull are glaciers – but in English it helps to know these are glaciers. The Faroes are the already the 'sheep islands', and can be called the Faroes or Faroe Islands (or Isles).

When the word 'hero' is used in these sagas, it is to imply either or both female and male characters or people, just as the preference today is for female actor or male actor as a descriptor of acting individuals (rather than actor and actress).

The sagas themselves are alliterative, and designed to be read aloud, or voiced inside as if spoken. Each line loosely has the same number of syllables each side of the caesura, the silent moment marked by a comma. The sagas are divided into verses each of eight lines. The stresses in each line do not exactly follow original Anglo-Saxon or Icelandic rules. There are deviations and distortions, the first half not always carrying the main weight of meaning. All do seek to be immersive, the story and rhythmic sounds quieting thoughts. We slip slowly inside each epic tale.

ON TIME, DISTANCE, WEIGHTS AND MEASURES

The terms for Common Era (CE) and Before Common Era (BCE) are used throughout the book as alternatives to the Dionysian BC (Before Christ) and AD (Anno Domini). The two notation systems are numerically equivalent.

I have allowed weights and measures to be mixed and flexible. Mostly distances are reported in leagues, but sometimes as kilometres and miles when referring to a modern measure; on a smaller scale, variously feet and ell, yard and metre; areas by acre, hide or hectare (a hide is 40 acres); weight in kilogramme and pound, tonne and also ton; and speed at sea as knots. The cubic capacity of ships is given in tons, as is the convention. This fluidity of terms, and inevitable apparent tangle, echoes many of the differences in name and identity that places and people on the sea and land experience.

In the end, we only really need to know if a journey was short or long, if a place was far or near, or if a rock was heavy and hard to lift. After the dark, comes the dawn. There are always shadows on a shining sea. This much we know.

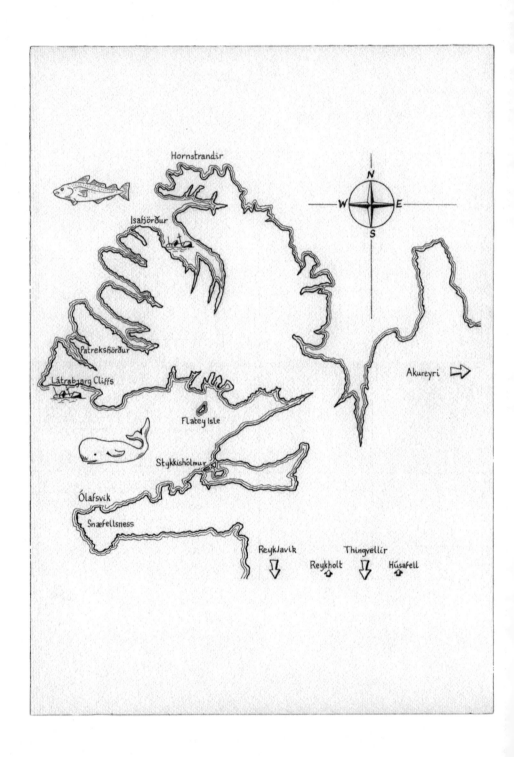

CHAPTER ONE

THE WESTFJORDS OF ICELAND

Krafla caldera, Iceland

Burning ice, biting flame. That's how northern life began.

To the south was a realm of dancing flames that seethed and shone. In the far north, there was ice and endless drifts of snow, a land of storm and lightning streak.

Where rime and warm breath met, life emerged in drops and took the form of frost giant Ymir. One-eyed Oðinn, the all-father of the Æsir gods, threw in the sky, the sun and moon, and they soon were chased by two snapping wolves called Skoll and Hati. The sun often has to hide, one day it may be caught. At the axis of the world was Yggdrasil, sacred ash which soared above the gods and people, over elf and troll. One root grew into Asgard, domain of gods, another into both people's world of Midgard and the Utgard citadel of giants, and a third to cold below in Niflheim where Loki's daughter Hel and dragon Niðhogg watched the dead. There was a rainbow bridge called Bifrost, linking Midgard to the world of gods.

They say the end will be a wind-age and a wolf-age, but no one wants Ragnarök to come, nor that seas might rise and all the realms be taken by the waves.

Listen. Who can hear the sound of grass growing?
The sound of wool on a sheep's back, growing.
Who needs less sleep, than a bird?

[Sæmundr Sigfússon, *The Song of Rig, Poetic Edda*, c1270]

Come then to this era. It was five to midnight, and fire was in the sky.

Sure enough, the sun dipped and rose. Cloud strata flamed beyond steep Kirkjufell, five hundred mountain metres up.

The port streets of Grundafjörður were wide and carefree, the wind thrashing at the shore. It had rushed in past the window frame, and in the distance a door had banged methodically. At the harbour quay of stone, the fish factory was deep in shadow of the church-fell. The sea was dark, the distant hills salmon in the sun. Gulls wheeled and a raven cawed. It was the top of the night, and all was stripped bare. Wave and wind, the chilly bleating of the birds. There was lava cliff, layer on layer of rock and ash, and a sunset that was now a golden dawn. There were no trees to bend before the wind, no shivering reeds. Boats strained at anchor, and each lifted grain of sand was sharp. No dancers danced, the village children were asleep.

A distant dog barked, beat against a fence. To the west were the glacial slopes of Snæfellsjökull, Iceland's cone volcano best set against an azure sky.

Yet this was the sun's last day, it was about to give way to cloud. If you could live for ever, you might pause to dream, just sit upon the dock and watch the early dawn. The beach was pristine, the water pure. Later the curtains still were dancing, and a chill had filled the room.

On distant polar-facing shores, there will be scattered trunks of pine, carried round the northern hoop by currents from Siberia. They arrive scarred and bare. And on each tidal line, far from jostle of the market, now are multi-coloured plastic pieces. Blue and green, red and white, stiff shard and frayed rope, net piece and packaging. It is a sorry tale. No place in Midgard, it seemed, could be exempt. In every village, there are some things talked about, some things never. Even the serpent Jörmungandr, the girdler of the sea, even sea-gods Ran and her husband Ægir, Njord and his wife Skaði, could not push away this new creation. Such modern magic was beyond them.

That same morning, clouds had caught the sun, and white foam was sketched on distant water, raw-boned horses out to race. The rocky shore of the fjord led to the fell's isle, and we walked across the hours and round the red string of time. The raven watched from a post, wearied sheep foraged on the shore for seaweed.

'Iceland summer,' shrugged the fishers' daughters at reception, smiling. Then came a call. It was the captain of the ship. He said soon, maybe.

On the far side of the volcano was the lava labyrinth, on a bluff in view of ocean roads. It is a *völundarhús*, a crossing point to home of elves. There is a beach with banks of gentian and yellow hawkweed, where men and women of Dritvik fishing village once laid on stones their clothes to dry before the sky. It is said the hidden people, the folk of rocks, those supernatural smithies, built the maze, and even gulls and other seabirds dare not fly above. You can walk one way in, and follow path to silence at the centre of the earth. On the beach of basalt beads are rust remains, pieces of the trawler *Epine* out of Grimsby.

Long ago, I waited once for a summer gale like this to cease. It was far beyond the west horizon, over ice sheet and a frozen sea, deep into the boreal taiga of Innu country. Wind battered that lake-shore, and we waited by the piled possessions. Our Innu friends strolled along and smiled. One said, there had been black bears at the village boundary that night, a worrying sign. Time passed and the moon set and rose, and then the wind yielded. The boat came to smack through the hard grey water, and it rained for days. At a forest edge strewn with stripped driftwood, a million blackfly flew and we caught salmon in the nets. We lay in the canvas tent by warm metal stove, drinking tea and telling tales. Nearby we found a birch-bark canoe had been stolen from a sacred site, and on return the storm struck, waves rising high. The boat began to fill, the engine strained, we loosened laces and all heavy clothing. The skipper Joseph and son-in-law Sebastian had never learned to swim.

After some time, the sea god did relent, and so our boat stranded on a sandbank. Waist-deep through the maelstrom we pulled the craft to a shore. On the long march home, birdsong filled the forest and the light was sharp.

> *There was great foreboding, so Ægir and Ran,*
> *Received the gods and elves, in the gleaming hill under waves,*
> *The hall was lit, with great nuggets of shining gold,*
> *The guests sat down on benches, and the cups filled themselves,*
> *And the hall was filled, with the peaceful hum of good talk.*
> [Sæmundr Sigfússon, *Loki's Flyting, Poetic Edda*, c1270]

The saga starts, as all do, with a resolute step, the deliberate dip of an oar.

Ahead lay the sea-road to the Westfjords, the places of an outlaw saga, and the settled lands of mountain, fell and fjord.

There was steady drizzle, air becalmed at Stikkishólmur. To the east of ferry port were mounds rich with wildflowers at the shore and a single bloodstone rock, this the site for the regional Thing, the open-air assembly where people met to make decisions. It looked out on a fjord of plenty, islands where the first settlers beached. It was days by horse to the Althing, at the wide plain ringed by basalt columns. Each summer, all of Iceland gathered, and the law-speaker by the Lögberg rock spoke aloud one third of Iceland's laws. Each family had a booth of stone with tent of coloured cloth and canvas. Flags snapped in summer breeze, trumpets called and horses grazed on the plains below. At Independence Day in 1944, even as all the people smiled, summer rain fell heavily, and Sveinn Björnsson was sworn in as Iceland's first president.

The northward ferry *Bardur* set sail early on this day. There was the smell of bilge and diesel, the currents smooth and lined out across the bay. Behind and south was Helgafell, the holy mount where Thor resides, and to the east Álftafjördur, the swan-fjord, still today a gathering place for flocks of whooper swan. We crossed Breiðafjörður past its three thousand isles, Snæfellsjökull to the west was hidden in the mist.

Once we had drawn up in Reykjavik in the drowsy sun of late afternoon, the harbour water was blue with sky. 'Everyone's gone mad,' beamed the taxi-driver, 'this is the first sun we've seen for three months.' The streets were thronging, parties ran all night, bottles crashed in alleys. Smiling faces every hour, were tipped toward the open sky.

It was here in Breiðafjörður, where the midnight child could pick the summer lice from off her shirt, it was here that Naddoð's longship beached. His angry crew had missed the treasure trail to south, the winds of Njord had blown them to a black sand shore. Yet his wretched men soon were open-mouthed, they waited, stacked their weapons, stood beneath the calling kittiwake. The raiding party pressed inland, it seemed an empty isle, they came to steaming pools, gathered forest berry, gazed upon a vacant lava land. This was not a kingdom reserved for only gods, nor was it ground of ancient ghouls. They fished and stocked, the ship hastened fast a thousand leagues to home. It was the late 800s, and the Vikings had discovered Island.

At home, Naddoð opened wide his arms, said it was an unstaffed state, all splendorous scenes. There were fine swans in every fertile valley, and butter dripped from all the fields.

Now this prospect sounded better than the annual scrap for meagre land for crops. So boat smiths built *knarr* cargo craft and launched a land-rush to this earthy summit by the Arctic. So it was that Flóki became more famed, sailing seventy summers after Lindisfarne was sacked. The boat was made of strakes of pine, and families were crew. Children stowed sour milk, they tethered sheep and breeding cattle, heaped dried cod and lamb, packed iron for nails and pine tar pots. Flóki sailed by star and swell, listened for the boom of surf, looked for clouds on land, steered west to follow gannet route. It was a tautly fitted ship, this magic migrant vessel.

Flóki brought three ravens, the wound-sea's wise black-feathered birds who cawed and coasted on the breeze. He claimed the empty land, the ground so green and water clear.

Now settlers streamed the sea-lanes, leaving the lands of the Norse, departing flatter isles of Denmark, sailed north from Ireland and Atlantic isles. Yet those sailors also carried elf and troll, god and dwarf, who slid into the spaces on the benches, endured the journey by the seasick families, jumped ashore at Iceland. An empty land lay ahead for all of them to spread and grow. Each farm put down roots, all was peace and promise. There was ample space for all. They had found a land torn by wind, yet washed by warmer currents. There was woodland on the plain, grass for all their sheep. There were fish at sea, bird and eggs on seaward cliff. They soon were found by Arctic fox, blue-white fur in winter, bronze in summer, yet they never saw a wolf. Their cats and dogs claimed homes, as did the mice and many fleas. Soon the axe took trees for timber, and homes were laid with stone, topped with turf for wall and roof.

And these very farms at settlement were listed in the Landnámabók, and no king claimed the best vale and grove, no noble took the fertile fields and finest views to mirrored fjord.

No doubt this explains in part, why people of the north rushed to take these ocean crossings, why they left behind the older worlds of sorrow.

The ferry docked at Flatey, two leagues of low rock and sheepy slope, and soon the ferry left the car-free isle. It seemed the worst of tern attacks were done, for the young were fledged, the adults ticking over sheltered bays. Snipe rose and dived, feathers buzzing over grass. On one shore was a wrecked and rusted cargo ship, and puffin dashing low. There were whimbrel and godwit, and snow bunting on the rocks. The sea surface crumpled, a school of fish leapt and flung themselves in air, racing this way and that. Under the surface loomed a dark shadow. An inlet thronged with spinning red-necked phalarope, and women and men were sweeping mist nets, catching birds. They held them in their hands, put them warm in bags to weigh. Yet Flatey was also isle of fishers, the first library of the land, and source of medieval treasure in the Flateyjarbók.

At the centre of the isle was the wooden library, a single room with two armchairs and view across the fjord to whale and dolphin. Here was once a monastery, and years ago illustrious monks and nuns inscribed saga and story on two hundred leaves of calfskin vellum. In those days, at the end of 1300s, they sat in scriptorium in the summer light, by candles in the winter, taking seven years to finish a manuscript. The Flateyjarbók was given, perhaps taken, a present for Danish King Frederick, and held in Copenhagen for three hundred years till returned in 1971. The Flateyjarbók contains the earliest Rímur, four-lined verse of hope and sadness, sung on winter nights in turfed farms, the fire blazing and rush lights on the walls, its recovery led in recent years by Steindór Andersen.

The wooden church was only a hundred years old, yet instead of austerity and pastel painted walls and pews, here was mural on the walls and all the vaulted ceiling.

The mountain theologian, Hans Urs von Balthasar said we should seek ways and places to bring peace to restless hearts, and observed sadly, 'We no longer dare believe in beauty.' And here was this church interior painted by the Catalonian Baltasar Samper in return for rent and food. A rich and textured scene of sea eagle and sheep, raven, fish and seal, and Christ preaching in a knitted sweater.

One day, a mate and deckie learner out of Grimsby walked this route from harbour, they had docked to have a doctor stitch the fingers of a fellow crewman, so the mate took the boy, saying bring a book. A girl called Oddný with fair hair watched them from a horse, and cantered over. She held out her hand. Give her the book, said the mate. He did this every trip, and so they sat inside the church, thinking of the news about the coming war. Here was peace, an escape from ship of hissing pipes, thumping wave, metal crash, skipper shouting down below. I'm going to live with this, thought the boy, this world of sorrow. I'm learning English, thought the girl, to read more stories, and so in time she would marry a farmer and live above the cliffs of Látrabjarg.

Under heavy skies, we sat with mugs of tea in armchairs at the port café. A layered cruise ship appeared, and brought ashore a crowd, so in they streamed and sat in rows, and local women in costume sang folk songs. The audience smiled and applauded, and then they quickly left.

We waited at the windows, by a vertebra of whale. The car had been driven off the earlier ferry, and the way would lie ahead, over mountainous Westfjords, where the sun shone for no more than two hours a week across the year. The narrow road would roll east toward the barrier cliffs of Látrabjarg, then north and up. From the pass, far below would be the port of Patreksfjörður on the north side of the fjord, and beyond the churning Greenland Sea.

This was land of fisher and the outlaw, of cod and catfish, of wreck and rescuer, where trolls went by mountain trail. It was also where was fashioned a wholly novel type of fish.

It long had seemed the brine was blessed, for the cod grew great, and their splendid elders lived a sweet and lengthy span. With every kind of beast, they coasted through the water column, swam with salty mouths agape. You could imagine, they assembled in fine cities, far greater than those raised by gods above. The elders grew to be a fathom long, they sensed no need for fear, for they could rule for ever. Over banks and darkest deeps, many lived a hundred years, and the cod grounds spread far across the shining sea. Those fish knew freedom, though beyond the fence might come a skirmish, a school of hungry orca. And the keepers of the upper watch, kept alert for arrow birds. One day across the sky came trailing lights. Wooden craft with sails had ventured far from Aljezur on Atlantic cliff, then came from North Sea ports. Close-hauled and tacking fast were smacks, a refuge well amidships to keep fresh the fish till men returned to port.

The cod were wise, they stalked and chased for dynasties. But they never could discern the prey that swam from those on lines, their eyes could never see a net of hemp and holes, a filigree of plastic.

Outside the fjords, the ocean spread before the fishers, flowing south along the Greenland current. These fish grounds were a great commons, yet fish and fisher soon would suffer tragedy. There was inflow from the Gulf Stream, nutrient-mixing, and the greatest seabird crowd in all of Europe. There were gatherings of guillemot, puffin and fulmar, kittiwake and razorbill, nearby on the sheer cliffs of Látrabjarg towering up a half kilometre. Fishing men and boys rowed out in sixæreen from the beach at Breiðavik, jackets waterproofed with oil of seal and skate, and set their long lines in the winter water. Later came the trawlers, from far and near towing nets inside the fish limits, and soon the days of rule of cod queen and king would be over.

Andri Snær Magnason has observed that Iceland experimented, they 'tried to see what would happen if everyone thought only about their self-interest. It did not go well.' In the town of Patreksfjörður was a mound on the promontory, overlooking western waters, where was found a grave boat, set in soil with amber beads and iron nails, and whalebone jewels for the Viking leader. And on the harbour front are two modern memorials, one to British fishers, a raised stone pinned to ground by four silver chains, one to French, a scarred rock hemmed by metal cables.

For on any day, storm winds can batter, careen and rip away all sound. Even so, you wonder, how could a trawler be so stranded, lives lost in blizzard and the beating sea, so close to safety at this shore.

It is said that the Westfjords were famed for sorcerer and wizard, shaman and witch, a counter-culture to the Christianity enforced on Iceland by Olaf Tryggvason when he had taken Norway's throne. The medieval sailors and their skippers depicted these waters filled with monsters. On the edge of maps were fish with wings, with serrated teeth, unicorn with serpent tail, beasts blowing plumes higher than a three-master.

Yet these reports and illustrations could well have been in error. The old cultures regarded the snake and serpent as sacred. Those wyrms and dragons knew, gold makes people lose their reason. And though Iceland won the cod wars, extended fish limits, the paper fish would soon destroy it all.

It was a still day in September 2001, so two inshore fishermen, Erlingur Sveinn Haraldsson and Örn Snævar Sveinsson, steered their small vessel, the *Svein Sveinsson*, out of Patreksfjördur to catch some fish. The sea was calm, so the invited journalists aboard did not suffer sickness. They wrote words and took pictures, and carried home the story. Small fishers long had caught fish in common waters, fish that belonged to all of Iceland.

Now a short silence followed, then came the fury of the court and chamber. Police were sent to knock hard on doors, 'Arrest those fishermen.' Erlingur and Örn stated again, the new management of fisheries was immoral and unjust, it had denied their rights to common fish. The authorities declared them guilty, ordered fines of one million kroner each or three months in prison. Their boat was confiscated.

How had it come to this, in a land where so much collective effort was spent in rescues? Where everyone had simply hoped each boat would survive the constant call of sea gods. And now this, a fishing craft was cut to pieces.

It all started with the magic spell of Individual Transferable Quotas. These were invented in the 1980s, at the time that selfishness had become a doctrine in the British and American cabinets, at the time that New Zealand leaders decided schools should compete with one another. Iceland had taken control of its water, so turned upon its smaller fishers. For these ITQs divided up the commons and awarded rights to existing fishers, according to their size of operation, and permitted trading of the quota. Now smallfishers could not choose to fish, for the cod that once belonged to all, and the large grew larger as they bought up quota. One bad year, one cash-flow crisis, and a fisher might have to sell for cash.

But only once, and anyway the price was the cutting up or burning of their boats. The game was up. As is the way, the large grew larger, and came proudly to be called by government, a breed of 'Business Vikings'.

Nobel Prize winner and economist Joseph Stiglitz later said at a meeting in Reykjavik, 'There you really blew it.' Norwegian social scientist Ottar Brox was just as blunt, 'Certain schools of economic thought are today more of a menace to coastal communities than foreign fleets, and parasitic middlemen.'

The second part of the plan was this: permit banks to lend and borrow against the paper quota. These were, after all, a guarantee of permanent income. You catch the fish, you sell the fish, you have money. The neoliberals were brazen, called their whole country an economic miracle, the financial sector was labelled as the Últras, they were the modern Vikings.

We walked to the town's outdoor heated pool to gaze upon these fishing waters. There was a silver stream, fretted water flowing from the hillside in and out of rock and pebbles, rushing over grassy slope. The light was grey, the clouds white and slate, cinder and silver, moonlit and exhausted at the long edge of midsummer. The waters of the fjord were clear as crystal. A family of eider burbled as they fed, their ripples spreading toward the far side, to the yellow beach, to the *Sargon* wreck. The sand was made by Atlantic catfish and wolffish, those crustacean-crackers, building beds of gold, and long has lain that ship blinded in the snows of forty-eight. Between water and the air, there were terns beating wings, gloss-black ravens calling, redshank piping.

At the hot pools, townsfolk rested after work. Beyond the fjord, it was clear enough to see the vale and cliffs of Hnjótur and Látrabjarg. That night, children played in gloaming edgelands, shouting and laughing. The sheep had fallen silent. To the north were high and low vales, the lands of outlaw Gisli's saga.

Gisli Sursson spoke this verse:

> *Bright land of wave's flame, goddess of gold I came,*
> *To a hall where seven fires, to my anguish were burning,*
> *On both sides men on benches, greeted me kindly.*

[*Gisli Sursson's Saga*, c1240]

There were once bodies in the brine, on the far side of the fjord.

It was forty leagues in and out of fjord, the high road skirting round the hill of Hafnamúli, steep slopes rising from the sea. The Arctic tide had ebbed, and there at the edge of Hnjótur's sandy beach, by a rock, was the hull of steam trawler *Sargon*.

A cormorant dried its wings, perched on rusty ruin. The road wound another twenty leagues over heath and past isolated farm and abandoned beach village at Breiðavik, and climbed toward the cropped turf by the light of Bjargtangar. Puffins stood by burrows, and rain fell. Away to east stretched a great wall, the long cliffs of Látrabjarg. Over the precipice was descent to scree and skerry and the silent waves below. Some years before, the sky just as low, we had climbed Hallsgrimskirkja, the concrete cathedral of the capital, seventy-five metres tall and forty years to build. It towers over Reykjavik. These cliffs are seven times higher.

It was a perilous path, at the eastern precinct of the cliffs, to the red beach of Rauðisandur. It was said, this was not a drive for the faint-hearted, for this road of rock ran down a narrow ledge. A tarred church stood alone at shore, tin roof rusty in the mist. There were calls of many waders, out on the wind-troubled dunes. The poet Steinn Steinarr was born in the Westfjords to utter poverty, the family broken up for adoption in the early 1900s. He was brought to the lands across the water, eventually east to Akureyri. It was a lonely life of misery, partly rescued by books and reading. He later found a welcome with a tribe of writer-artists in Reykjavik, one was Halldór Laxness, and he wrote of this place:

> *A wave breaking, on copper sand,*
> *A breeze rustling, the tall blue grasses.*
> *A flower that died.*

I hurled a stone, at a white wall,
And the stone laughed.

[Steinn Steinarr, *Time and Water*, 1948]

There is a museum in the vale at Hnjótur, where on display was the film that brought fame to Látrabjarg. There was display of breeches buoy, medals and a silver cup. There was sixæreen and shoes of catfish-skin, worn to measure distance as the counted shoes wore out. It was brimming with objects, as is every village museum in Iceland, each filled with tool and utensil, with every kind of way of local living, and not a single thing looted from another land. The tale on film was told in black and white, the late 1940s cold and bleak, snow drifts deep, the waves and spray too high it seemed. There were men on that ship who froze to superstructure. Ran and Ægir and their icy nets, they were busy on successive winters.

It happened like this.

The Látrabjarg rescuers were invited into Iceland's soul. In many a coastal parish, church bells rang for every wreck, wood rustled up for coffins regardless of the sailors' home. It was what they did: wade into the frozen waters. There was a kindness, not just of strangers but of competitors. So grateful thanks were offered back by crinkled eyes, as women of the farms fed fish stew to crews, as farm men had already circled round to milk the sheep. It was the second year of peace, the third of Iceland's independence. In the faint daylight of winter, a layer of cold roofed earth and sea, all the treeless slopes and fields were bleached.

The farmers of this bluff would now discover how it felt to wear a national halo. One tarnished trawler was stranded by the gods of sea and wind, then another one a year later.

You might think those early settlers might have chosen deeper soil, where a plough could turn the turf. Yet here was bird and egg on ledge, here were many fish at sea. On a land unclaimed, they settled farms at Breiðavik and Hænuvik, at Hvallátur and far Kollsvik. And this was why these fearless farmers, sure-footed as sheep, could drop a rescue party straight off the cliffs from sky above. So one spring day in 1948, the farmstead men and women brushed clean each suit and dress. They shone shoes and carried coats, for they recalled four years before, how each witness at Thingvellir had stood in rain, how they strained to hear a single word spoken by the President. Now at banquet in Patreksfjörður, Bjorn Sveinsson and his nobles gave to Þórður Jónsson a sil-ver-handled trophy. He pinned gleaming medals on women and the men, forty-five in all, and to some surprise, five honours sent by George the King of distant fishers. That night, they danced in the hall, and for a few hours quite forgot the rescue on the hellish cliffs.

Earlier in the hall, all had been hush. They wished to hear their leader. Iceland flags and those of Britain had been placed side by side on each tablecloth, and the President said to Þórður he could find the funds, if they could tempt the famed director to film their rescue of the crew of *Dhoon*. Wise leaders in ages past knew how such annals might depict a story, how people might feel a common pride, how it might define a country from its past. So the farmer-actors for the movie met at Þórður's farmhouse at the shore. Þórður wore his cap angled, his left eyebrow often raised in smile, ready as a leader. So they trod again ten leagues, took the film crew to the cliff-top meadows. As the heroes spread on grass, Óskar Gíslason scoped the set, lay out flat and crawled,

CHAPTER ONE

gazed below from brim, and said to Þórður words like these, 'We will film your great descent, and then return in winter for the colder scenes with snow.'

That prior December day, coastguards had received a mayday call from sidewinder *Dhoon*. The Fleetwood ship had once been named the *Armageddon*, two years earlier near St Kilda isle a wave had ripped away the wheelhouse, splintered wreckage on the deck, two crew were swept away. This trip the *Dhoon*, she had mineswept in the war, now set sail with replacement skipper, a captain from Hull's Hessle Road. They steamed to Iceland's western waters, would they sneak inside the limit, or stick to deeper grounds? To the fishers, these cliffs and clashing currents were both a draw and nemesis, riches undersea but deadly too.

Well, in this winter storm, all nearby trawlers helpless, facing waves of forty feet, now their anchor did not hold.

One growler sheared again the wheelhouse, popped the planks of ship, swept away the skipper and a crewman famed as fairground boxer. His son a decade later was also lost in another trawler wreck. The bosun Albert Head, a Lowestoft boy, marshalled the crew for tide on tide, thirst was now a fear. He broke off ice to suck, they huddled in the whaleback, he kept them talking.

Night gave way to dawn, and dark returned again. Was there hope, what would they promise, just to go and tell their wives and mothers how much they missed them? What would they give, to sit in winter sun on promenade, and watch the children skip and play? Snow fell without cease, along this bitter sea road. Outside was black blizzard, so Þórður called each neighbour. They fetched horse and rope, brought rockets and the rescue gear. They did not know where exactly was the ship, nor that the crew would be shackled as three whole tides washed in and out of wreck. They tied the tackle to the horses, called happy hounds to heel, strapped on boots with nails, shrugged rope around their shoulders.

There were many leagues to march, across the moors of ice. For these rescuers had already suffered loss. One daughter died of fever, a son drowned right in this sea. They knew well of Egill's Saga, could recite the verse on winter nights before the fire.

'Me the sea has robbed of much,' had spoken author Snorri Sturluson. Egill's older boy was buried in a mound, a bee-ship town, drowned in the fjord in sight of land. And at last, from snowy peak, the rescuerers spied the tiny stranded *Dhoon* where waves were pounding at the reef.

It was not a simple task, a descent they did each spring, taking many thousand birds from warm embrace of nests. There was razorbill at base, kittiwake and fulmar from the central shelfs, guillemot from sheerest bluff. This was winter, so with heavy hearts they tied twine around their waists, and six men dug their heels in ice. The first slid over, abseiled through the borough of the birds, a plumb line to the dark below. They hoped they might attach a breeches buoy to stranded ship. They knew it could be bad. At that time, they would seem as gods in clouds to the English fishers holding tight. Þórður and his fellow farmers swung down the wintry cliff, kicked off from crag, and ten of them arrived at the cliff base, while the others anchored ropes at top. Oddný Gudmunsdóttir dropped, so she could to talk to them in English. Yet they still did not know if they would find a single fisher still alive.

Now in spring, the men and women of the founder farms, pointing to the route, showed Óskar and his crew how they could drop camera bag and tripod, all the kit and batteries.

By and by, they dragged the living fishers in by breeches buoy. Twelve sailors had been waiting, two days soaked by freezing sea. Their hands and feet were useless, the farmers gently put lit cigarettes on each lip, broke flatbread into pieces, slid mittens on their hands, the fishers' eyes showed thanks. Here was relief, smiling rescue. All would be fine. 'Swing your arms,' said Oddný. 'Have you come by boat?' they asked. Her news stopped their hearts again, there was half a league to climb. The farmers formed a chair from rope and tied in fishers one by one, each still wearing a lifejacket made of cork. Árni Helgasson scrambled up to tell them at the top to pull, so seven crew slowly rose, and crawled and rolled on snow, staring at the cloud above.

But the night drew in too fast, and they could only fetch the other five halfway to the icy ledge of Flaugernef. So Haflíði Hardórsson and his crew took off outer clothes and caps of fur, wrapped the fishers up, and waited for the distant dawn.

Some seamen muttered, they would never go to sea again. They were stiff with fright, carved up by guilt, for it was they who had survived when friends had drowned below. At long last the dawn came, they strapped the men on horses, and trekked the winter fields to nearest farm. No wonder Albert Head fell six times, since he could not grasp the reins. The women tucked them smiling into beds, spooned hot broth for each. None before had tasted coffee mixed with schnapps of brennívin. Their eyes were glazed, yet they soon were gone. They sailed by trawler south to Reykjavik, took a plane to Glasgow, a train to west-coast Fleetwood, where a grand reception hailed them home for Christmas.

'Oh good, you're back, fix the back gate would you.' Before long, they were on the ships and sailing for the cod again.

Not many people know as much about endeavour in the face of disaster as Óttar Sveinsson. He has written 70 books, a fisherman surviving days in polar water, a plane crash high on glacier, rescue parties in a storm, people lost in open boats. Yet he says, taking off his sunglasses one winter day, 'This was the most remarkable.'

Óttar said, 'We were taught about them at school, and Þórður Jonsson is often mentioned, how so many people of Látrabjarg were given medals.' It was perhaps the bravest rescue ever, the English crews from two stranded trawlers. 'We never heard about this,' I say, 'just the cod wars and how coastguards embarrassed the navy of a fading empire. How our brave fishers were stopped from trawling in the Iceland waters.' But said Óttar, 'Many rescuers suffered trauma all their lives.' Anna, the daughter of Haflíði Hardórsson said her father never spoke about that time, stuck on ledge all night, for he was struck several times on his head by falling rocks. She stitched together his story from other sources. Her father thought that dawn would never come.

Yet this was only half the tale, for Óskar did come again in winter, when the farmers put on hats of fur with flaps, pulled on roll-neck jersey and extra coats, saddled up their horses, took out rope and rescue gear, shouted to the dogs. They posed, waved goodbye again to children, for the crew needed camera shots in mist and snow. And now in gale force east, entering watery stage

CHAPTER ONE

from west, again the weather blind and grim with cold, another antique trawler the *Sargon* once of Grimsby was on the search for shelter. She had steamed into the fjord on the northern side of Látrabjarg, soundings with a seven-pound lead called by second youngest deckie at the bow, the skipper blindly steering, hoping for the snow to cease.

Just across the fjord was the safe harbour and town of Patreksfjörður. Did they know, did they have inshore cod on ice below? In *Sailing Home*, Norman Fischer has written, 'One of disaster's most disastrous features is that it always surprises us.'

That was the first dawn of December, and now their anchor dragged. The crew were all from narrow streets of Hull, the mate and bosun, engineer and spare hand, the oldest trimmer born in days when Grimsby sent its boys as slaves aboard the fleeting system. Only six would see again their homes, the frost giants took the rest. With a grinding screech of metal, the ship was stranded at the base of Hafnarmúli. This rock now held the *Sargon*, so close to safety. All was dark ashore, so on deck the crew launched flares, burned each mattress. And from a turf-farm a woman out to check the sheep saw the flame and phoned the coastguard, and soon a lad on a horse from Þórður's house clattered over slatey slopes to find the film set. The crew and actors were amazed, they drew out charts, and saw this was a lengthy walk, north around their tongue of land, twenty leagues to plain of Örlygur.

The formal inquiry court in Hull would later certify, 'The conditions were appalling.'

The judge voiced admiration for the shore party, coming over testing country. For Kenneth Carpmael knew this was not the only wreck where rescuers had been so willing. Yet to Iceland he sent no special message, neither thanks nor medal. He settled that the stranding and the loss of life was 'not due to wrongful act, or default of skipper or the owner.' It seemed he did not know, these were the very rescuers of the *Dhoon*, sent medals by the king the previous spring.

All was wretched, by the clamour of the waves, for Þórður's team could not attach the rocket line to ship. The icy waves thrashed on deck, set solid over every metal surface. Six of crew were in the whaleback, the other ten and skipper back at bridge, the wind too ferocious for them to leave. Óskar's camera kept jamming, yet after dawn the breeches buoy was fixed to hull, the first crewman strapped in. The farmers scampered into waves, and pulled him from the salt. Six ashen crew so cold were soon wrapped upon the shore. Yet none from the wheelhouse could escape, even as the woodbine funnel still stood straight.

It seemed not far from bridge to bow, so Þórður and Árni hauled themselves aboard, slipped on ice, grabbed at frozen metal, slowly trod in the gale to search for survivors.

At the bridge lay the skipper, all the windows shattered. Ice had clasped the ship. The door was broken at its hinges, they found eight other bodies, squeezed into the space. Two were plainly boys, they were Henry aged thirteen and Edward seventeen. Þórður and Árni shouted out with joy, for here was one man still alive. He fluttered eyelids, but they could not free his fingers frozen to a metal post. He died before their eyes. Time had scythed the men on *Dhoon*, and now had taken second gang of fishers. Each had died still full of days. That year was bad for Hull, three trawlers drowned, sorrow in all their sinews. Yet in those very months, Iceland lost sixteen, and they would soon extend fish limits further out to sea, as would Norway and the Faroe Isles, sowing seeds for later wars of cod. So the coastguards fought for fish, yet also rescued stranded fishers.

Days after the rescue, Þórður and the local sheriff, the sea now mirror calm, commissioned a boat to cross the fjord. They were dismayed, for they found open tins and bottles lying on the *Sargon* deck. A man must have been alive, at the time of rescue from the shore, down below in dark. But he was gone, snared and taken deep to the Hlésey hall of Ran.

There the rusting wreck lies still, rising up as ebbs the daily tide. In Fleetwood and in Hull, mission men were feared silhouettes at the glass front doors of wives and families. When each door was opened, death slipped in. Those men had roved from port to port, across the rime-cold sea.

So at their funerals, heavy stones were laid inside the coffin boxes, to give some heft for bearers. But still they stumbled as they walked from church to grave.

> *Generous people and brave live best,*
> *Seldom nourish sorrow.*
> [Sæmundr Sigfússon, *Hávamál, Sayings of the High One, Poetic Edda*, c1290]

———

When settlers came to the Westfjords, the empty land was waiting for a story.

They travelled fifteen hundred leagues from Norway, yet it still was two hundred more to the port of Isafjörður, over high plain and pass, in and out of seven narrow fjords, north and north and nearer to the pole. Alpine flowers bloomed by waterfalls, and the sea eagle looked down from roost high on cliff. In recent times, there had been a slight revival, more inshore fishing boats in village ports on Dyrafjörður and Önandafjörður. New tunnels have been burrowed into hills of elf and dwarf, though old tracks still wound up and over slope and scree. Set upon a spit of sand was the town of coloured wooden houses, fish-port and trading post. Each January end brings a special ceremony of freedom, as the Ísafjörður townsfolk gather in the cafés, sit outside in icy streets. For this is sólarkaffi, a time to sit and share the sun-coffee. The town lives in shade for a month either side of the winter solstice, the sun swallowed by the winter wolves.

The people gaze, too long, at the notched mountain profiles on the rim around the town. One day, the sunlight reaches windows and walls of the café.

The winds always seem to blow in Ísafjörður, pulled this way and that by nearby glacial caps. Yet one day the surface was a mirror, and in the fjord was the *Preziosa*, a cruise ship seventy metres high, layer on layer of cabins, its engines rumbling night and day and the diesel smoke flattened in the fjord. This acrid air, far from any city or factory, the polluted breath of ship. On board were as many passengers and crew as live in Westfjords, strolling up and down stone piazza and crystal staircase. The ship never docks, so avoids all harbour dues. Beyond the mouth of fjord, some-where in the mist lay Hornstrandir, the pure land at the far north-west of this northern sea. Once a territory of small farm and troll, it had been abandoned in the 1950s, people defeated by another winter too severe, by the lack of overland connection.

Today Hornstrandir is without car and horse, no fishing or hunting are permitted, you carry out what you bring in. Arctic fox run free, sometimes polar bear. It is a land that drifts in every distant dream.

One tunnel to north opens to the cove of Bolungarvik, the northmost village of the Westfjords. Here were reminders, how at times you have to hang to life by fingertips.

It was from Bolungarvik that the trawler *Heidrunn II* disappeared one night of the savage storm of '68, six men were lost, three were skipper and his two boys. Above the houses of the village can be seen defensive structures to divert each winter avalanche. Up concrete steps between two shops was the adult polar bear. The Natural History Museum had two hundred types of stuffed bird, trays of eggs from cliffs, the jaws of largest ever blue whale, ravens on a nest. When the settlers arrived in Iceland, the land absorbed the sheep and cattle. Yet there would come on the floes in the cold Greenland current, those great white giants, thin and hungry in the summer, they could charge faster than a horse. In the early sixties, four Ísafjörður fishermen were on Horn-strandir to gather eggs, the fog was thick and they were lucky. They saw the white hummock on the beach, crept up and shot the polar bear, carried its fur back to fame.

Big animals like this bring reputation. In ancient times, Audun from the Westfjords captured a young bear, and sailed it east to show to Norse and Danish kings. In the far north, the bear is sacred, called honey-paw and chunky-paw, grandfather and apple of the forest. Norway's King Harald wanted the bear, but Audun gave it to Denmark's Sveinn. Gifts and giving were the moral of the tale, happiness came from giving, said Audun, it increased his reputation.

On the eastern side of cove was Ósvör, a wooden fishing hamlet set on turf and stones. The roofs of huts were grass, the walls were wooden slats, living places half underground. This was the kind of setting for Jón Kalman Stefanson's *Heaven and Hell*, a fishing village on the stones, the boys and men rowing out to challenge wind and storm, the certain death if you forgot your sealskin waterproof, ice on face and beard, frozen mittens, fish lines baited and waiting, breathing in and out the cold, throwing cod two ells long into base of boat, flipping till they had frozen solid. Jón Kalman's narrator says, 'There was hardly anything as beautiful as the sea on good days or clear nights. But the sea is not a bit beautiful. We hate it more than anything else.'

At Ísafjörður log-museum on the harbour was knife and hook, bone saw and axe, handles wrapped in string and smoothed by sweat and oil. There was displayed the feared anchor-device, it was used to cut the warps of British trawlers. That was the era when coastguard vessels clashed with naval frigate, then on another day rescued British fishers.

Further along the fjord east of Ísafjörður was Súdavík village, torn apart a century ago by closure of the whaling station, then again by recent avalanche. One January day just 20 years ago, the snow slipped slowly, gathered pace and crashed down, swept houses out to sea. Children died, adults died, the village was rebuilt either side of empty scar. At the waterside was the old Norwe-gian whaling station, operational for twenty years from the 1880s, employer of one hundred lo-cal people, all to kill the whale. In old times, *hvalreki* was a gift from gods, a whale carcase washed ashore. There was meat and blubber, keratin and bone.

Now the *Fengsæll* whaler was hauled ashore, the clouds dark, snow still on mountain-tops, the fjord dead calm and reflecting each hill and fell. The whale could not stand this active hunting, and now machinery was leaking rust to soil. On the skerries out to sea were basking seals, and we could hear, at southern end of village, the sound of yip and bark. In an enclosure, at the rear of the Arctic fox research centre, were youngsters in their summer fur, running and tumbling, jumping over rocks, rolling in the grass. The museum laid out all the contradictions of identity, sheep and predator, winter fur for sale, the whale to eat or watch.

At the periphery of settlement, there always seems to be a troll or monster, ready to jump in and change your day. The wild, too, was the place where human laws did not apply.

On the route north to Ísafjörður, on a high heath was an outcrop of bronze rocks, tall above a plain of slate and moss. Far below was Arnafjörður, the eagle's fjord, and we had looked down upon a single eagle circling. The water seemed still, and the cloud was low, clinging to the slopes of scree. This was the place where outnumbered Gisli Sursson died, and his wife Audr poured scorn on their opponents' show of force. Gisli had been a caring farmer, a Norse settler who had built by hard work the free-farm at Haukadalur, the hawk-dale. In a dream, he was told to be kind to those who were deaf and poor and helpless. He was a wringer-of-verses, yet was declared an outlaw, and took to wearing shape-shifting cloaks of green and brown to fade into the land. For many a year, he and Audr stayed ahead of spy and mercenary, helped the poor, and so his honour grew.

Yet, he had said of opponents, the end you want will come.

It was the last night of summer, the air still but heavy with frost. Gisli had hidden in under-farm passages, lived happily with Audr, even though their winter food was lichen stewed in whey. But Helgi and Eyjolf the Grey still sought him, and one day Gisli said, 'I suspect fate will take its course.' He had dreamed of loon birds fighting, their hooting calls from lakes at dusk, and so he knew that soon 'the dew of bows would be descending.' Fourteen strong men came with spear and sword and axe. Eyjof had been paid three hundred silver pieces by Thorgrim's brother Bork, and Gisli, Audr and their foster-daughter Guðrid raced up the ridge to this high point, not far from the seven cascades of Dynjandifoss. The band attacked, Gisli and Audr standing high on rocks. Helgi was cut in two, and Ejyolf stepped back. Two men grabbed the women, Gisli fought the others with an axe that shattered, then sword, then rocks alone.

Audr wearing rune-bones struck Eyjolf with her club so hard it took away his strength, and he staggered away. She spoke the famous words, 'Remember, you wretch, for as long as you live, that a woman has struck you.'

Gisli wounded badly spoke this verse, his last:

> Goddess of golden rain, who gives me great joy,
> May boldly hear report, of her friend's brave stand.

Gisli leapt down upon attackers, and thus his life was ended. All the mercenaries, each one wounded, gained nothing but dishonor.

Gisli's farm had been on Dyrafjörður, beyond the eagle's fjord and raven's pass. It was said there were evil spirits, on the pass ahead. Just when you think you are in the clear, a strike might come from far. It swooped from sky, the beast. The ash track had angled back and forth up mountain-side, wine-coloured and narrow, there were no barriers. Ten breaths from summit, a lumbering troll appeared, a long club held out in front, swinging left to right. Full beam headlights shone, and it came down fast. We halted, a span of single hand from precipice that fell away to charred ground. The car began to scream, one alarm then all. The truck and construction crane drew up beside and stopped. It could turn and nudge, clear the way.

It roared to life, scraped past and was away, growing smaller in the mirror. The alarms ceased and silence fell.

At the summit were snowfields strewn with blackened stone, and beyond was a green valley and blue water far below. A gyrfalcon rose by the roadside, turned to stare and with stiff wing-beats was gone. The clouds seemed brighter as they raced across the sky, and that night in Thingeyri wind buffeted at the windows, and we turned up the radiator despite the summer light.

White horses were racing up the fjord, the clouds grey-white on cinder-black. No boat left the port, no fishermen drew up to load their empty crates. Nearby was the local Thing, grassy mounds by the wooden church where Gisli and friends made a pledge that later was betrayed. At Haukadalur was a French monument, even though France had toyed with a plan of building here an army base. The white walls were inscribed, *always lost at sea*. Ahead was the very farm, the hay meadows and fence lines that had stood for eleven hundred years since Gisli farmed this vale. Gisli had worked day and night and the fire room of the farm, the extended baðstufa, was 70 ells long and 40 wide, the floor covered with soft rushes.

It was here that Gisli crafted cargo vessels, a man of many talents, said the saga. In the farm were held great feasts. One winter, a storm hit the house and took off all the roofing from one side, and rain poured in. In the autumn, when the moon shone, there were games in front of great crowds by the mere, wrestling one-on-one, horses racing, ball sports played in teams. All Gisli's guests were bestowed with gifts. Yet others craved his success. It was the death of Thorgrim, Gisli's brother-in-law, that caused Bork to summon Gisli to the Thorsnes assembly. He could go and be outnumbered; he could refuse and live out-of-law.

And so thirteen years as outlaw lay before him. This was the core of Gisli's saga, how fate gives us at times a choice that is not a choice.

The morning fog was dense. There was neither shore nor cliff.

The boat edged out of Ísafjörður's harbour, where many a trawler has safely docked in Arctic storm. In these waters, three British trawlers were lost in '68, Hull's triple trawler drowning, and the crew of the *Notts County* rescued. This was the very spot, where crowds of giddy citizens gathered to watch a single English sailor carried ashore, the stretcher tipped to one side then the other, three days after the *Ross Cleveland* had gone down. It was also where the *Notts County* crew had stumbled ashen and icy, yet formed a guard of honour to clap ashore the crew of *Oðinn*. The Iceland life-saving service said there had never been such force of wind, and Þórður Jónsson, still at his farm on Látrabjarg, called coastguards to say farm vehicles had been overturned, their farm doors quite impossible to open. This was a country where you might smile indulgently, the car hire booth saying always park to face the wind.

A mist-bow appeared off to starboard, a Bifrost bridge set out by gods. From the blue water, it curved out and in, and now the sun began to burn the fog, a spreading blaze of light.

Patches of Midgard sky broke through, and there were puffins circling on the glass of sea. There was a hint of colour on the bow, and now the sky was cobalt blue. Tube-nosed fulmars glided round the boat. Crags were vertical and a sunway shone on sea, the light sparkling in the boat. The boat sped fast, for Ægir had cancelled swell and wind, and a white wake of froth raced at stern. Between two table-mountains was the lush green bay of Adalvik. The white wooden summer huts of Sæbol, roofs red or green, were scattered cross the bay. The engine stopped and a dead quiet followed.

The rib puttered ashore, and we vaulted onto black sand beach. This light, this place, far above the known world, perhaps this was a part of Asgard. A whisper of breeze invited us in. It seemed, on this pure land, that the world had somehow been rerooftd. There was a ringing silence, over stands of lyme grass and tall acid alexander.

The path was up from Adalvik, fishing village facing west to Greenland, over the pass and down the old way to Hesteyri, the last settled village on this land. This was the wild land we get when the people and their grazing animals go away. Half a thousand bibionid flies descended, twisting and swarming round our hands and faces. Later in the meadows, I stood on a nest of wild bees. One stung me on the jaw, in this tranquil land. There were no sheep on all six hundred square leagues of Hornstrandir. There were close to one hundred species of flowering plant that day, it was a paradise for orchids, yellow stands of buttercup and mauve cranesbiil, white hemlock gently shivering. There were the haunting calls of whooper swans from a lake below the church. A layer of fog lay across the plain. The Stadarkirkja church had been freshly painted, red tin roof and white wood walls. Outside were polished gravestones, one for a fisherman out of Patreksfjörður.

Sunbeams shone inside on white pews curved in semi-circles. The only sound was the humming of the insects.

High upon the pass was a tall cairn, and a view far below to salty sea. The headlands overlapped into fading distance, and beyond the rock pavement the fjords were filled again with cloud. We were looking over to the Drangajökull glacier and all its regional power, cool air locking in the mist. In those hidden waters was the stranded hull of *Notts County*. Here the Hornstrandir slopes were white with *fifa* cotton-grass, each said to be a child's soul, at home woven into wicks for household lamps that burned the oil of seal and shark. The landscape was webbed with ponds the colour of sky, with hidden ditches under flower meadows. There were white moths, and the feathers of eaten birds, large mushrooms on the slopes of sundew.

It was eight kilometres from the Arctic Circle, and there were mountains hidden in the mountains.

Down at shoreside, the sea was still. An Arctic fox rounded the rocks, and foraged in the mounds of kelp. It ran low to the ground, its tail was brushed with frost, and it trotted south. We walked north to the doctor's home at Heysteyri. On a line, clothes snapped in the afternoon breeze, and we drank tea on the wooden veranda. At any time on such a land may be heard the tinkling bells of distant church, as if underground or from the sea, and people may be seen riding in coloured clothing, stopping at an old farmyard expecting to ask for buttermilk. But the elves had been abandoned too, even as they walked to church inside the rock. Two whaling stations lay distant on the bay, long closed, their buildings in the past used for aerial firing practice.

A fulmar flew silent as a moth. What did the bird know that we did not, on this wild and untouched land? Still the blazing polar sun shone brightly.

Last week, said Kath our guide on this deserted strand, she drove five hundred leagues with all the family, all the way to Akureyri, just to catch the sun. The campsite was full, yet nothing was missing.

Iceland poet Kristín Svava Tómasdóttir has written:

> Dolphins jump in the bay,
> The sun is shining,
> Nothing is missing.
>
> It is so warm. There is no way to wear black.
> There's no way to stay inside half-lit houses.
>
> The sea is blue.
> The sun is shining.
> Nothing is missing.

['Austurvöllur on the Day of the Wake', 2018]

The feast had finished, the harbour water somewhat calm. The open-decked oak trawler *Láki* plunged east. It was cast up high and raced down iron wave, then simply ploughed ahead. We were in the sky, then down so low. A sleet of cold froth poured over the prow, white and radiant. To the north, there were dark clouds over the Westfjords. The sea was black, metallic blue and green, slate and slushy brown. The wind tore away the water, and still the search continued. Our eyes were pinned, legs bent, absorbing each shuddered thump. The eyes of captain and his crew were roaming. The shore was sheer cliff and long waterfall on the thin strip between the sea and sky.

People pointed, for a line of blue had appeared. It advanced across the sky, and all the clouds cleared. Now green bubbles from the boat crushed outwards. The ship paused, wallowed and yawed, and the captain said on the Tannoy, 'At eleven o'clock.'

A sperm whale blew, and a rainbow formed in air above the long brown body lying in the water. Snæfellsjökull shone beyond this beast of 50 tonnes. The whale arched, and dived, and the tail fluke rose and cut into the water, the deepest diving mammal in all the seas. There came another, in the glittering light, it wallowed and huffed, tipped its fluke. Now many a whaler sang shanties about these kinds of fish, they thought them fierce and savage to the seafarers, great jaws ready to snap around a boat, leaping from the sea to fall with fiery splash.

Yet the polar light sang on the sea, a forge of glittering fire, a magnesium surface burning bright. The bow wave rolled outwards and white droplets, fell back to green again. The whales, it seemed, had the power to gift us sun. How to find the good times, many a saga might ask, what became of that fine horse. How would you describe a sea to someone who'd only ever held a glass of water? Someone, say, born in a desert. It is a hundred colours, black to silver and metal sheen, fiery and foam. It is mountain of solid water, cliff and crag and no safe path, it is evanescence into light and smoke. It is a bird that flies and floats, fulmar on a locked wing, puffin circling on the surface. It is frightful waves that are only chop from far. It is remains of trawler dashed on rock, rusted pieces scattered on the pebble pearls. No amount of gold, it seems, could ever save a sea-wearied crew. It is the polar light upon this sea. It is the sun that stumbles, and comes to fade as shadows travel north.

We came gently to the harbour, the song of the sea had ceased. This Midgard world came close to saying, goodbye to every whale. Whale watching began a generation back at Húsavik, the former herring port. Now many thousand people walk up the gangways, bringing each year more income than the whale ever did as food. This day all were wind-beaten, wet and lifted up, salty by this polar shore.

Only death will dry your feet, the old folk said. The whales had come, where in later months it will be dark and hope encircled. Birds will have flown, and fishermen will lean on harbour walls to talk. That day the sun hung in sky, when the wealth of world seemed wasted.

The mead halls had begun to crumble, and it seemed one day the skyscraped works might soon be standing idle.

CROSSINGS

The first saga happens at the north and west Iceland, in the mid-900s. Ingimund sails from Norway, builds a temple and is a wise leader. They give names to places, and the clan grows. But harsh Hrolleif and his wife Kör become a menace, and are banished to the isles of Flatey. Skaði is the daughter of Ingimund's son Egil, and becomes a fine swimmer and rescuer from wrecks. But more clashes come, and Skaði's mother fights a night battle with Kör. Both disappear, and Skaði casts a spell to bind the troll-son. She walks over the mountains to the Althing. At the plain, flags snap and a herald blows his horn. The throng opens up for this single curer girl, and she takes her place at the booth of her mother.

At a Norse king's banquet, three Lapp shamans,
Had predicted the fortune, of each man present in the hall,
One said to Ingimund, he would settle on a fiery isle,
Live to great age, and sure enough he tried each way,
To remain beside the king, yet it was impossible,
To fly from fate's decree, so he sailed for Iceland,
And raised with Vigdis, four tall girls and a boy called Egil,
They named the valley Vididal, it was overrun with willows.

Ingimund raised a temple, one hundred strides in length,
On the river's western bank, and sure enough they found,
As the shamans had foretold, a silver amulet of Freyr,
And in the tenth autumn, walking out on frozen floes,
At the river mouth, he found a dead white bear,
With her crying cubs, which the girls now raised,
And when some pigs went missing, they later came upon a wild herd,
So they named the nearby pool, the swine's lake Svinavatn.

Yet even in those early years, there was insufficient wood,
To build another hall, and so he sailed,
The sea roads back to Norway, the white bears in the hold,
As gifts for the old king, who offered him the ship,
Named *Stigandi* High Stepper, designed to race upwind,
Ingimund filled the hold with timber, plank and stave already cut,
And when he made landfall, where the ship was beached,
To this day at Vatnsdal, this place is called Stigandi's Shed.

So stages passed, and the clan of Ingimund grew settled,
The livestock fed themselves in winter, there were fish,
In nearby lakes and river, and the settlers felt entirely free,
From the attacks, of criminal and king,
In summer it had seemed, there were cloudless days,
And Ingimund and children, daily helped the valley farmers,
He was wise and voted speaker, at the Hunavatn assembly,
Yet now came the family settler Hrolleif, to break their hearts in half.

Hrolleif had broken teeth, a red scar cross his hairline,
He seemed to have a heavy foot, was yet nimble with a sword,
With his compact brother Thorolf, they claimed the upper slope,
And it soon was clear, Hrolleif was harsh,
He wore a wine-red cloak, and he walked through other farms,
As if he owned them, calling insults at the daughters,
The valley people soon suspected, there must be robbers,
On the pass, for no one came back safely.

And as the sense of menace spread, Ingimund's younger brother Odd,
And three fellow farmers, were found bleeding by the river,
So Hrolleif and Kör his wife were outlawed, fleeing west to isles in fjord,

Ingimund by then was almost blind, attended by his youngest daughter,
Who guided him on horseback, steered him in the farmhouse,
And when he died, he was burned in a longship,
Built from timbers of *Stigandi*, and the news toured far,
So the valley farmers felt, this was an honour for them all.

On Flatey lived the girl called Skaði, it was a windswept isle,
A ferry-stop in Breiðafjördur, where much later would be built,
A library on the hill, from imported timber,
To house an illustrated book, of sagas of those isles,
Her mother's name was Fenja, she had countless skills,
She could heal the ills, dispatch disease and sores,
Egil was her husband, the son of Ingimund,
He had become, a goði of the nearest Thing.

Skaði had been water-sprinkled, when she was named,
And from an early age, she had lovely eyes,
A fair complexion, hair more shiny than a silken scarf,
She walked the land, learning of the lives,
Of plant and bird, and Fenja taught her skills,
How each leaf and flower, should be ground or mixed,
How to treat the ill, and everywhere she walked,
On her arm was a wicker basket, separated into sections.

Skaði would live to elder's age, and it would be said,
Even though she lost her sight, she had turned most noble,
And extended lives, of so many settlers and their children,
Yet all the while, new farmers had been laying out,
Tún meadows by each house, gathering stone for sheepfold,
They needed labour, and so evolved the use of slaves,
Brought by traders, who raised on shore their tented camps,
In which men and women sat silently, each trader holding scales for silver.

Skaði was a skilful swimmer, living by the shore,
As were many men who carried oars, who rowed for pay,
On great ships that slipped, between the rolling waves,
At their isle and distant kingdoms, of Denmark and the Norse,
She won countless challenges, when many a man,
Would push her underwater, and hold her there,

And then she'd press them down, stronger than their struggles,
Till bubbles ceased appearing, and then she let them free.

If any ship was wrecked, on the skerries round the isle,
Then their laws on strandings, dictated all belonged to nearest farmer,
Once a ship approached, struggling in a storm,
And all on board had thrown away, everything to keep them light,
Yet a giant breaker rose, where no one could recall,
Having seen the rocks, and rammed the ship,
It capsized all at once, smashing planks to pieces,
Skaði swam in wreckage, three times she towed a man ashore.

Yet no one dared ignore, the news of Hrolleif's deeds,
And when the wicked Kör, was seen walking,
Backwards in the gloom, the people warned their shepherds,
Watch the sheep, this said they also counted,
Twenty cats at the house of Hrolleif, each fortified by magic spells,
So neighbours could not check, why possessions often vanished,
It was well known, that all wyrms are enticed to treasure,
Yet still Hrolleif seemed to draw, more gold and goods to him.

Hrolleif had built his fire-hall, longer than any settler,
Had ever seen before, and on the wood of gables,
And in the rafters, ornamental tales were carved,
So well crafted, many thought them better than a tapestry,
And the son of Hrolleif and Kör, the unruly boy,
Who grew wide as well as tall, who could swing a sword,
And sling stones with precision, Slídr he was called,
Now the local people feared, their worlds would overturn.

One dusk a shepherd boy, saw a force in dark tunics,
With no slowing pace they rode, past his shieling,
One with saddle brightly coloured, another on a gilded horse,
Outlaws and robbers were by now, much in evidence,
And so here on Flatey, no man with axe or pike,
Could find a way to challenge, the men at Hrolleif's farm,
So they turned to Fenja, pleaded that she call on elves,
To cleanse their isle, to rid them of this tribe of trouble.

Egil had a fearless herd, horses bred with coloured manes,
And one late day in spring, when a thick fall of snow,
Had covered fields and fell, he and Skaði voyaged,
Across the isle, and were stranded at a farm,
As the storm resumed, and blizzard and severest wind,
Prevented anyone it seemed, for many days from travel,
And now Fenja was left alone, to fight one night the evil Kör,
Local shepherds were disturbed, by thunder crashes from the hall.

When the storm had cleared, the people found,
There had been a rock fall, from the nearby cliff,
It fell on Hrolleif's hall, they searched and found no bodies,
And at Egil's house, their shepherds also found,
The badstufa silent, the fire cold in grate,
Fenja too had vanished, yet not all had died,
For they found the hulking Slídr, stunned upon the shore,
So bound his hands and feet, and dragged him on the cloak.

Some summers long before, the goðar farmers met,
To build a platform, a special place to forge agreement,
It was a mighty Althing, at Thingvellir where earthen plates,
Ground and fought by basalt columns, from one horizon to another,
There was plain and lake, feed aplenty for the horses,
And in the open air, the goðar came each June,
All equal to each other, they sang and set the laws,
Swapped sheep and corn, it was their common court for ruling.

So Skaði and her father, took the son,
On the ferry south to Thorsnes, and she prepared the trip,
They retied his hands, with strips of leather,
But had he wished, he could not run,
Nor escape his captor, for Skaði's spell,
Had fixed a leash, invisible to all,
On Flatey at the crumpled hall, she had recently released,
All the cats from bonds, and they had fled into the fields.

Egil was bent though not yet broken, so he spoke again to Skaði,
'Take him to the law rock, bind him with more spells,
You will find, a hundred flags are flying,
On the plain, beneath the rocky row of pillars,
Our childhood days, are filled with wonder,
As the world unfolds itself, to our waiting empty mind,
So take these polished pebbles, they will slow you down,
Leave each at a chosen site, and cairns will build with time.'

Egil stood aside, looked once more into her eyes,
She was wearing pleated shift, apron clasped by bronze-owl brooch,
Around her neck, an amber pendant from the eastern sea,

Her hair was knotted, now she would do the healing,
So Skaði took the blackest stick, pulled from raven's nest,
One that flowed upriver, and she cast another spell,
And Egil tightened troll-man's hands, the killer could not struggle
The men of stone awaited, by the ferryboat to hell.

The sun was hot, yet shadows served another season,
Hare's tail bobbed on cotton meadows, banked at ponds of sky,
At bilberry slope a whimbrel burbled, the goggled plover,
Sang insistent warnings, snow lay on the taller ridges,
She whistled out a call, a gloss black raven cawed,
And perched upon her shoulder, in her basket,
She had stowed her potions, in her mind she held more spells,
Now they bent their steps, past sulphured banks of bedstraw.

The polar light was brilliant blue, water glistening over riffles,
At the pass it still was summer, the bee-ship towns were bright,
From a cliff a fan of shale, spread a thousand steps below,
It was the month for cutting hay, and distant men and women,
Swung their scythes, singing to the vernal grass,
Every farmer aided every neighbour, as wind and rain awaited,
They hurried now in sunshine, it could be winter in an hour,
Yet Skaði knew this troll, had never helped with hay at any time.

He shouted at her, called for help from beast and troll,
Threatened they would kill her, so she detached his power of speech,
As we all have heard, Skaði had learned her mother's magic,
She plucked the purple butterwort, these for treating lice and sores,
Into bag went campion and gentian, dancing blue of harebell,
For healing skin was bedstraw bunch, lady's mantle for an ulcer,
She stripped the bark from willow, it would numb most pain,
And walked on over mossy meadow, her feet were sodden now.

They crossed a plain of steam, heated water gushing into sky,
And stood upon a rocky hill, ahead was the plain of snapping flags,
At booths of stone and turf, were waiting goðar and their thingmen,
On stokks of wood, cod dried in polar wind,
A herald blew his horn, the lowing echoed,
Off the rocks, rolled across the flats,

Even eagles flew to eyries, perched and looked below,
To see the throng was opening up, for this single girl.

She knew the path, their plot was by the Lögberg Rock,
Where the Lawspeaker would be calling, from memory one third of laws,
At the Althing, to succeed you needed charm,
Skill with words to manage feuds, this she had inherited,
Her tent was pitched, before the colour riot,
Yet servants bowed their heads, for in former years,
Here had stood Fenja, helping each in queue,
Skaði stepped inside, looked around and clapped her hands.

The men and women cheered, called out Skaði's name,
She was keeper of the magic apple, spoke to Oðinn's dark seagull,
The flags on spears were wind-fed, in those warriors' hands,
Swords were thumped on shields, they pointed to their ill,
She smiled and nodded, soon would walk from booth to booth,
She would leave to them the task, justice for the killer of her mother,
Who was fixed to a post, the roped man's final crossing made,
Now would start a saga, of celebrated curer Skaði.

SAGA II

SETTLEMENT

This saga happens centuries later at a north Iceland farm of stone and turf, in the early decades of the twentieth century. The shepherd lad called An always had wet feet, and had lost his mother and sister to illness, so was fostered. The sons of Magnus the farmer had also died of drowning and the fever. They travel by horse to the new town of Akureyri for supplies, past falls and boiling pools. The farmers had set up a co operative, and a steamship is being loaded with herring in barrels. They meet the skipper, the nephew of a famous author who had stayed at the farm when Magnus was small. An comes to be trained as a doctor in Copenhagen, inherits the farm, stitches the wounds of English trawlermen, and stands in the great crowd at Thing-vellir on the day of national independence.

His feet were soaked, this shepherd lad called An,
He clicked his teeth, trampled over tussocks,
The sheep ceased grazing, and lambs looped out in line,
By a lake aged with sky, a white tern lanced the shallows,
In his pocket was a book, a gift from distant fishers,
Ahead in a hollow was the farm, long and low inside the ground,
And beyond the smoky lava field, at a sheer cliff sprinkled white,
Side by side in a grassy mound, lay his mother and his twin.

'Only when you're dead, will your feet be dry,'
Long ago his mother whispered, yet she had to sell him,
And for every slave, their friends were mainly lambs,
His teeth were black, yet his book had bursting tales,
Of warmer worlds, with wooden house and lamp-lit street,
Children daily at a school, allowed to sing and laugh,
He longed to leave, dark for him might mean at best,
Rímur tune and saga song, a board set out with tafl pieces.

An the black gazed from the gate, again across the plain,
His mother had told how this coast, was filled with Lakí ash,
How sand was shifted by the polar sea, how they hauled,
From far below on anchored sailing ship, the hawser tense,
Pulled up coffee sack and flour, barley bag and sugar,
How one drenching day, fulmars sliding through the cloud,
The cable tore, lashed a hundred metal metres,
It killed her winchman brother, and horses clattered far.

An crossed the rippled sward, came inside by cattle byre,
The floor was bare, fretted flagstone set on soil,
The walls were dusty turf, braced with salvaged timber,
He chose a ladle, took the wooden lid from churn,
Set an alum kettle on the range, lifted from the wall,
A limb of lamb, dried maroon and marbled fat,
He spooned out curdled skyr, sunbeams shone through glass,
Up the narrow stairs, were four cribs crammed together.

The wind whistled, the dark turf walls were warm,
Yet in the sooty shadows, many ghosts were skulking,
For this very farm had featured, in sagas from the Landnámabók,
Farmer Magnus had also suffered loss, his older lad had died of fever,
The younger boy drowned off the beach, there in sight of sand,
One lay in a mound, beneath a bee-ship town,
The other down amidst the cod, caught fast by Ægir's mesh,
Their mother Anda murmured, we the sea has robbed of much.

In years long past, when Magnus still was young,
A wanderer and traveller, was welcomed to their farm,
His father was a Rímur singer, the reason why this man Sabine,
A young song collector, had asked to stay and listen,
For soon he would compose, a tale at swampy creek,
Set on England's eastern shore, how the lass Mehalah,
Was deserted by untimely deaths, and when he sent his book,
By boat and post for Magnus, then An was first to read it.

The tale to him was strange, 'an extensive marshy tract,
Veined and freckled in each part, with rents and patches,
Of shining water, dappled in all directions.'
It was written, a land more desolate,
Could scarcely be conceived, this caused An to smile,
He read of thrift that mantled marsh, how stands of aster,
Fringed those living swamps, how countless waterfowl,
And flocks of sheep, grazed beside the curlew of the fleets.

He read about her shack, built of tar and wreckage,
Roofed with pantile, twisted thorn that offered shelter,
From the cold sea wind, and how the cruel landlord,
Demanded rent from them, while her aged mother,
Shivered with the ague, and how the girl Mehalah,
Wore a knitted jersey, taken from the body of a sailor,
This was a world and saga, that An could recognise,
Yet it seemed all filled with gear, so different to his own.

At his English school, Sabine the teacher had learned Icelandic,
Enough to translate epics, into living tales for students,
So he wished to seek the scenes, depicted in the stories,
To fill a folio, with water-coloured drafts,
He rode past skogar forest, ate fish and lichen,
Poached in milk, yet had he come some years before,
He might have taken, alive or dead a great auk bird,
And received the museum prize, of a hundred silver pounds.

He wrote of fair-haired children, their bright eyes blue and grey,
How some people, even spoke to him in Latin,
How at the farm of Magnus, the ceilings were too low to stand,
How set in walls of turf, were tiny panes of glass,
The floors were partly boarded, on the trampled earth,
How they sat by fire, and talked of tales and sagas,
How he slept with family, all climbing up the ladder,
Where in pairs for warmth, they shared each wooden bed.

The English teacher, had travelled next to Akureyri,
This the northern capital, fetched deep in Eyjafjörður,
An inlet forty leagues in length, wide at entry to the Arctic Sea,
And so one day An and Magnus, pushed at the outer door,
Led three hardy horses, over slatey stone,
And Anda simply stood, watched them growing small,
She would wait, for the sound of hooves,
For clogs and sack of fish, for the taste of town at harbour-side.

Farmer Magnus and the boy, rode past falls of roaring water,
There were few crossings, in this lava land of canyons,
They paced by boiling pools, of opalescent green,
From jagged rock poured smoke, the land forged far below,
At Mývatn they cantered, for the sky was darkened by mosquitoes,
By dawn they climbed the pass, gazing down to bright blue fjord,
And there at anchor was a metal vessel, smoke drifting from its funnel,
It had steamed from far, to load the silver treasure from the sea.

They were staring at success, for ten years past,
Magnus and the fellow goðar farmers, had fixed a new cooperative,
A place for trading fish, and opened up a simple merchant store,
Set among the wooden shanties, each with glass in windows,
Out on fjord were herring smacks, additions to the fleet,
And many circling sixæreen, green and blue with gunwale stripes,
On the far side, a hot spring splattered into salty sound,
He wished to look his best, so Magnus switched his horse.

By the steamship, were a thousand herring casks,
And rows of gutting girls, filling kegs with fish and salt,
Herring once was food for poor, for horse when hay was short,
Now the town was trading, such headway for this treeless land,
Magnus soon will drink a brennivín, and talk of noble plan,
How to green their Akureyri, how to make a garden city,
How to raise again, Yggdrasil to link the land to sky,
He tied the leather reins to rail, left An to listen to the laughter.

Inside the noisy shop, mud and slush upon the floor,
The farmer-fishers were drinking beer, to celebrate the ship,
'Come and look,' waved cousin Lars by wooden counter,
'American shoes that bend, and spring to shape,
Dry feet will be our future way,' so Magnus paid for clogs,
And dipped a little deeper, for three pairs of rubber boots,
So the farmers ate fish soup, shared the smoky flatbread,
And all sat back and smiled, outside they saw the children skipping.

Yet it always happened, the men turned to talk,
Of drink and death, in storm and distant from the land,
Deep in bone and gut they knew, was recollection of a father,
Of a son, the little hearts that laughed,
The hands that tickled children, so sorrow leaked through turf,
On walls were placed a single lamp, and after silent days,
They would find the wood for coffins, speak fine oration for the lost,
Whether bodies washed ashore, were theirs or distant sailors.

An now assembled, all the blinkered horses,
For the farmers raced, out to furthest house and back,
Along the dock, voices bursting in the sun,
Past shoreside meadow, the drying hay in stacks,
To a church that stood alone, inside its walls were heaven-blue,
The men recovered hats, took another drink,
And strolled across to check, the barrels with their stamp,
Herring for the Baltic ports, to them the silver in return.

There came a cry in English, a short man from the bridge,
Of this sleek trading ship, he shouted greetings,
'Come aboard and bring your friends, see how the furnace works,'
Magnus turned to An, 'that is the nephew,
Of your favourite author,' so they walked aboard the metal ship,
And smelled the barrels stacked below, the sweating scent of coal,
And when Magnus rode home with An, they were wearing rubber boots,
And Anda soon became, the toast of all her friends.

In those bright fresh days, of the newest century,
There were so many fish, taken from the sea,
So Iceland declared home rule, shook off more shackles,
And in the decade after Fourteen War, before his illness,
Magnus sponsored An, so he sailed to Copenhagen,
Where he packed in years of training, and took his place,
As doctor on return, and by then An's hair was mostly grey,
And the farm and sheep, had been left to him in legacy.

Yet An decided, he would rent out the farm,
And take a post on Flatey, the very isle,
Where would dock a Grimsby trawler, and An would stitch,
The ripped fingers of a deckhand, and from this isle,
His daughter Ólíni then would travel, north to nurse in Ísafjörður,
She was an English speaker, so worked in harbour hospital,
For she had sat upon his shoulders, in the smiling crowd,
At Thingvellir in ceaseless rain, on their day of independence.

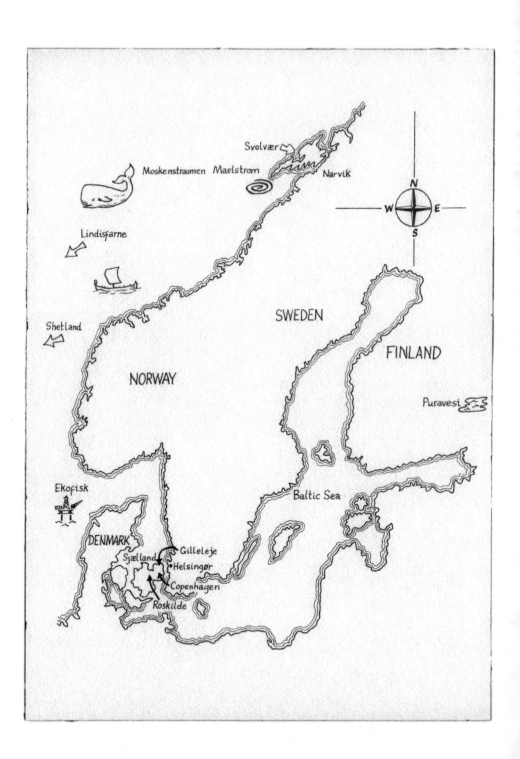

CHAPTER TWO

THE SJÆLLAND GATE AND LOFOTEN ISLES

Roskilde ship museum, Denmark

Over the waves, with the wind behind her,
And foam at the neck, she flew like a bird,
Those seafarers sighted land, sunlit cliffs and sheer crags,
And looming headlands, the landfall they sought.

[*Beowulf*, transl. Seamus Heaney, c700–1000]

The longship had been tacking, and now heeled towards the shore.

The square sail filled, the hemp ropes straining on the blocks. The clinkered hull cut across the shallow sea.

Ahead now on the skyline were two towers, the Domkirke cathedral on the hill. The ship raced south. The sun shone and the sea glittered, the clinkered planks creaked. Gulls cried, and there were other sail-steeds on the sound.

For two million tides, ships such as these have sliced through seas, propelling once the empire of the Vikings. The whispered breeze invited settling deep, and in days gone by a coastguard would have been watching, wondering what this ship was bringing.

Once this kind of hull would have been stacked with war gear, axe and sword, a dragon painted on each linden shield. Now ahead was a low land, no part of Denmark higher than three hundred ells. The supreme invention had been vessels with overlapping planks, made watertight with moss and wax of bees, ships that strode so fast. These did not rise and plunge, and in the hull were rounded stones of ballast granite. On the longest ships, the bow and stern flexed a yard sideways, the ship shifting energy from the sea to forward movement. There was no keel, the crew moved from side to side. Long ago at Roskilde there once had been a chief's hall, a long-house placed just so, its two tall chimneys when aligned pointing to the safe lane into harbour.

At that time, too, protective barriers had been built across the fjord, wooden piles and chains, a single place where inward ships could dock and pass across their goods. It was a healthy country, there would have been smoke from many fires clinging to the hills.

These days the fjord banks of Sjælland were thirsty fields and stands of ancient oak. This was no isle of sheep and shieling. It was patched with golden corn and dappled grove, with heath and airy birch of satin bark. On a mound was a copse of pine, the kind of place where longships were entombed and dead kings laid on fur and finest thread, a sword in hand, a shield laid beside. There could have been gold interred, and from the fjord below sailors would have looked up and steered a little nearer, their sails stiffened by the breeze. The wanderers would point, for the outcrop shrine would have been named after the buried man.

All around the circled northern sea are such mounds, some marked with stone in oval shapes of ships. West across the brine and up one estuary, not as wide as this, was found the longship of Sutton Hoo, half a league uphill and laid in one of twenty mounds. The king's hinged helm of tinned bronze, a dragon stitched across each brow, was such a find, such a golden Saxon burial, that many felt he must have been as famed as Beowulf, the Geat warrior-king himself.

All that longing, it seemed a struggle for silver and more gold, only to lay it back in soil. All that digging, the rush to rivers and to mines, and today the modern banks send it back to storage underground. A thousand Viking hoards of silver have been found across the lands of the Norse, all fetched from other countries across the gannet's bath. It was a chore, caring dragons tried to keep them hidden, protecting people from themselves. Now the canvas sail stitched in strips was hauled down, and the varnished boom laid on top.

The skipper smiled, 'Oars up,' she said. Painters out, and rattle of pine in oarlock rope. A girl and small boy sat on the harbour wall, watching from the shore. Silence, then dip and splash, and creak and splash again, and the ship glided into port. The breeze dropped and the air on land was hot.

Some leagues south and west of here, this an isle of white sand and beach hut, myth-tale castle and seaside resort, a short march away was Heorot, once the court at modern Gammel Lejre.

And in these low-lying lands of Sjælland was many a mere and marsh, perfect lair for troll and ogre, the underwater rocks of wilderness, a home for every kind of harrower. At olden Lejre, dy-nastic home of the Scefings and the Sjoldungs, the people of the shield and sheaf, were folk-halls fifty paces long, outbuildings for craft and prayer, the rich burial mound of Grydehøj.

In the Heorot hall would have stood a huge tree with branches and blossom growing through the roof. Clouds could form in the rafters. The hall had tiered side-benches where people sat and slept, facing cross the fire-stones. There would have been huge treasure chests. The roof was shingled, and there were covered walkways under eaves. In the soil has been found a silver Oðinn, the god on a throne with his ravens either side, gold rings and bars, and a single feathered-wing of eagle. A stone ship long ago was shaped on turf by standing sarsens, nearly two hundred ells in length, and fully fifty graves were laid inside.

At this very place ruled Hrothgar and Hrolf Kraki, the most magnificent of kings of ancient times, and here too came the bear-men, the bee-wolfs, named Beowulf and Baldar Bjarki.

At the Roskilde shipyard were men and women with magic in their fingers, fitting perfect mortice joints, smelting iron for nails. They were constructing longships, as did the Danes in ages past. In the modernist museum of shuttered concrete, the sea slapping at the base of windowed wall, were the five Skuldelev ships, propped above a floor of stones. The wood was bog-black. There were sweeping lines from stern to prow, on one of which was placed a golden dragon's head. These were found twenty leagues north, raised from mud fifty years ago. They had been sunk as defensive barrier to prevent attacks from sea.

This may have been an act of desperation, or perhaps of love and respect, for such a longship could take a year to build.

One was a cargo vessel, built from planks of pine in western Norway, later patched with oak and linden lime. *Skuldelev 3* was the many-splendoured ship, constructed here in Denmark for short trips in local waters, through the sound to Baltic. *Skuldelev 2* was oak-made, a seagoing warship thirty metres long and built at Dublin. It could carry sixty rowing crew, and was blueprint for a modern replica, the *Sea Stallion*, that sailed up Roskilde fjord, out through Kattegat and into salty North Sea, south and round to Ireland.

A thousand years of silence seemed wrapped around each ship.

Those shipwrights took forest trees to spread an empire from the Arctic to Kiev. They worked ash and oak for plank, birch for joint and beech for longest keelson. The mast was made from pine, or fir if true trunks could be found. Rope was bonded up from hemp and linden bast, shrinking when wet on board. For shroud and sheet, for brace and backstay, horsehair and walrus hide. They carved peg from willow wood, splashed pine tar on every plank. Those famed shipwrights wore brooch with gripping beasts, each axe and adze was clear of rust. Those horses-of-the-sea, they galloped through the waves. From this very place, the mouth of Roskilde fjord opening into narrow Øresund, longships surged out to salt, a drummer thumping, and each trading ship came about, yielding tax for passage.

And so this narrow Øresund fed the Danish treasury for centuries. It linked the Baltic Sea and ports of fertile plains of central Europe to North Sea and the western markets. The Sound Dues had an elegant rule. The king could choose to buy the cargo at the value stated by a captain, discouraging him from going low to minimise the tax. Long after the Vikings had settled into other countries, those Dane and Norse and Swede taking on their lands and language, the Danish empire had been great. In 1380, all of Denmark and Norway had been merged, much of modern Sweden too. The North Atlantic empire was the crown for Greenland, Iceland, Faroes and the isles of Shetland and the Orkneys. It later took on trading posts in West Africa and India.

Then came defeat, to Sweden in the Kalmar War shortly after *Hamlet* had been written, to Britain after choosing France as ally in Napoleonic wars, to Germany for the most humiliating of all, the loss of Schleswig-Holstein.

It is also said, Denmark has adjusted well.

It was large and now was small. It did not mourn for empire losses, so much, for it looked inward. They form a club, it is said of Danes to solve a problem without involvement of the courts of kings. There emerged thousands of cooperative dairies and farms, cooperative purchasing societies, health insurance groups, the folk high school movement for young adults to encourage self-awareness. And lately the commons of universal welfare for the old and young, and a solidarity of togetherness for all.

Skiðblaðnir was the fastest ship in Asgard, built by the finest craft:

> *A good wind blows whenever the sail is raised,*
> *No matter where it is headed.*

[Snorri Sturluson, *The Prose Edda*, 1179–1241]

The train hissed toward the island capital.

Copenhagen grew great on the Sound Dues, yet it is rare for a national capital to end up at country's border.

It was fiery, the hottest spell for Copenhagen since the 1920s. Were the Norse gods pulling strings, were they still diverting arrows with a buckle? Who was in control, we might wonder. The city had become in recent years geared to outdoors, to activity and well-being. More people cycle than in other cities, it is easy to walk, there is clean water in the harbour. And along each dockside were crowds of people. A single white cloud was in the sky. There was laughter. Art galleries had emptied, the indoor zones of cafés too. There were outdoor yoga groups, dancers round a music box, groups on the water with sail and kayak, and others leaping from the dockside. No one had felt the like of such city heat before. This was in the days, remember, when you could just travel on a whim, and walk freely through a throng milling in a city. There was clamour, and people did not have to choke on dust.

This was not by wyrd, nor by fate. There had been concerted effort.

Harbour baths were designated and opened all days and hours, free to all, at Brygge and Feskertorvet, and sand laid out for beaches. At the same time, the greened city around the clean harbour had grown in reputation. More than half of commuters cycled to work and school, in those days before the pandemic shifted city life. Many others walked. Again, this was no slip-up. White crosses had been painted on the streets where cyclists had been killed by cars, then cycle routes constructed and more curbs placed on motor vehicles. This rapid growth in cycling happened fast, just in twenty years. Other cities still consider the car as far too important. Yet take away the noise and air pollution, keep the spaces green and blue, ensure it is accessible to all, and cities soon can change their character. They can help, it seems, bring better health for all.

This active life of the capital has coincided with a revival of an older word suggesting choices about how we might live. The Danish term is *hygge*, related to the good life.

It suggests contentment and well-being, a life with meaning and a sense of purpose, a life good for us as individuals as well as for others, and implying doing good through trust, reciprocity and obligations for people and nature. It is seen as a key component of happiness. The good life has analogies in Bolivia, Ecuador and Colombia as *buen vivir*, in Japan as *ikigai*, in China as *haoshenghuo*, *kalyankari jeevan* in Hindi and Sanskrit, in Spain and France as *felicidad* and *bonheur*, in Netherlands and Norway as *het goede leven* and *koselig*, and in Germany as *Gemütlichkeit* and *das gute Leben*. It refers to how we might feel at particular moments, eating together or cosy by the fire for *hygge*, and across a whole lifetime guided by a spiritual framework such as *ikigai*.

It is now well established that the growth in Gross Domestic Product, the golden child of economists for far too long, their measure of vigour and country-triumph, matches poorly with average life satisfaction and happiness.

Over the past fifty years, GDP per person has tripled in Denmark, in the UK and USA too. Each person now has on average three times more stuff than their grandparents. But average happiness has remained flat in affluent countries, no better than in the 1950s and 1960s. For poorer countries, more is good, for the people need essentials: food, schooling, safe water, health care. Over the past century, the consumption economy of affluent countries has sought to create an image of the good life being achieved through having certain goods and services (a car, dishwasher, handbag, holiday) to achieve comfort, luxury and status. Advertising has used utopian imagery to manufacture desire for a life filled with material comfort and luxury, suggesting that a good life is accessible for all in a world where hardship, suffering and death might no longer exist. Yet for some, happiness stays low despite all the stuff. For others, something seems to have happened.

Five of the top six happiest countries worldwide are from the same region. They are Denmark, Finland, Iceland, Norway and Sweden.

At the Happiness Research Institute in Copenhagen, Meik Wiking has researched and written of *hygge*. He's not saying the country is perfect, but is sure they have got some things more right than not. *Hygge* is happiness, giving value to cosiness, friends and togetherness, equality and gratitude. It is sharing food, baking cakes and lighting candles. It is also co-housing, it is volunteering and looking after neighbours, it is being in nature, and feeling you have a meaning in life. In the northern latitudes it is always waiting for the sun. And all these activities, they are low in material consumption and low in carbon emissions. Meik writes *hygge* may be bad for market capitalism, yet is already good for personal happiness.

The aim, says Meik, is to change the story, 'How to make cities great, how to make them liveable again. By working on happiness, we are doing more now to change the city.'

It seems a good life could help save the planet if it centres on, at the very least, healthy food, being in nature, regular physical activity, social togetherness, craft and cognitive skills to keep the mind active, and a spiritual wrapper of meaning. All are in our circle. And nature itself, the very planet, could stabilise within some self-imposed limits. Alas, this ethic of care might dawn on us too late.

In a village across the Baltic and east to Russian border of Karelia, my friend Tero was elected mayor. It is a lake-scape of ice-fishers, winter now burning up at both ends. We had met onstage at the American Museum of Natural History, right by Central Park. Tero Mustonen stood up and said, 'Tell me this, where is the escape route from this destructive modern world for my people?' The silence of the panel was instructive. At his home in winter, the snow a metre deep outside, he also observed, 'People living in Karelia have witnessed both colonial onslaught and full blown modernity; these have caused critical impacts on our landscape, tradition and spiritual practices.'

And paused, 'However, we are still here.'

He and Siberian friend, Vyacheslav Shadrin of the nomadic Kolyma, had pressed the museum for permission to see artefacts recovered by famed anthropologist Franz Boas. In a hangar underground, they were taken to shelves containing birch bark maps and shaman drums. It was imprisoned magic, and Slava fell in a faint. The spirits were angry, he whispered. The maps were the only examples known, yet here they were underneath one of the world's most famous cities. The museum would not return them. How fortunate that five hundred million indigenous people worldwide have survived, often only barely, the depredations of colonial and extractive economies, and bring to our modern days an awareness of the watchful world, their traditions and truths, their ethical and moral obligations, their respect toward nature.

What a contrast, with modern selfishness. Cultures and civilisations spanning millennia found coherent ways of living that were good for both people and their own pieces of planet. Their terrains were nourishing, they were attentive to nature and cared for people, their lives were interesting. A healthy country was a good country.

At home, there had been bats flying at dusk, the snicker of their wings audible as they dashed above.

> This is why, the Æsir gods called gold,
> The metal of strife.
>
> [Snorri Sturluson, *The Prose Edda*, 1179–1241]

———

On the coast of Sjælland, the red sun flared and slipped into the sea's embrace.

There was no green flash, even as the western sky was clear of cloud. We had taken to two wheels, for the liminal precinct between the sea and land, on the island edge, and two hundred kilometres lengthways on the coast of the Sjælland Riviera. Beyond the narrows was Sweden, Copenhagen linked to Malmö by the bridge. Mostly shores of the North Sea and its inlets do not have a beach of sand. They are sandstone cliff, marsh and salting, fen and lowland river, raised sea-defence of concrete, channeled river estuary, black sand and rocky rubble. Yet, when the sun rises into a summer sky, we know where we'll be drawn.

Along this coast was wild habitat beside industrial, stands of ancient trees on headlands and chemical works on the far shore, marram dunes with hips of wild red rose, and a rusty cargo ship passing beyond the swimmers standing in the waves.

The grass was humming, the air clear, it was a sea of blessings, even though on those hills had spilled blood as well as happiness. This beach of escape, the place that authorises doing nothing, allows watching the march of waves and the playing children, the listening to wind snapping flags and canvas. Inland there never seems the time for leisure on the land, out here all hands were doing nothing. The beach has created modern pact. On the north Norfolk coast, facing this way toward Denmark and the Netherlands, are old fisher cottages with no windows on the sea-ward side. The last thing sailors wanted on returning home was to look again upon the sea. The first thing we might do today, on thinking of a spell at the seaside, would be to check the view from landscape windows, check the chairs on timbered terrace.

We each are vessels for a ghost or two, a fading memory of place or person. It is just that those of king and queen always seem to carry heft, look to fill a story.

There was one, so well famed, who lived at Kronborg, at this north-east edge of Sjælland. The square curtain walls are brick, grasses growing from the tops, and the castle roof all tarnished copper. In the narrow sound, white-sailed yachts leaned and sped, and a ferry was heading for Sweden's Helsingbörg, four leagues over the Øresund. At Helsingör's harbour-side was the Little Mermaid's slender brother Han, silvered on a stone and reflecting castle and the trawlers in the port. It takes, too, the image of a watcher, for some have said they do not care for such a man. Yet if you wait, this thin merman winks, at a certain hour.

The citadel was beyond the moat, yet all was wall and angle, and sun reflected from the roof. The fortress seemed devoid of human scale, less defence than symbol. In its grounds, each year since the 1930s, a Shakespeare play has here been staged.

For this was home to Hamlet, Prince of Denmark, written in the year 1600, just as Denmark was about to start to shrink. A tale of ghost and madness, and a skull. The king Hamlet dies, and there was an empty throne. An invasion from Norway appears imminent, and his brother Claudius snatches both crown and Hamlet's widow Gertrude. On an icy night, on those very ramparts, sentries see the ghost of king, and tell the grieving Prince. So the boy Hamlet meets his father, overlooking Øresund again, who said he'd been murdered by Claudius. The Prince resolves revenge, and chooses to act as if mad, to put on an *antic disposition*. That's about it, for when the father-ghost appears to the Prince, no one else could see him, and so the Prince looks more in grip of madness. At a graveside, Hamlet picks up the skull of Yorick, a jester from his childhood. By the close of Act V, the entire Danish royal family is dead, and in marches the Norway king unopposed.

The trail inland was narrow. A pale man appeared, saying nothing, and pointed to the path. At Gurre Slot, a castle wall and four tower ruins from the 1100s, was another trapped ghost, this of Valdemar the King. The castle was in a mere, bounded by healthy trees of ash, hawthorn growing from the walls of brick and mortared stone, the ancient thorn and flowers with the scent of death. Nothing remained of baroque turrets topped with pointed roof, their ancient views across the still lake, a drawbridge on the inland side. It was a castle for a princess, so here lived Valdemar's mistress Tove Lille, until she was slain by Queen Helvig. The three inspired myth and song, the *Gurre-Lieder* cantata, and it is said Valdemar gallops out at night to hunt, calling on his dead vassals, and horses can still be heard snickering under moonlit skies.

A frog might jump, into those ancient ponds. Imagine how Valdemar feels, to have seen his walls fall, and moss grow over all the paths.

What could have gone so wrong for such a king: Valdemar said God could keep his paradise, if only he could keep his Gurre. No wonder he roams the marsh and field at night, trapped for all eternity, for the wronged were both the queen and mistress. The queen now lies in quiet grounds of Esrum Kloster. We sat on walls, on the castle isle. The sky was clear, and tall reeds rustled in the marsh, there was no mist. Nothing stirred in summer heat. There were stands of white bedstraw in the grounds, and from the wood came the sound of doves, soft-cooing. Close by was the white-brick Gurre church, austere save for a griffon on the pulpit. There was a silver font, and orbs of light hanging by two votive ships, barques from days when Denmark had so many craft to sail.

Sunlight slanted through the glass, and a handsome hawk flashed across the churchyard, its feathers of a golden hue.

This too was set in landscape of small fields and swidden clearings, tall beech and emerald ash woodland, heavily barked oak, butterflies dashing in the dappled light. There was resinous heat inside the stands of pine. There were dairy cattle and painted cottages, marten and swallow swooping over village roof and lane. A fallow deer, ears pricked and wide, bounded through the long grass golden in the summer sun. It sprung up, was gone, leapt up again, sped toward the Fredensborg palace and the formal gardens.

My college friend's mother grew up in a renaissance castle on the isle west of Sjælland. Valdemar's Slot on Tåsinge was built by King Christian IV in the 1640s for his son, but he died in battle so the castle and land were given to Admiral Niels Juel after a naval victory over Sweden. Janey's mother said it was a gilded life growing up in the 1930s, a precious idyll of sailing between the isles, and travelling to school by ferry. She came to England in the 1950s, married locally and settled in Scotland where the Danish words in name and place made her feel at home. Each Christmas they travelled back, the long trek by ferry and car, finding the castle decaying more each year.

The running and laughter of young children brought the corridors to life. Yet curtains and tapestry carried on crumbling into dust.

Of all those ghosts of admirals and kings, the most famed was Hrothgar. He was a wise king, but nothing he could do kept the monsters in the mere. Hrothgar did not blame his people for their misfortune. He could not protect his hall from Grendel, yet he did not lose their support.

Hrothgar spoke of the dangers of all power, especially as there will come the time when the old powers seem only paltry:

> *A man in his unthinkingness forgets,*
> *That it will ever end for him.*

[Beowulf, trans. Seamus Heaney, c700–1000]

The author of *Beowulf* wrote that the Spear Danes of Sjælland isle had courage and greatness, and Hrothgar the King believed gold did no one any good. The dragons knew this too, for they could be soundless for centuries until disturbed by raiders. The warrior, the bear-man Beowulf later ruled the Geats well for 50 winters, and 'Grew old and wise as warden of the land.' Yet beyond the border were massing enemies, waiting for the fall. A robber stole a goblet from the dragon's lair, so the hoard-guardian scorched the ground, burned homesteads bright, the sky-winger left nothing in its wake. The *Saga of the Volsungs* tells of Sigurd hiding in a ditch, on the heath with Regin's twice-forged sword.

He stabbed Fafnir, and that winged wyrm queried Sigurd, 'Who are you, and who is your family?' and then stated with his final words, 'This gold that once was mine will be your death.' Sigurd took on the dragon symbol for his shield, yet the gold did indeed bring only greed and vengeance.

Beowulf too came to kill the Geat dragon, and was poisoned by its blood. He was buried with his ship in a mound by the sea. The laments of old women and men, who had seen so much, reminded those at the funeral byre that there was more to lose than just this wise king. The desire for gold could bring down a kingdom too.

In later years say the sagas, there came to Sjælland one of four kings who made the year of 1066 famed, the one who won one battle and then lost the next, who died in the bloody clash of Stamford Bridge, an arrow in his throat. This was Harald Sigurdsson of Norway, later known as Harald Hardrada, feared by all the northern states. When he was young, King Olaf came upon him playing with woodchips in a muddy creek, and the king declared, 'I can see a time, when you will command real warships,' and the lad avowed, 'All I want is warriors and weapons.'

This Harald came to be five ells tall, fair-haired and handsome, an ash-blond beard, one eyebrow higher than the other.

You wonder how he came to be defeated by the English, perhaps a fatal flaw awaits those who never seem to stumble. On Sicily he crushed a town, ordered shavings tied to wings of birds, smeared with wax and sulphur, and set alight the sparrows that fluttered back to nests. At first the thatch was smouldering, then the town was all ablaze. In a second siege, he sunk a tunnel, and took the town at night. In a third his death was faked and so his men walked stiffly to the gatehouse, the coffin full of stones, which they jammed between the posts. At Nissa River on Sweden's coast, he defeated ranks of Dane and Swede, the enemy wiped away by waves of stone and arrow.

When Harald's golden ship, sails stained with spray, scudded up Roskilde fjord, they plundered and burned the villages all around, and in soundless grief the survivors fled to hide in the ancient forest. This explains, in part, why Harald was so detested here, for apprehended women were hauled away in shackles, and only would only see their homes in dreams. This was why the Danish women later mocked Harald with a show, they carved out anchors from their cheese, saying how easily they could hold the Norway ships. But Harald, like many a man, could not resist the whispers that he deserved a greater crown. He listened much to the exiled brother of Harold king of England, this Tostig was a bully of a man who had been promoted to Earl of Northumberland well beyond his competence. It was he who saved Sjælland, for he had sailed to Norway, and persuaded Harald to invade England rather than pursue protracted war with Denmark. After sailing over Humber sands, up the smaller Ouse, Harald's pavilion was impressive, there were many cloaks lined with ermine fur. Bowls were lathed from maple, coiled with gilded silver, and torques carved with runes were placed upon an altar.

And around his tent was assembled all his shining force to take the English crown. They flew banners embroidered with Oðinn's ravens.

Fifty years before there had been a wise king, and he had united all of Denmark and England, took on healing after reign of terror led by Æthelred. Some say Æthelred was unready, others that *unrædy* meant ill-advised. His mother put him on the throne at nine, disposing of his brother first. He became an expert of the court and corridor, a ruined king who quite ignored the world outside his court. If anyone spoke ill of the cloistered king, and no one heard, all well and good. Otherwise the court would act. He gathered silver from the people, paid Danegeld to each invading Viking force, and was safe as king for forty years.

The annals say Canute was sturdy, with fair complexion, handsome all except his nose, thin and high upon his face. His eyes were sharp, and light shone on all his ships. He seemed a wise young man, who carried many scars, bringing thane and jarl across the shallow sea. All his force were freemen, not one crew was still a slave. They all recalled those friends they lost, years back on St Brice's Day. For when it seemed Æthelred's reign could get no worse, he and Archbishop Wulfstan turned inward, and ordered all the settled Danes be slaughtered. They were butchered, cut down as blue corncockle weeds bright in summer wheat.

Canute sailed two hundred longships, steered through shallows to the Saxon shore, and the rule of Æthelred was ruined. For two decades, the Danes and English were united under Canute.

The brothers of Svipdag once asked their Swedish father Svip what was King Hrolf Kraki like, the wise king of Sjælland isle?

> I have heard he is open-handed and generous,
> He withholds neither gold nor treasure,
> He is fierce with the greedy, yet gentle with the modest,
> He is the most humble of men, so great,
> His name will not be forgotten, as long as the world remains inhabited.
>
> [Snorri Sturluson, *The Prose Edda*, 1179–1241]

At the centre of the Viking world was Yggdrasil, the tree that held up the world and sky.

The sagas of Finland also began beneath a tree, the giant pine at Hummovaara meadow. Here a district doctor sat with the seine fisherman, Juhana Kainulainen, also a hunter and tietäjä spirit man. Elias Lönnrot was dictated more than two thousand lines of oral poetry by Kainulainen and other folk poets in the midsummer of 1828, and wove these into *The Kalevala*, an epic that came to mould national identity. At the time, singing matches were held in villages, and Larin Paraske came to be nationally known for her repertoire of eleven thousand lines. The great pine stood alone on a rise, taller by a half than any other tree nearby. To the west the winter sun had paused above the distant forest, and the pine was fiery pink. Tero Mustonen and I tramped through deep snow and the long cold, the silence endless. We stood by this ancient tree, relic of the primeval taiga, perhaps four hundred years old.

It was said, Kainulainen on a fishing trip could sing all night without repeating a verse.

According to Finnish tradition trees are animate, their spirits strong. Before cutting, it was right to knock on trunk with the handle of an axe to ask the spirit to leave. Some trees are sacred, others signifiers of messages. Another practice was to cut branches in a set pattern so as the tree grew, the gaps would always remain. Some were memorials to the ancestors and the dead. But when the Lutheran mission pushed its way east from Sweden to meet the Orthodox Russians advancing towards the west, sacred trees were called *suspicious trees*. Edicts were issued by both church and state to destroy them all. In the north, the Lutherans also burned Sámi shamans at the stake. They wanted to make people of the forests and lakes see sense, become proper Christians. This was why Lönnrot ended up etched on the heart of every Finn: he stopped the oral traditions from being forgotten.

In mid-winter, when the days are short yet dawn and dusk are long and low, you can walk out from the fishermen's cooperative on the banks of the great lake, and be in light of shattering intensity.

The sky could be hard and endless blue, the tracks of skidoo curving out from shore in sheen of snow. Another day could be just as cold, tens of degrees below zero, yet bring driving blizzard. This was the weather for fox-fur hat and reindeer mittens. The forest bears were slumbering. Throughout history, the bear was given many names, to avoid the use of bear itself: bruin from the harsh land, apple of the forest, honey eater, handsome one. 'Welcome honey-paw,' said old Väinämöinen in *The Kalevala*. Both Beowulf and Bodvar Bjarki were men as strong as bears, growing faster than the weeds when boys, and it was they who dispatched the forces of chaos looming in the shadows.

To succeed as an ice-fisher, you need to know the lake-bed, the water column and its layers and currents, the under-surface of lake ice, the ice itself with its leads and secrets, and the air above carrying wind and weather. For the fish will be brought up from the dark below the ice.

Esa Rahunen knew more than a hundred fishing sites called *apaja*, and on the kitchen table he laid out the secret maps, passed with care across the generations. It was ancient knowledge, rightly closed. Each night, Esa dreamt up the best location, where the fish would be. He kept a logbook, like all skippers, all the weather records, every catch on every trip. And at a certain place, a long-bladed chainsaw roared to life, bit into ice. A rectangular hole was cut, and dark water bubbled up into the harsh light of headlamp and head-torch. Frozen machinery was unwrapped from cracking tarpaulin. There were no stars, no lights from the distant shore, no birds quarrelled. Nylon nets and robot torpedoes were slipped into the deeps to guide the net away for half a league. Hours later, when the time came to create the pulling hole, skidoo and sled bogged down in sludgy ice and surface water.

'It's too warm,' once shouted Esa, waving his arms. Too much slushy snow had fallen that winter on the lake, pushing down with weight, forcing water up through leads.

At the new ice hole, the fishers peered carefully at the ice. Too many air bubbles to be strong, too many warm periods this winter. Then in the dingy penumbra of dawn, snow started to fall. It pelted into faces, covered everything in minutes. It was to be a day sunless and moonless, quenched of any kind of shadow, the lake dark and teeming below. The night before, we dipped in this very lake, scampering from the shoreside sauna. There was a hole, a floating cover of wood, where a muskrat rose to breathe. The reeds were thick, and there was no other way but to jump in fast. Now the fish were treasure from the deep. They crowded in the blue net, leapt and flipped. From the inky water, the shoal of vendace was raised into the air.

It was a kind of miracle, these fish were given to the fishers. The wind angled hard as skidoos slewed across the snow and slushy zones. We raced to the factory to pack the fish for market. On the way, the lead skidoo slid and clipped a bank of ice. It tipped over, and we leapt away. The sled with a tonne of fish tottered, and righted.

Local people waiting at the factory door were handed bags of fish by Esa. Tero also carried to his village, strings of fish to give to friends.

The father of Tero's wife was a merchant skipper whose ship was sunk by ice. The *Finnpolaris* was the other side of Greenland, in heavy wind and swell, it struck an ice floe that ripped a hole in starboard flank. The zinc ore turned to slurry, and the ship listed so fast they could only launch one lifeboat. Matti Pulli and the crew were fifteen hours aboard the lifeboat, and watched the ship go down.

''Tis memory on the waters / for a boat, a craft to cruise / to make the wider waters green,' said old Väinämöinen.

Said Kaisu's mother, when the phone rang in the night, 'Dad's ship is drowned, he is OK, everybody is OK, go back to sleep.'

She was never afraid for him, said Kaisu, for he was not afraid of the sea himself.

The ship went down in mist and blue polar light, the ice pack closing in. It had been one of forty thousand ships that passed through the Øresund that year. And he returned, another time, across the Baltic in an open motor-boat. He accompanied a driven friend, Pekka Piri, on a crossing to Iceland, three and a half thousand leagues over Baltic and the Kattegat, to North Sea and the North Atlantic. They packed fuel and radio, sea chart and survival suit, food and GPS. It was a thousand leagues before they even left the Baltic. There was the colourful warren of Nyhavn, white breaking crests, thick fog, exploding waves, not much time to talk. Do you want to raise the bridge, yelped the startled speaker, expecting more than an open boat far down on the waves. They passed the coast of Sjælland in late spring, and Pekka called his trip *The Call of the Sagas*.

'He was a man whose thoughts had a thousand arms,' said Kaisu. It was for him a flight, an adventure to escape what mid-life brings.

But her father had a calmer view of life, a skipper who had been through a thing or two at sea.

Looking over to the Sjælland shore, Kaisu's father would have seen sandstone cliff and broad dune, the flank of one of the largest forests in Denmark, entry to fjord and stone harbour.

Looking ahead, Beowulf and his fourteen men sailed this swan's road, the wind behind and them flying like a bird across the Øresund. The seafarers sighted sunlit cliffs and looming headlands, and over the side the Geats vaulted onto the sand. They walked a paved track across the heath, hurried through the forest of Gribskov, onward till the timbered hall of Heorot rose before them, radiant with gold.

Gribskov is still five thousand hectares of ancient forest west of Esrum, a woodland once of green stream and common ownership. A mix of wood-pasture, coppiced trees, pond and bog, swamp and spring, passage grave and chambered tomb. It has been forest since the last Ice Age, since the time when the North Sea itself was steppe and plain. There are bottomless lakes, deep in darkness, one swamp that swallowed up a monastery, its bells still heard on quiet evenings. These days the land was burned up, the heathland fried, wheat golden and barley bales in lines on hill-top fields. The oak forest was cool, lanced with light and mottled shadow in the emerald green. Hooded crows cawed. The grey-black birds continued calling. At the chocolate factory there was an air-cooled café.

Inland from the castles was the Cistercian abbey, the cool stone of Esrum Kloster set in swidden clearing, near to the inland lake.

Here was walled herb and vegetable garden, meadows stretching to the river, cool vault and halls filled with cycle-songs and chant. It was a centre of learning and manuscript illustration for centuries, yet as with sister English abbeys, it was taken by the crown with the adoption of Lutheranism. A quote from Kierkegaard was on the wall: 'the moment is where time and eternity touch.' In a side room were medieval wall paintings, the riches of fruit and vegetables from the walled garden. The Kloster walls were three feet thick, and the windows deep-recessed. Dragoons were barracked here, stone stolen to fortify Kronborg, it was held by military until the Second World War. Now all was quiet once again. From the nearby heath tops, there were views across the fields and copper statues to the sea beyond.

At the seaside, the sun blazed. The Louisiana Museum of Modern Art was built on grassy slopes, the window pictures framing blue. Many bicycles were parked outside, and the landscaped gardens were filled with families, ahead the Øresund and Sweden. On the plateau of ancient trees, children raced around the Henry Moores and Giacomettis. Inside Warhol was abandoned to the day outside, for this was hours of sun and sparkled light. At such coastal places, the light falls from the sky, bounces up from the sea. The breeze was cool, inland all was cindered. At Gilleleje harbour, there were many small boats. Catches had been unloaded, crews had left for home, and visitors eaten at the restaurants. Britain has a wartime tale that plays into identity, into care for others. The allied army was beaten, thousands of Belgian, French and British soldiers were on the beach, the call came for every kind of vessel, sail across the southern sea, bring home your men from Dunkirk. A thousand little ships carried the troops across the water.

And here at Gilleleje, three years later, small ships saved Jewish Danes from terror, crossing over the sea to Sweden.

Migrants and refugees can tell of their own great escapes, and who opened up their hearts to help. They know, too, of the shadows cast by those who die. Syrian refugees fled conflict, arrived on Greek islands and had to swim the final metres. A young infant lay face-down in the waves. Frozen tourists sat on the beach and watched. Denmark had for the twentieth century sought to remain politically neutral. It did not enter the first war, in the second Germany simply occupied the land for meat and butter to feed its cities. The model protectorate resembled stability until August 1943, when the Danish government was forced to stand down.

Suddenly, time was tight.

Playwright Jonathan Lichtenstein's father had escaped Berlin on the *Kindertransport* route. Hans was twelve years old, and travelled unaccompanied to arrive at Harwich on the Essex coast. He carried only a suitcase tied with string. In his nineties, he travelled back with his son, back through their own traumas. In *The Berlin Shadow*, Jonathan wrote they talked more than they had ever done. They found an angel serving in the coffee shop at the Sachsenhausen concentration camp. He had said, 'People come from all over the world to visit. Then they come in here and they are all in such difficulties. All I can do is get their coffee right.'

The shadow had been cast across generations, the silence of unspoken loss. Jonathan came to realise his father's furies had been partly because he wanted to toughen up his son. To cope, not with what *might* happen, but what eventually *would* happen.

In Denmark, an uncooperative government had gone, and under direct and martial rule the Nazi occupiers began immediate deportation of all Jewish Danes to camps. The German diplomat Georg Duchwitz leaked the plans to Danish resistance movement, who alerted the Chief Rabbi. The next morning, Rabbi Melchior urged all to go into hiding and spread the word. Sweden had already been receiving Jewish Norwegians, but had not wanted to make any welcome public. Greta Garbo called King Gustav V of Sweden, the physicist Niels Bohr escaped and demanded to speak in person. On the 2nd October, on Rosh Hashanah, Swedish radio broadcast it would receive all Jewish refugees. Now the resistance called to synagogues, go now.

The lines of exodus were from Copenhagen, from south and west of isle. Travellers swiftly moved, in boots of cars, in railway trucks.

The target was the fishing village of Gilleleje on the northern shore of Sjælland. And now the fleet of small craft carried over Øresund eight thousand people. In autumn seas, the journey would take an hour in a motor trawler, yet some were taken across by rowing boat and kayak. The *Gerda III* of the Danish lighthouse service was skippered by Otto Hansen and crewed by three other local men. They could carry ten refugees on each trip, so they pretended they were on lighthouse duties. They carried three hundred people across to Sweden.

It was a stunning success, the flotilla crossing back and forth the busiest sea lanes to and from the Baltic. Yet also this: the eighty people hiding in the loft of Gilleleje's whitewashed church, were betrayed and deported to Theresienstadt concentration camp. A single boy escaped and watched, hiding by a gravestone. The charges made by some fishermen, fees twice the monthly wage. The capsize of some vessels, the suicide of others as the Gestapo forces moved in. Yet several thousand resistance and non-resistance members aided the escape, organised into small groups, mostly kept anonymous or known by fictitious names. On the Yad Vashem list in Jerusalem they are honoured for this collective effort, and in the gardens also by a single acacia tree planted in Denmark Square.

As with Denmark, Norway was occupied primarily for resources. At the narrowest neck of the country, north of the Arctic Circle, lies the port of Narvik connected by rail to Swedish iron mines. Exports pre-war were to the UK and Germany, and during the war Germany obtained eight-tenths of its raw iron for military machines from this one port. It became a centre for conflict, an allied victory in 1940 and temporary occupation then retreat, and the raid on nearby Austvågøya isle on the Lofotens that sank ten enemy ships and destroyed the manufacture of glycerine from fish oil and kerosene. The resistance movement, meanwhile, grew to thirty-five thousand strong, supported by training and supplies from Shetland on the secret fish-boat route known as the Shetland Bus.

Snow fell heavily at Narvik airport and on the route west to the Lofoten isles. It covered every fjord and field, every piece of jagged history.

By the morning, it was a metre deep.

The Lofoten isles are a lynx foot long in Arctic Sea, warmed by the Gulf Stream, this was Valhalla's backbone. There were hooded crows, grey-cloaked jumping on the ice, crying in the old air of winter, the sky low and the sea black. At Harstad harbour the ferry silently approached, coloured lights shining on the fjord, it docked and sailed north again. All sounds were muted. A hammer sounded on metal in the shipyard, a car hushed by, there was the padded feet of a man running for the bus, huffing in the cold air. We walked up to the church on the hill, but the doors were locked and so we cleared snow from a seat, and watched the town below.

Somewhere great cods were being pulled from these seas, they had swum down from the Barents Sea to spawn. Gulls wheeled above the harbour edge, but did not make a sound. Our feet crimped on soft snow, and the wind snatched at hair and frozen lips.

When the crew had made ready, the yellow and white former-whaler edged out of the flat-calm harbour of Andenes. It passed flocks of eider duck strung out in lines. Sharp etched hills dwarfed the town, black rock and white snow, larch groves without leaf. Above the sea, the cloud was charcoal, the sea itself green-black. Twenty leagues away the mountains of the mainland were white and the clouds pale and lenticular above the peaks. The ship steamed up and down the swell. We drank coffee, but by the time the soup was ready, there were few takers, most passengers grey and some had leaned over the side. Summer in Lofoten brings two months of constant sun, winter just one of darkness when the sun stays below horizon. Now the cloud broke, and the sea turned molten mercury, it glittered black and silver, the bow-wave ploughed aside a surge of bubbles.

Over the Tannoy the skipper played the pings from echo-locator. There were whales singing.

There was a huffing plume, and another, and then the bent dorsal fin and rounded back of a fin whale, the second largest beast upon the planet. The sperm whales then appeared, brown in colour, outbreaths from their only nostril on the left. They watched with steady eyes. The skipper clicked, *diving*, and the fluke of one then another flipped into the cold air, bent and they tipped into dives. They left on surface a slick of oil, gradually spreading and suppressing waves. On route along Kvaefjord south, there were reindeer browsing in the snows of a low saddle, and in birch woodland were two moose, ears pricked, white-legged and prancing over snowdrifts. They stopped to look. There were sea eagles circling over fjord, and at some places the water was a turquoise green, a colour that seemed imported from the tropics.

So that he could be a sky-traveller, looking down on the fjords below, the god Loki said, 'Lend me your falcon skin.'

Norwegian explorer Erling Kaage described sailing toward Cape Horn in the south Pacific, alone on watch in the darkest hours, and hearing a long deep sigh just west. A whale was swimming alongside, sixty tonnes of fin whale, and the deep sound of breathing filled the air above the ocean.

He wrote, 'The world was not quite the same, from then.'

One Lofoten day, the temperature rose, and water poured off slopes, and then promptly froze again. The ground was ice, the air frigid.

We slipped and fell in slow motion. At Svolvær, the rorbuer fish cabins were rust red with white window-frames, stilted over water chuckling on the rocks. The wind poured around the loose wooden windows, whistled in the roof. A black mountain rose above the harbour, the huts and shipyards and the thin town spread at the narrow base of land. Fish boats with mizzen sails pushed through the currents round the offshore isles, and on return the crew gutted and cleaned the cod beneath a thousand screaming gulls. The cods were laid on long triangular wooden frame, the stokk fish drying in the polar wind. There has been winter fishing for cod from Lofoten shore since Viking times. The village was home to one of Norway's finest landscape painters, and the Gunnar Berg gallery was opened as a good turn, and here were original paintings of these isles, ragged mount and trollfjord, and every kind of coloured clinkered boat, crammed in harbour, pulling in the nets on open sea. They seemed a dreamlike people, fishing under sail.

The rorbuer were once crammed with fishers, and we pegged the windows open at night to let in air and sound. Tonight, it was said, it would be clear. A group had gathered in the restaurant, wrapped in every kind of padded clothing, and headed out to search for light. The alarm rang at two and four, and I stood outside in starshine, staring at the northern sky. But there was no aurora, no curtains came of neon green.

Far to south-west, not quite at the final town of Å and the seething Moskenstraumen maelstrom, source of inspiration for Edgar Allan Poe's tunnel cataract as smooth as ebony, was the chieftain's longhouse on a hill at Borg. The wind still was bitter, cold enough to rot a tooth, the fields frozen.

This was a ninety-metre hall, vast on the hill, greater than those of Ingimund and Hrothgar. A fire was blazing at one end, smoke rising to the rafters. There was sweet stew bubbling in cauldrons, swinging on chains. A man played a lute and two women stood in costume singing a folk song. There were sub-rooms in the longhouse, for carpenter with lathe and tools, for cook with vegetables piled on tables, for sleeping bench each covered with sheep fleece. It still was cold enough to bring people huddling round the wooden bowls of food.

And here, too, was something greater. For a group of boys and young men had come. They were thinly dressed, and each had a mobile phone. I talked to one lad from Afghanistan, another from Syria. They had taken pictures, they wanted to send them, but there was no one at home. This was now their culture, their new home.

Down on the shore was the harbour and shipyard, where longships had been built and sailed across the north sea-roads on raiding trips to Britain, the route made in reverse by the Shetland Bus.

Later at the Svolvær restaurant, the owner seemed to contradict the whalers up at Andenes. 'Oh yes, of course, we still will catch a whale, would you like a piece of minke?'

> Cut wood on a windy day,
> Row to sea in fine weather,
> Murmur to friends in the darkness,
> Many are the eyes of day.
> [Sæmundr Sigfússon, *Hávarmál, Sayings of the High One, Poetic Edda*, c1290]

At the top of Roskilde fjord was the smell of diesel on the Hundestad harbour, the ferry bell ringing and the waiting people eating ice-cream. Yet above the busy port, on a headland of droughty grass was a lime-washed cottage with dark thatch, pine trees bent by winter winds, the home of Knud Rasmussen, polar explorer and friend to Inuit people. Rasmussen was born in Greenland at the time Britain was making slaves of boys to work the fishing smacks of Grimsby, and crossed the North West Passage on a dog sled. The house inside was silent, dark with panelled wooden walls and polished floor. A polar bear rug was on the bed, its head upon a chair. In the main room was a huge silvered stove in the centre, and many seats and desks, places for visitors to read and write.

Would Rasmussen and friends have sat outside on summer nights singing ballads, the wind in the pines? That would be the way to settle into the world. Nuuk from here was more than three thousand leagues away. The curator happily talked of his vintage bicycle, propped against the wall outside.

The Far North long held an attraction, fatal for some. Monks travelled toward the summer sun in search of isles close to heaven, seeking paradise and mystic places of perfection. When Naddoð came back from discovery of Iceland, he said it was a land of rich meadows, even though sheep and cattle had not yet made the journey. And polar explorers, too, sailed to find extremes. Norway's Fridtjof Nansen sought the North Pole, travelled in a wooden ship locked in ice, then overland by dog-sled; Roald Amundsen was the first to South Pole, beating Britain's Scott by a month. Rasmussen survived the polar ice, yet died aged 54; Scott and Shackleton searched for the navigable passage beyond Greenland. Shackleton's ship the *Discovery* now lies at whaling port of Dundee, in dock by art museum. Yet here in Sjælland the thatched house was cool despite the heat. The bay windows looked upon the sea. In the distance cargo ships passed freely south toward the Baltic.

A white bird flew across the frame, all was calm by sapphire waters.

Robin Hanbury-Tenison says his definition of exploring has always been, 'It changes the world.' People travel in order to see and make sense of the world, often wanting to be first, to be where no other human has been before, certainly where they had not been themselves. We could count in this class explorer and pilgrim, long-distance walker and tourist-trekker, astronaut and deep-sea diver, none are so very different. Equally, they might also have been searching inside. Norwegian solo explorer Erling Kaage has written about silence, not just in polar landscapes but internally to soothe the mental chatter. 'The quieter I became,' he wrote, 'the more I heard.'

Rasmussen was a rare northern explorer, for he could speak the language, talk to people in their country. He was schooled in east Sjælland, and set out on his first expedition aged twenty-three as the new century started. He wrote as he travelled, recording Inuit folklore. The fifth Thule expedition yielded ten volumes on ecology and cultures of the far North, one dog-sled trip, two Inuit friends, three years to reach Nome in Alaska, and twenty-nine thousand kilometres travelled.

Wrote Rasmussen, 'The greatest peril of life lies in the fact that our food consists entirely of souls. All the creatures that we like and eat… have souls that must be pacified lest they revenge themselves.'

In a clearing on the cliff to the east was a granite erratic, a memorial stone. Long ago here sat Soren Kierkegaard, gazing at the wind.

It was carved with this inscription, 'What is truth other than living for an idea.' Kierkegaard also wrote of how we should live our lives: 'Prayer does not change god, but changes those who pray;' and that, 'Life is not a problem to be solved, only a reality to be experienced.' He died after falling from a tree. At dusk, the cliff top had been pink with willowherb and yellow tansy. The cliff dropped away sharply to a narrow beach, no place to be in an onshore winter storm. Yet that day, the far crystal waves lapped at the sand, and all was silence.

This was the very place where Hrothgar's coastguard stood, and called down to Beowulf, 'My job is to watch the waves for raiders, any dangers to the Danish shore.' He guarded their ship as it rode on water, bound by hawser and anchored fast, and received from Beowulf, striding along the sandy foreshore, a sword with gold fittings that guaranteed a respected place on the mead-benches. Such care for others is the *xenia* valued in the Greek epics, always feed visitors, welcome outsiders, listen to their stories. Rescue them from danger, too, if the call came.

That evening, white tablecloths were laid on tables and we ate outside on the cliff top looking at the sea. Swifts dashed madly in the updraft, swerving round the diners. The sun went down, and all the ways were dark. To the night light, moths still later flew.

You could sit lazily, sleep a little, in this house of fresh sea air.

The world began with flood, and could end with flame at the red string of Ragnarök, the burning of the world with heat that never ends.

Long ago, before Ymir gave birth to giants, before Buri brought on gods, the middle land of Midgard was empty of people, and great forest trees fell and were compressed, layer on layer.

Oðinn still had not made people, he was waiting for the ash and elm to grow. Those ancient trees became crushed carbon and what happens, you may well ask, when you put them in a hearth or forge: they burn. This carbon was rock of raven black, some was liquid, and still it burned. On the cliffs was the white Nakkehoved light, square tower and red roof, once coal-fired, warning ships caught in a tempest. The lighthouse had arched windows with lace curtains, and photographs of every keeper by a walnut desk. It was a shore and skerry-land where gales blew direct upon the shore. On such a night, hard to hear and rain plastering at the windows, the keeper would have stood and watched, hoping not to see the lights of ship. The steps spiralled up to the light and lenses, and far away was southern Norway and western Sweden, across the blue expanse.

The sea was crystal clear, and white hulls and sails were dotted to horizon. To the north-west too, Skagen stretched out from Jutland, where meet the North and Baltic Seas. 'I have spent many winters on the ice-chilled sea,' said the Seafarer, 'on the exile's roads.'

It was ancient carbon, discovered under the prairies of ancient Doggerland, that transformed the northern economies.

Gas had been found, in small amounts, oil extracted from shale, but no one really believed in the big one until the late 1960s. The list of locations sounds like the names of fish grounds in a her-ring skipper's moleskin notebook. West Sole first, then Viking, Leman Bank and Hewett, all large gas fields. Several hundred wells were dug by US companies out of Texas, but all were dry. On the eve of withdrawal, Norway changed for ever. Oil gushed from one well in Ekofisk in December 1969, three hundred kilometres south-west of the fishing village of Stavanger. And the North Sea world now pivoted. Here was cheap energy that flowed in pipes, for which consumers and countries seemed willing to pay regardless of price. When there were shortages, the prices leapt, perfect for producers. At its height, Ekofisk alone would produce three hundred thousand barrels every day, some forty thousand tonnes.

And who would pay to clean up any mess, the tanker wrecks and tar-killed birds? No one was even thinking, might this burning of ancient carbon put something in the air?

Now came migrant workers, and work opened up on rigs for men of Norway and of Britain. And half decade after oil discovery, to our home territory in the east of England came oil families from the plains and nodding rigs of Texas. It was a time of three-day week and dark malaise, only twenty years after food rationing had ended. The oilers imported culture, and hatched a plan to set up a football team for their children. The colonel of the four local US airbases saluted, you can join our league, and the new team turned to local schools to fill the roster. Lawrence Elkins was the coach, the Hall-of-Famer who played for the Oilers and the Steelers in the 1960s. He seemed old and chiseled to us, but had only just turned thirty. It was an exciting time, he said, looking back a half century later.

'You all were good, my English boys. Those big old running backs from the air bases, all of a sudden they'd disappear, you boys wrapped around their ankles.' None of the team, Texans or locals, had ever put on pads before, yet he turned us into league winners, even though the Alconbury air team had won fifty-nine games in a row.

And on each sporting day were great barbecues and smoke drifting cross the grassy field. There was burger never seen before, imported root beer and coke only imagined. It was exotic, the taste and allure of migrant culture. Lawrence came back to Yarmouth years later, walked around hoping to see someone, but he did not recognise a single face. That broke him worse than waves of sixty feet.

Then came a time when mice ran after cats and all the oil was gone.

The restorative symbol all along the Danish coast, on hill and ridge inland, was now a row of turbines turning on the skyline.

Denmark installed the first offshore wind farm in the North Sea in 1991, soon followed great arrays, and sandbanks had a new purpose. Denmark now produces half its energy from wind. Portugal leads the way in certain months, with wind, solar and hydro. Norway reinvested income from its oil, and now all their energy comes from renewables. Yet, you have to say, this is for free, once they have been installed. And there is no hidden cost that others pay, for air pollution and the climate crisis. Now are plans for floating arrays in the deeper waters, a new job for Dogger-land. On the seashore, where the gannet's voice and curlew's melody are louder than the laughter of men, it seems that doing nothing does not feel like the dust of waiting, even for a throne, as was said in *The Kalevala*:

> The village waited for the new moon,
> The young ones for the sunrise,
> Children for a land of strawberries,
> Water for a tarry boat.

[Elias Lönnrot, *The Kalevala*, 1835]

Listen, I will tell you such a story, might have said the old skippers, the grizzled guardians, not embittered by troubles of a life.

Yet beyond the whale's domain and sea lanes, where skerries sank sailors and their ships, grim jaws still await their prey. At the finale, our lives will be no more than flights of sparrows, flitting though the great halls, vanishing from sight. Sweet sirens call from the days of old. It was said Sigurd could put on wolf-skins, and listen to the language of all the animals. It could be if we wish to sleep untroubled dreams, the same might today be needed. The days might be numbered.

Another evening, the sun set orange in the north-western sea, and a single fishing boat crossed the sunway. Everyone stopped eating, and there was silence as the sun paused and vanished.

Now the harvest moon was due and mist would soon be creeping cross the haunted meres.

It is said of Ragnarök,

> *There will be a wind-age and a wolf-age,*
> *Before the world is wrecked.*

VIKING QUEST

This saga happens at an Arctic village on a Lofoten island shore, at the start of the 790s. Longships had sailed under Leifr's grandfather and father, but had not come back. Grim learned a new method of shipbuilding, and after two years three long-ships were ready to leave. Some mothers are crying, a grandfather hides the family axe and shield in the granary, but the lad still takes up an oar. The slave boy Sigi could sing, and joins the Wyrm, and the sightless Cædmon warns him to be careful of Leifr. Only the Wyrm makes it to the western shore, where they find a monastery at Lindisfarne filled with gold and treasure. Valliant Grim sails back over the whale's domain, but some waiting mothers tear at their hair. Many years hence Grim would come to be buried on a promontory, in a mound with his ship.

Come now beyond, this swirling northern sea,
Yonder to the Arctic loop, where the winter sun lies low,
To Valhalla's ridge, a spine of rocky isles,
Three hundred leagues, a lynx-foot long in icy sea,
It was a land of fjord and slope, of god and ghost,
It could be where commenced, the empire of the Norse,
So gather by the fire, fill your wooden bowl with stew,
For this is a tale of longships, leading quests across the briny deep.

When lazy days had passed, and western storms washed out,
Men tarred planks, rigged pine for mast,
Packed holds with stockfish, stowed hornless sheep,
And milch cow bound, in well between the benches,
They gazed at ragged peak, at pulsing choppy swell,
At seething salt beyond the sound, and longed,
For fertile field, for orchard trees and pasture,
To gods again they prayed, assent and let us pass.

Three ships square-sailed away, with ring shields,
Shining bright, a glaring serpent head above the swell,
The parish people stood on stones, watched them slowly part,
Nor were there any tears, just the gentle creak of oar on oak,
And wet-dipped splash of blade, they watched the vessels vanish,
The lad Leifr's grandfather, fair and tall with torque,
Around his neck, had knelt to eye and pledged,
He would return with silver, yet solemn was the silence of the lost.

The fair boy's father Hrafn, followed next as raven chief,
And one year later, again in month of lasting light,
Rain streaming out of sky, the cliff tops lost in cloud,
He steered two dragon ships, away from safety of the strand,
The boy's mother stood, wet on rock and stone,
Tight were clasped, Borghildr's hands so cold,
Concealing hope for safe return, for a winter shorn of worry,
Beneath the scarp were all the watchers, thinking too of silent summer.

Deep or shallow, the sea has no mercy,
It traps them all one day, sailors swimming with the fish,
Yet we hear the sobbing souls, perhaps in squall a single dove,
When falling on the fields, would flutter autumn snow,
Two gloss-black ravens cawed, some wise advice for sailors,
Back at the longhouse, swinging on a chain,
A cauldron bubbled, outside the cold so bitter it could rot a tooth,
Now day was night and wind was moaning, through the wooden walls.

At the folk-moot morn, now spoke Leifr's uncle Grim,
Hrafn's younger brother, stood by birch and willow bush,
This was the promontory, on a mound by row of pines,
The precise place in years to come, where Grim's famous ship,
Will be entombed, his body laid on fur and finest thread,
A sword in hand, and from the straights below,
Sailors will look up and steer, sails billowed by the breeze,
Pointing to the shrine, called Grim's Outcrop to this very day.

The early autumn sun, shone on courage of the crowd,
Here was keen-eyed Borghildr, captain now of longhouse cooks,
Whose sole surviving child, Leifr harboured hope,
One day soon he would be chief, and here one step behind,
Stood the slave boy Sigi, holding arm of Cædmon,
The mentor whose advice to Grim, our ships were much too small,
And to the side, was sombre Dísir wife of Grim,
She felt the looming trouble, land to feed them all was lacking.

Grim clapped his hands, two shots across the sound,
Looked upon the waiting crowd, 'we will build our warships,
The longest ever clenched, fit for strength and fastest speed,
Come men of craft and wood, come weaver and you magic smithy,
It will take two winters, then our voyage will begin,
Bolvik and his shipwrights, will search for standing oak and pine,
Each should wear, a brooch of gripping beasts,
And ensure their axe and adze, are sharp and clear of rust.'

Now came summer, malice gone from sea and air,
They readied for the gannet's bath, this pond would not defeat them,
Grim prayed to Njord, cast runes to let them pass,
To Freyr's ship *Skiðblaðnir*, with its perfect wind,
To spearman Ægir whose daughters, had devoured other quests,
So end to end for ceremony, they set the longships out on blocks,
The length of longhouse on the hill, and named the ships,
First the dragon *Wyrm*, then serpent *Niðhogg* and the giant *Hymir*.

Now the holds were packed, with pickled fish,
With bread unleavened, baked with pea and bark of pine,
They stowed fresh tubs of sour milk, skin bags tight with drinking water,
Sheep watched from on the hills, they neither took a cow,
Instead packed cabbage head and apple, garlic clove and hazelnut,
In the longhouse blazed a fire, smoke rising to the rafters,
One last stew was bubbling, loom and lathe were set aside,
For this was day of Norse departure, for the loved ones of Lofoten.

Crews had come from far, to admire these ships,
And some agreed to take an oar, in return for share of treasure,
Grim appointed cousins, as captains of the other ships,
His inner fear, was returning empty-handed,
He saw Dísir smiling, perhaps she thought,
Their future was secured, and Cædmon gripping Sigi,
Now leant and whispered, 'In a storm you watch for Leifr,
Tie yourself on tight, do not wander like a wolf.'

Finn wore only bearskin, carried giant axe,
For all the other arms and armour, had been hidden by his grandfather,
In the longhouse granary, hoping this would stop the lad,
Thorkel's mother cried, 'I shall be left to tend,
Our empty crib, I will wither when he sails,'
Sharp-tongued Steingerd, let her hopeful boy Halldor join the band,
He chose to crew on *Wyrm*, 'If they strike at me,
I will be a hostile ram, who shames the hungry wolf.'

The crowd of giddy citizens, gathered round the ships,
The heroes strolled as sunlight, shone from summer clouds,
Women fetched the clothes, laid on stones smoothed by storm,
The rosy sea was shattered, to a thousand pieces,
Grim called for order, the men stowed their gear aboard,
And settled which of them would take, which bench by drawing lots,
'We now will trust the ocean, and what the wind shall offer,
Let us cross the beach, and launch our latest ships.'

The sightless bard, calm Cædmon sang a lay,
Tall and grey with age, he stood by Sigi's side,
Whose piercing eyes, were sight enough for two,
Who daily showed the scald, how to find with hands his bread,
Who in return had taught, the boy to sing,
Now Korval commanded, his crew to *Niðhogg*,
Hymir waited for captain Thorvald, and fate now decreed,
That the boy Halldor switched his ships, he preferred the *Hymir* crew.

Bolvik gripped the sanded tiller, the men stepped up the mast,
Pulled the forestays taut, bent up the sail,
They secured the sheets, to polished bollards on the deck,
And so the longships, slipped away from home,
South and west their bearing, they sculled from shore,
The breeze was thin beneath the blue, and mothers and their daughters,
Waved again from sunny strand, they saw the sails were swelling,
The crew could hear the hissing, round the sterns as vessels gathered way.

Inland the fields receded, and islands rose ahead,
Fish large and small, ushered fleet to sea,
At their time of death, all sailors hope they can rely,
On the gown of ground, to be drawn around them,
Yet one dawn the clouds flared red, first came cat's-paw riffles,
The sea wind rising fast, they reefed the sails,
A sheet of rain grew near, they were sucked inside a raging gale,
Hailstones piled upon the decks, all the boys were baling fast.

Nor had Grim suspected, two ships of three were doomed,
Bolvik had the helmsman's skill, the poise of old,
As each wave was raised to strike, and swamp the deck,
The *Wyrm* would glide away, unscathed to face another roller,
Of all the watercraft, that ever challenged ocean,
The tightly fitted *Wyrm* would show, it was the most reliable,
And it was the rudder man, Bolvik who guessed each gust,
Who kept their swift-hoofed steed, afloat for later days.

But the surface of the water, now was ripped by storm,
Squall on squall, came racing from the depths,
Once again the men were shouting, the tackle shrieked,
The air was lit, by lightning flash,
Hymir took a sea on beam, the bow was shorn away,
Fragments of the wreckage, floated on the waves,
The *Niðhogg* sprang her timbers, the cracks now widened fast,
The baling was in vain, none could save the shattered ship.

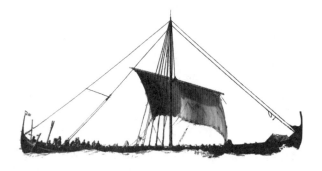

At next grey dawn, light leaked behind the *Wyrm*,
The moon was grey, the oarsmen sick,
And those alive now grimaced, a tail-wind snatching breath away,
The mate swayed his hand, staring at the diving gannets,
The sun stayed hid, but all was still,
Two ships ahorsed, no return for them with purses full,
Grim spoke to Bolvik, 'An underworld awaits us all,
And will not take us yet, on we'll sail the stronger.'

They loosened wet-hemp rope, it would tighten once again when dry,
'You will find your treasure,' gritted one silver-bearded thane,
He was black-eyed, a leg snapped in storm,
His journey soon will start, with sword they'll tip him overboard,
Bolvik sighed to Grim, 'No single thing is easy,
On this earth, over whale's domain,'
Called Grim to crew, his arm rings glinting bright,
'Leifr the stock,' but now a silence struck.

'Come now slave boy, what did you see?'
Sigi stepped up, bruises on his arms and neck,
His eyes were hooded, 'I fell over,
In that great wave, Leifr was there then not,'
Fierce was the quarrel, now erupting from the crew,
Who was looking after Leifr, that boy was meant to father,
Many sons and daughters, now he's taken to a depth,
They knew that Asgard, was always domed by cloudless sky.

Whatever happened now knows Grim, bereft will be Borghildr,
Life has taken colder hue, and now the slave-boy,
From shaking hands, passed sour whey and stockfish,
The sun grazed on ripples, a summer day had come,
And so onward forged the longship, wavelets slapping,
At their prow, the clinker planks still resolute,
Two porpoise raced in bow-spray, no men would wish,
To cast a spear, fixed they were to safety of the ship.

Now chanted Sigi the singer, his olive skin was shining,
'Ho,' growled the men, a whale now led them on,
This ship seemed to know, by instinct what the crew,
Were thinking and also how, the helmsman held the rudder,
They saw a coastal land ahead, flat and wide not narrow,
As at home, there were level fields and moors above,
They slipped south on rising tide, fetched up by a ridge of dunes,
The sailors stumbled, lay down caked in brine.

On the beach, Grim struck a spark from flint,
A man climbed up the dune, called back it was an axe-shaped isle,
Surrounded by the salt, yet over on the southern side,
Was a hall with sunlight, glinting from its steep-pitched roof,
They did not know, this was a healing isle,
Or that an ancient pilgrim's path, crossed its flats beneath the tide,
Yet no watchman saw the *Wyrm*, saw the tired men spread out,
None had even thought, that such a force could end their ways.

Yet years later, these very sailors will have adopted,
The cult of single god, and on this isle a priory pink,
Of sculpted stonework, will be raised,
For here on Lindisfarne, soon the crew were curious,
How so much wealth had gathered, was this single god so much wiser,
They launched the *Wyrm*, rowed out and round the isle,
Grim stood tall upon the deck, stared at the shore,
There was a coloured cross, set in grassy sward.

The monks stared at the longship, saw the northern soldiers,
Who seemed to laugh, thumping ship with axe and sword,
Now they carried flashing shields, gleaming war-gear,
Down the gangway, not one stood to oppose,
The spacious vessel *Wyrm*, and so it rode on hawser,
And Grim and men loaded, their arms with silver chalice,
Books of jewels and torque of gold, silver pin and plate,
This had become a crossing, it would pay the Norsemen well.

The walls were strong, but the sculpted rood and screen,
Were burned and so too, hung the doors on broken hinges,
Wondrous singing would no more, fill the luscious hall,
Those windows of a place, of sacred learning,
Had been closed, prayer cushions would long remain unclaimed,
None will hold the lamp of learning, lit two hundred years before,
One older monk, all incense now abandoned,
Had scratched on pillar as they left, how had it come to this?

So Ægir granted wishes to the sailors, for they were worthy of his help,
They had slaughtered sheep, provisioned boat from spring,
Some had prayed at island grove, for their fleet of one,
To pass through soft days, and creep into the fjord of home,
Now a competition spirit, came upon the heroes,
As they left the isle, over dormant waves,
They rowed and heaved the *Wyrm*, across the sea,
Faster than the stallions of Freyr, could pull his famous ship.

They hoped they would arrive, just at the hour,
When ploughmen walked their oxen, out to break the soil,
They expected they would see, women laying out the washing,
Who would shout to longhouse, holding hands of waiting children,
There would be smiles on men, at oars and tiller,
Yet as they came ashore, some women had already seen,
The fleet was only one, for they'd been spinning yarn,
For clothes that missing husbands, would never claim or wear.

Soon Grim stood before the people, 'Let me show you,
How our quest was so rewarded, how this *Wyrm*,
Will soon to be judged, the most famous ship in all the ports,'
A crimson carpet now was spread, on wooden longhouse floor,
And a pile of golden gear, glittered in the candlelight,
'Our swords and axes hummed, in the smoky hall,
We had all the heroes, who won this famous hoard,
And bore this treasure back, bright in boxes to the *Wyrm*.'

Under a cruel king, many a warrior crouches,
Filled with sorrow, waiting for an outer threat,
Often wishing their kingdom, might be overcome,
But this was not the case, for the men who followed Grim,
Now Cædmon's hands had guides, and Sigi sang a final lay,
'This candle was made, to become entirely flame,
Friendship and loyalty, have brought us home again,'
And Cædmon smiled as he heard, these words from distant desert lands.

Now this saga of the quest, will end beside the ragged rocks,
Valiant Grim will stay, a skipper all his life,
Borghildr's hopes had been raised, when she saw the *Wyrm*,
Yet now were dashed, and amongst the waiting crowd,
Stricken Steingerd was tearing, once again her hair,
Yet Finn's grandfather, clapped his boy on shoulders,
And took his axe, to prop beside the door,
If only other ships had come back, safely to their island home.

All could see on Dísir's face, her deep relief,
She knew the future, for her children was secure,
And though Steingerd shouted loud at Grim, he spun away to Borghildr,
'You should adopt, that boy Sigi now,
Cædmon needs a guide, he grew clever on this trip,
Even though it seems, he takes on many bruises'
And so the sailors from the ship, seemed altered by this trip of treasure,
Each had grown a little taller, and smiles were on their faces.

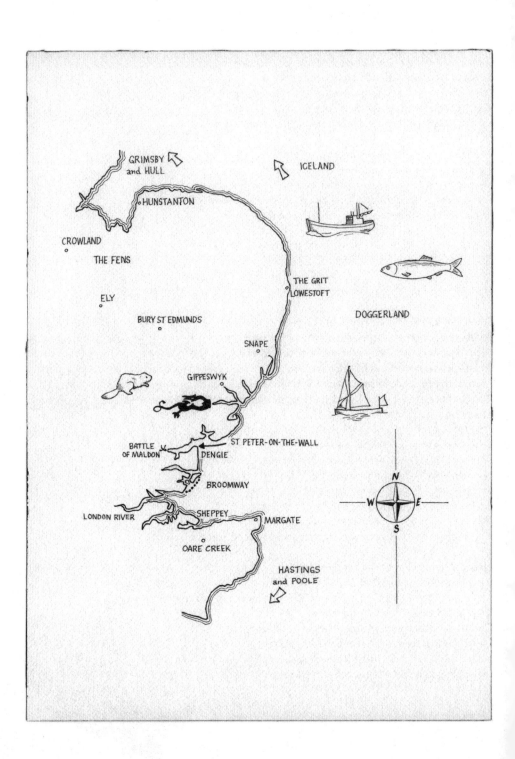

CHAPTER THREE

THE EASTERN SHORE

Pakefield Man, Lowestoft

It started with a flooding of the land, a drying then a drowning.

The tall figure had paused as the tide eased over steely shins. To the east was the sea, to the south and north too.

It was the night of summer solstice, at a verge that once was dry. He faced the land, and seemed to give a sideways glance, in his left hand was a staff, ten ells long and ending in an orb of straw. It fitted well his grip.

This was the place of first light, a festival for stories. Night breeze snapped the canvas of the tent, and assembled folk settled onto wooden chairs and all could hear the waves crump on the beach below. By the darkest hour, the tide had ebbed, and the crowd was drawn back to the long-limbed god. The moon had risen and it shone a silver path upon the sea. Those who summoned all these people strode with blazing torch, the crowd breathed in, and stepped forward. The straw was lit inside the giant's frame, golden grass that had been green in spring, packed tight as if a target for an archer. There was light inside the dark, it seemed, and he began to flicker. From the sandstone cliff, he had seemed slight at water's edge.

Yet down here, this Ægir lit each lifted face, the wind spinning sparks and shards of straw. This burning man, he silenced all the people.

Such hush on land, it can quieten inner noise. Yet that year, living figures had crossed to this coast in hope, fifty leagues to south. The migrants were in a sealed container, they wept and called their families. Batteries and air had drained, but the driver had already sold his soul. In court, there were no words of sorrow. So swiftly does all the world come to be a ruin. The giant no longer burned, so I spoke of a saga from the marsh, one thousand years ago, when friend and cousin, men and women, swung sword and axe, and some fell and others fled the field on stolen horses. And how in the court of the cloistered king, the ermine-clad had one concern, how to stay upon the throne.

On this eve, back on every Denmark beach, a sail's stretch and a wind's whip away, bonfires would be burning. It was a night secured by flame, and all would share in sadness for the fleeting nature of our lives.

Once four decades and more before, we too had strode from the surf and serpent-circled sea, north beyond the harbour, where had been the fishing village of the Grit. It had been midsummer, the two hundredth anniversary of American independence. Down the cliff path was carried food and drink in crates, and search parties walked the beach, gathered driftwood and timber pieces, and we dug a pit in the sand and piled stones around the edge. Across the night's short hours of dark, the light flamed and flickered.

Then we swam in neon fire. We rose dripping from the salty water, streaming falling phosphorescence, green girls and boys walking out from shallow sea.

This day the sky began to brighten, well before the rosy dawn. The water was molten mercury, the wind brisk and cool.

From the harbour wall to north appeared three clinkered boats, six oars in each that dipped and strained, dipped again. The boats swung in the swell and thumped through waves, beaching by the cold colossus. They were bearing gifts to share. Trestle tables in a line were set back upon the sand. A pale stillness spread across the shore. The crews stowed oars and jumped onto the sand, and carried fishes smoked and cooked, set the feast by rolls of bread. The people gathered now, bleary in the pale light.

The sun eased from dark horizon band, the crowd stood together eating, and the light lit the blossoms on the hill, blazed from windows opened to the salt. It shone through the ribbed and graceful god, waiting in the waves.

> He has no mind for harp, nor of receiving rings,
> Or for any other thing, but the rolling of the waves.

> [*The Seafarer*, The Exeter Book, c970]

And so begins this tale, where the North Sea in flood washes up at Kent and diverts to every dune and slack of Flanders and the Holland lowlands.

The standing wave of tide gathers by the Faroe Isles, funnels south past Shetland and Orkney, and comes to spin in three counter-clockwise amphidromes. At each hub is a still point, at the spinning edge the tide washes into salting and swatchway, up creek and over causeway. It laps at sea wall long-since raised, it carries salt far up river. This is no open sea, it is shelf-shallow and treacherous as a province, there is fast-flowing river, currents changing hour by every hour. When tide and wind oppose, now comes steep curling wave, a black nor'easter booming full on shore, swirling slack and eddy, surf bark and seabirds flighting fast to landward, wicked seas with white-capped comber.

Then stillness, not a breath, starshine on the water.

The herring fishers said, we're going down to Shetland, as they drifted north on falling tide, then back up on rising water to the Goodwin Sands. Their world was on this sea that was often not a sea: sandbank freed, wind screaming in the rigging. In pitch dark, a ship could be stranded by striking the bottom of the sea.

Yet looking north from southmost shore, it felt like north was up. On the Kentish coast, there is creek and beach, marsh and river. Once barges with five thousand square ochre feet of sail laid up the Medway, along the creeks of Oare and Faversham, hulls scraped clean each winter. Skippers and their mates waited in the fleetside pubs for news of work, at the Three Mariners, at the Plough and Sail. They had crossing tales to tell, to ports and far-flung places, how they met strangers and shared food, returned with cloak of kindness, black coal one trip, straw piled high another. The dairy maid and ploughman took home these tales, shared theirs of cold cattle shed and the old enemy of winter clay.

At the height of days of wind, there were half a thousand sailing barges and more, top speed eight knots with lee rail underwater, often then becalmed. A single passage could take weeks, or just a single tide.

Now it was a graveyard, this coast for the working barges of the east.

On the trade roads of the northern sea, there had been brigantine and buss, boats clinker-built and carvel-planked. There was coble, cockler, collier and cutter, dredger, drifter, ketch-rigged bil-ly-boy. A schooner, lighter, half and halfer, sloop and smack, a hull hauled upon the dunes, tied to rotten quay. There was painted transom, lugger, yawl and wherry, mulie barge, stackie barge, spritsail barge, London mixture for the fields, coal for city gas lamp.

Let us just declare, at this ring of sea, you can be sure of wind. Breeze and puff, roar and zephyr, a gusty gale. A wind will howl with rage, hearts a-flutter; a sough will only ruffle moonlit water. Yet wind gave way to coal and oil, craft set to thumping rhythm. Sail was slow, no longer modern. And soon in cities on the land, vehicles would move no faster than a horse.

One day we walked east from the tarred fisher-sheds of Whitstable. There were oysters up on racks in the sea, and ranks of turning turbines. That night a storm had beaten at the glass, and rain had run and blurred the glittered lights out on the estuary. On the far side was the south Essex skyline, beyond dark water, and the isles and lowlands of the Dane's Hundred. It was days after the winter solstice and fishing boats had risen high in harbour. The tide had flooded cottage basements by the shore. This was a coast for city migrants, retired to live in light. Yet there was decay, a shadow of abandonment and good days long departed. We walked on promenade and shingle bank, and turnstones flickered by the waves, crowds of crows watching from the grassy slopes. Heavily the rain fell on Herne Bay and the route to inland station.

Across the River Swale lay once-hellish Hertei Isle, the limed longhouse of the Ferry Inn up from red hills on the brine. A causeway led from Oare marsh, dipped under white horses on the yeasty sea. The route was marked with posts, and in the sediment was a broken hull. Godwits fed, lifted wings to dry. On the Horse Sands was a red trawler, the *First Freedom* out of Faversham, straining at its anchor, one crewman looking back at shore. There long had been a threshold guardian, a ferryman of old, for this was halt where in the late 800s Viking Danes over-wintered, in the second year of Alfred's reign.

A lamp would shine, at the Inn, a guide for reed-cutters ferried home. This wintry morn, all the windows were dark and every soul had fled.

The path turned round the Oare meres and pointed south inland. A flock of lapwing lifted, the fleets were watery silver. Horned cattle grazed in reeds. Above the susurrus of sound, the clouds dashed away, and light burned inside the panicles. A host of knot was gathered on the scrape, waves splashing at their feet. In the distance could be seen sails furled on main and mizzen masts, one last barge black-hulled, lettered still with gold. A flock of Brent geese flighted in, and circled looking down at wrecks. For in the creeks were many ancient horses-of-the-sea, in twos and threes, once their planks polished till they shone, now only rotting timbers tipping into sediment. North of here, the London River had been black and bleak, no curlew burbling over flats. There was broken wharf, waste upon the tideline, oil on water, smoke and smog to breathe. There would have been chaos at the docks, the noise unbearable to crew who lived by wind and sail.

Blow after blow, winter paused and summer faded, and on the northern edge of estuary, now clean enough to house a run of salmon, you will find the least safe wetroad of all this circled sea.

There are a thousand wetroads crossing Britain's isles. Inland they are ford and watersplash, on the salt are strood and causeway, revealed and drowned twice daily by the brine. They link old drovers' routes, they wander out beyond the seawall and its safe defence.

On the Maplin Sands, where a sailorman in days gone by could cut a route in a draft of half a fathom, on those sands is the ancient Broomway, ten leagues long a path laid with hazel wattle.

The way from Wakering Stairs once was marked with mapples, half a thousand switch-brooms set in sand, their heads lifting with the tide. In a sea fog, you might not know which way was left or right, and it is said one hundred people have been lost. I walked it one blazing summer day, container ships rising in a heat mirage out beside the Shivering Sands. I returned as winter solstice called, one mighty day of sky, the sea a layer on rippled sand. It was a world of wonder out beyond the marsh and on the surface of the sea. How time had passed. Guides Brian and Toni Dawson took out photos, their daughter still away at college. Time had drained to the sea. The winter light was bright, in the pale sky stretched trails of cloud. At the Heads, the entries back to land, pebbles were stained green with chlorophyll. Walkers splashed and slick mud drew down on boots. At the coastal battery, the red paint of ten-foot shell had faded. It was quiet, there was neither bee nor grasshopper. Fifty years ago, a London airport had been proposed. Wash your mouths out, say the Foulness islanders. It took an age to fight away.

For a thousand years, this was the isle's front garden path. The postman rode on horse and cart across the sands, bringing dryland news to archipelago. He passed rotting wreck, and stopped to gather plaice and sole from the traps of a Saxon fish-kettle. Barefoot was the way to walk, the sea warmed in a thousand sparkling pools. Once the Reverend Marsh of St Mary's on Foulness, returning home shoeless and carrying books, stepped from broom to broom, and saw green lights glowing in the fog. A marsh ghost, smugglers heading for the shore, something leaking from the soul. We walked back south-west toward the setting sun. There were teeming wild duck and charcoal geese, and as the sun fell further, wigeon arrowed cross the heavens.

These were the isles where illness once was endemic. Have you had your ague, people asked in spring, and then again in autumn.

It is often said, the tide comes in faster than a running horse. In days of yore, the last of the barge sailormen, Bob Roberts, wrote of sailing over Maplin's rip and slack, and there before them was a man aboard a swimming horse. The mate thought a buoy had been untethered, but here was an Army officer, cut off by running tide. Out from Shoebury, a gallop on the sands, and now awash and lost. They threw a line and towed him in. Oðinn in his dwelling hall taught spells of battle, could drive away a storm, directing Valkyries Hildr, Hlökk and Guðr to sink or spare a sailor.

Near the shore were skeletal timbers, a cruiser sunk in sand, the remains of trawler that never floated off.

The sun dipped fast, long shadows cast by ripples on the sand. Far away was the land of people. Out here were figures walking on the dry sand, bunched up and staying close. Black-backed gulls wheeled and cried. We turned west to head for land, the tide already speeding past the path. We stepped up at Wakering Stairs, and stood upon the fortress wall.

> West I came over fishing grounds,
> And I carry the sea of Oðinn's heart,
> That's how I sail.

> [Egill Skalla-Grimson, *The English Poems*, c950]

People sometimes murmur, you can never walk the same shore twice.

Whatever the gap of tide and time, the liminal place of wet and dry will shift, across lifeways, far to other eras. At the harbour-side you might hear the creak of oar, at briny dusk the taste of fragrant oak-smoked fish. By noon heat, there could be tarred planks blistered by the sun.

Fifteen years before, I walked all this Saxon shore and Angle coast in and out of a year. Some days the vault of sky was vast, on others mist locked in the land. Yet heading east and north, the sun was ahead and on the starboard side, reflected up from water as it fell from sky. On one side, the world seemed luminous, and my sight became bleached, as if old fading film. For half a moon, the sea washed back and forth inside my right eye.

How long is a coastline? Well, this of the East Saxons is lengthy, yet it is hard to say what is one thing or another. Should we measure round each cliff or pebble, each salting isle, and where does the brine cease as it flows up each river on the tide.

One thing is clear. All low-lying lands have long been under threat, maybe more so now. The land sinks and sea rises, and every century has brought breach and inundation of the stronghold. In the bleak winters of 1949 and 1963, the raw sea round the Dengie froze, yet the scars of savage flood of '53 were deeper. No one saw it coming, a full moon, hurricane-force winds piling water south, a deep depression pulling up the sea. All three, that winter night, brought waves working at the sea walls, filling badger sett and rabbit burrow, loosening cracks in clay. With thunderclaps, in a hundred places, they just let go. Three hundred people drowned, the sea stealing cross the land and flooding houses from the back.

People woke and gazed from upstairs windows, they thought snow had fallen, gasped when they saw it was water in the moonlight. It was a stunning triumph for the sea, refugees housed for months inland, the sight of slithering eels stranded on the marsh and clogging up the fire hoses. Sea walls were raised and widened, hard defence against another flood.

And so they circle back, landscapes pivoting on memory coming round again.

Middlewick Farm lies on a rise, five metres up from sea, the defended Dengie lowlands spread out below. To the far south was Kent, the horizon blue this summer day. We gathered the code from Janet and Pip Thorogood to open farm gates on the plain, they stood at farm door and waved, and we returned hours later hot and dusty. The corn was in, the wind turbines turning. They have farmed here since the fifties, Janet's mother migrating south twenty years before in search of fertile land. They packed their Ayr farm on a train, machine and cattle, plough and table. We sat in the front room, cool breeze blowing through the farmhouse. There was plaice for lunch, fresh from the Blackwater that very dawn. A copy of Isabella Tree's *Wilding* lay on the kitchen table with the papers. Pip had converted his farm to regenerative practices, a test of learning and redesign. All was well, the crops were stronger, and there was many a swift and swallow. The old ploughs stood idle, and there was carbon building in the soil.

Herbert Tomkins in *Marsh County Rambles* of 1904 felt these flat lands east of Burnham were a country made for smugglers, cut by half a hundred creeks and outfalls. It was a marsh pasture for sheep-wyke dairies, tall bulrush round the star-shaped decoy ponds, a bell on posts at each river ferry. Samuel Bensusan, laureate of the marshes, wrote of a land where silence was profound, and moonlight flooded landscape, where there was otter, but also hounds and hunter and a waiting butcher.

He was friends, too, with tramps of the road, grizzled wanderers with tanned skin and laughing eyes. 'It's a good life,' said one, 'the tramping, the weather's the only trouble, cold rain and east winds; but give me a barn and I don't mind.' This would have been the time, in days gone by and the harvest in, when great stews were cooked at marshy farms. Men were drawn from far for work, some on the run and seeking shadows. Each laid out an offering: hare and oxbird, eel and swede, fish and turnip.

We had walked out to the seawall, and faced south. The sun shone, there were straw stacks at field boundaries and skylarks singing over stubble.

In Bensusan's days of the thirties, this was a land of bosky elm and nightingales in spring, red squirrel and immense flocks of fieldfare and yellowhammer, sighing turtle dove and droning bees in clover. I once walked this route in thick fret, the wings of a thousand starling rushing in the fog, and then came the strained sound of a small plane searching for an airstrip.

An established custom requires you sit on the lichen-crusted seawall, and watch the sparkle on the sea, the waders at the waves, waiting for nothing happen. A flock of sparrows chattered in the elder by a drainage dyke. Swallows dived, fluttered up, taking insects from the yellow grasses. In the mud by Holiwell Point was the fossil of the car.

It had been here years ago, windows out and now the roof was gone and struts eroded. Bladder-wrack had swarmed up, and one day the car would be gone, as too a billion other fossil-fueled vehicles worldwide. A sailing barge was tacking, out from River Crouch, and from the far side on Foulness Isle was a sudden flash and flame, smoke pouring into morning sky. A heartbeat later came the thunder cracks. On this side was the double-decked war tower, angular concrete and narrow eyes, raised to watch for mines.

'I've never seen it,' said farmer Pip, a reminder the home territory is often hidden by the daily toil. Years ago, all the Essex archipelago was field and farm, or ringed for wargames. I had stayed over on Foulness in the pub's dying days, the George and Dragon, the rusting sign depicting George and the slain serpent, a small room made up above the bar for writer Ken Worpole and me. The diocese had called time, and inside the church cobwebs were thick across the aisle, the silence deep. We walked Wallasea Isle, flat and featureless some would say, the stubble sharp on stony soil.

So it was we looked back, from the choppy river on an autumn day of sun and spray.

At the marina, the pontoons were low, the tide out and boats on the mud. Skipper Selina said, we just took on the business, at the beginning of the year.

But the old fishing boat could take only six now, facing outwards. Yachts heeled, dinghies dashed. On the south side was wetland Wallasea, the seawalls breached and salt inside the land. It seemed a risk, yet time had been reversed, marsh and salting had appeared. The land now held the tide, providing flood protection services. Mother Redcap lived out on Wallasea, at a farm called the Devil's House, and at Canewdon, where Canute came ashore, there were six witches, three wore silk and three wore cotton, they rode down the hill to offer help to people at the river. The fish-boat motored up the Roach, toward the place where Darwin's *Beagle* was stranded in the silt. To the north was the riverfront of Burnham, when once I sat in box window and watched a lifeboat dedication.

The crowd sang to those in peril on the sea, and volunteer women and men stood to attention, the hymn to an eternal father, an Ægir under waves, to hear us when we cry to thee.

A flock of fifty avocet flickered on the foreshore, a bird extinct, so recently, yet here it was again. On the Foulness mud were common seals lazing as do people on a beach. The sun shone on the water, on silvered sand and silt. On the north side of the Crouch, wind turbines turned steadily, and we could see the distant straw block at the shore, where we had stood and looked this way.

At the northern Dengie edge is the stone chapel, St Peter-on-the-Wall, raised by Cedd in the 650s CE, the Christian migrants sailing south to raise a stave church on the Saxon shore. This Lindisfarne of the south was built of stone and red tile, harvested from Ythancaestir, the shore fort built by Rome. Here you may stand, at the eastern end and look upon the saltings, small groups of people lying in the heat mirage over the strip of sandy beach. Sails raced in and out of white horses, the shore strip of county far beyond. The oaken door was open, swung on iron hinges. Inside was the silence of deep time, rays of light focused by the three high windows.

Saint Cedd stood at this door, a tall man with sloping shoulders, like Aidan of Lindisfarne he had a disregard for the traps of wealth and power. Here was a place of sacred stone that had survived many an insulated king. On the path of crushed flint was a single piece of red Roman tile, a glaze on one side.

At this foundling place, three hundred years later in 991 CE, a water fleet of one hundred handsome sails came on the inward tide.

There were whale ways to follow, in those days, up and down the shallow sea. Stood alone in leading longship, at crimson prow, was Olaf Tryggvason born in Orkney, his helm bright as glass, pointing out the water path to royal mint. Dolphins were common enough in those days, shapeshifting rescuers of sailors, they would have leapt in bow waves, and children would have stopped their games, looking out with wonder at the ships. Would some crew have waved, as they bent their oars near breaking point? Did Olaf stop at Cedd's chapel, was he inspired by three centuries of longevity, for in only eight more summers he imposed on Iceland, adopt the Christian God or trade will cease, hostages be killed. On this day, away flew Olaf to Northey Isle, under skeins of geese, to demand a tribute from the cold King Æthelred.

And here would be composed the saga-poem, *The Battle of Maldon* (Mældune), for Maldon was the mint and he sought the silver to buy the throne of Norway.

A thousand years and more had passed, and grey clouds turned green, a blizzard tearing down the long platform. All sound was dampened, and snow covered wood and plastic bales, lay on cars and concrete. The writer Andrew Simms had asked, 'Come to our city book club, we are reading this books of yours.' It was a tall house in a terrace off the Holloway Road, and the group convened around the kitchen table. And so land met mind, and words had taken hold. Rosa said, 'I know you already, I have had your voice in my head for weeks.' They discern things I hadn't seen.

Yet a late train was cancelled, the land still was frozen, and there was a squeeze for space on the last stopper. That short night, before dawn, I drove with my brother to listen to ghosts of this battlefield. In those few hours, the wind had poured from west, rattling roof and bare branch. Ahead was the wet causeway, and the air rushed through a stand of pine. At the seawall by a raised field of kale had stood Byrhtnoð and his East Saxon army. The sun rose across the cold Dengie and shone along a red thread of cloud. Light glinted on the town to west, blazed upon the mudflats.

The causeway arced left then right toward a grassy hill and hawthorn thicket on the western side. We had guessed the ships of Olaf would have pulled up safely on the far side. But here was beach and turf, a perfect setting for a force to pose in full.

A barge was stranded in the mire, and a flock of knot went up and flickered, drifted down again. We stood on Olaf's promontory, and faced the town and waited. The birds flew again, and twisted, but we could not see the hawk. It was wet underfoot, and the isle farm dark. The pasture was poached by hooves, yet was a perfect vantage point for the Vikings. Surely, you would think, they scoped this place in advance. Here would the shields have been laid, here sword and axe, then arrows fletched and flung ashore.

The causeway was not narrow, yet it was written Wulfstan, Maccus and Alfere fought back the Viking army for a tide. The land seemed to say, this was a choreographed battle with start time, with shared rules and pitch marked by hazel poles. On the eve before the battle-day, soldiers would have slipped across the wetroad, sat by meat crackling on the spit, passed mead from hand to hand, shared stories with those they soon would fight.

On both sides were female warriors, dressed as men, fighters skilled with lance and sword.

Some say the Earl of Essex, white-haired Byrhtnoð, old and hoar and five ells tall, somehow blinked to let the Vikings come ashore and win. Yet he was trying feint and trick, to force invaders back to brine. From above, a sea eagle viewed the battle lines, stretched deep and far. For soon was raised a riot on this stage. Byrhtnoð stepped forward, and some men on either side leant on spears, set down their shields in stacks upon the soil. From home in Viking village there were mothers who had not wanted their sons to go; in nearby marshy cottage, there was wife of smith and cooper, mother of some rangy boys, who watched them rush to sign for the Essex fyrd.

Yet it came to this: a grandmother waits, she had seen so much, clapped her last grandson on the shoulders; a mother collapses under sorrow, tears at her clothes.

Yet sure enough, the reign of Æthelred was far from done. Byrhtnoð lay dead, Olaf was given ten thousand pounds of silver. It would be twenty-five years more before Canute sailed to this shore, pressing up the Crouch to claim the crown, the first to join the English and the Danish threads. Such a king, he often said, as did Heorot's Hrothgar, should not eat, until all others at the feast were served.

And on one occasion, Canute sat before the rising waves, an instruction to his courtiers, there are certain things a king can never do.

Frost shall freeze, fire melt wood,
Earth grow, ice bridge over,
Winter shall be cast off, good weather come back,
… A good reputation is best.

[*Maxims I*, The Exeter Book, c970]

Animals know much more than we do.

Out on these isles was seen a marvellous hare swimming in the water, rising up with wisps of phosphorescence. No wonder it had magic powers, this runner who could see a storm.

Three rivers north, up the Stour and beyond the site of battling dragons and on the route to Fens, stands a wool church with a tiny stained-glass window of the Tinners' Rabbits, three hares sharing three ears. How was this pre-Christian symbol adopted by the church, how too so many green oaken men in the rafters? It was Anglo-Saxon goddess Eostre's favourite animal, one poem of the 1400s declaring seventy-seven names for the hare: the way-beater, lurker in the ditch, fellow of the dew, the looker to the side, the springer and the jumper, the intuitive hare with leaping mind. Owd Sally and Owd Sarah, and good day to you, Sir Hare.

It was the dark before dawn, the hour of the rabbit at the equinox, at the upper reaches of the River Pant and Blackwater. The dewy path wound up the streamline, and all was silence. This water would flow over wetroads and out to sea at St Peter's. Those Saxon masons would have known a land rich with beasts, yet the migrants' chapel also witnessed losses, over the years. Now from copse of willow and alder came living sounds of bottomland, splash and chuckle of the water, then a slow expanding stillness.

You could be tempted to sleep with windows open, to hear such timeless music of the marsh.

The pools were faint before the dawn, growing silver. The land was dark. Into silence sang a robin, a wren flitted by our feet, a frog was croaking. There was a wavering hoot of tawny owl, a youngster calling back. Time passed. More light fell on water, and a lodge of woven stick and mud appeared. The water surface undulated, and an adult rose, ripples slapping at the shore. There were midges, that autumn morn, where these water architects had been working, a night of building almost done.

For this beaver family, now two kits and two adults, was the east of England's first for a thousand years.

At the time of Gawain's encounter with the Green Knight, the beaver was a favoured creature. Such an intent worker, that animal, each day altering home and habitat. The Green Knight's beard was *beaver-hued* with a red glow, his face as fierce as fire. Yet he was also a green man of oak forest and the wilds, so lived by courtesy and good manners.

By the hour of the dragon, the extent of their design was clear, twenty dams of latticed branch and mud, two lodges with entry porches under water, willows felled and stripped for food, ash ignored but dying now it stood in rising water. The next spring, shoots will sprout from willow stumps, and the beavers will have grown fresh food again. In times past, such rural pools could bring danger, for the mere-maid and the bugbear lurked to drown a passer-by, as did Grendel's mother, dragging children into darkness.

You can see, these beaver think in abstractions, and have filled this patch of land with power. They are carers for the water. Where had been a ditch at margin of a corn field, now were ponds on several levels, slipways of mud, many wetland plants. Archie Ruggles-Brise had led these wild-architects to his land, and has plans, enclose a longer stream, rewild fields that take too much to farm. Beavers work for free, after all. Could this use of land for food find a way to make the wilds work, could this redesign change the way we think?

Now the beavers slept, safe from predator and hunter, and soon the cocks will crow down in village, and people would be stepping out to check for eggs.

Soon yellow leaves will fall from oak and poplar, the autumn thrown down and winter once again ready to stand over mere and swamp.

South of beaver watershed was another reservoir. These are the country's driest lands, right by salty sea, and every village claims a sunshine title. Yet how to keep the towns and cities from a drought. To the region's north lie the Fens, the great common wetlands inhabited once by a stilted people, dried out by drainage engineers. Water today is piped to upper Pant and Stour, transferred overland by river, piped again and so the reservoirs are filled. There is footage of post-war demise of Peasdown village, in black and white with heroic commentary. Progress was coming, and the Sandon Vale of South Hanningfield would be flooded, farms and village gone underwater. It was conceded, civilisation was, 'Washing its hands of the tiny hamlet and its once green valley.' And so each house was flattened, each tree uprooted, a farm family and four children carried out chairs and one doll to a flat-bed truck, a dog racing round their feet.

But on their mostly flat farm, a clay and gravel dam was raised, puddled by the feet of migrant labourers. 'We could have taken our time,' said Farmer Froob of the 1950s, 'The wheat looks good this summer.'

We walked around the western lake, Simon Lyster born in the nearest farm to avoid destruction. There were bones of birds on the concrete dam, and overspill ponds had been filled with reeds. Yet from a pine copse came a wondrous sound, the grating call of guardian raven. Two supernatural ravens, Huginn and Muninn, thought and memory, sat on Oðinn's shoulders, spied on Midgard's lands for the one-eyed god. Ravens have long been absent from the east, yet here was a pair, returned to the site of drowning

Had the ravens flown the thirty leagues from Tower of London, had they doomed a kingdom now to fall? They laughed from highest branch, looking down upon us standing far below.

We need the drinking water. Yes that, and the glaciers and cooler seas.

When land is lost, whole villages razed, then some wisdom of the wild is gone for good. Fond farewells may be said, to lowest lying lands. When Maurice Beresford in the 1940s had an inkling there were deserted medieval villages, historians scoffed. Whole village depopulations were rare, plague-driven if at all. Beresford wrote 'no traveler comes easily to a lost village; you must be friends to mud, to green lane and rotting footbridge, to broken stile.' No one wanted to check, yet he discovered more than three thousand lost villages.

He found an answer: those who wrote the history also cleared the land, and villages and their commons were enclosed for sheep and corn, fields seized for sculpted garden, woodland felled and heath ploughed.

You still can find, hillsides with house platform and remains of croft, hollow-ways of street by stream, ridge and furrow under grass. You cannot find, the stories of those people.

And since that era of enclosures, the whole coast has warped. Dunwich port on the Suffolk coast, three churches and a monastery, is mostly underwater. South of Aldeburgh on an empty shingle spit was Slaughden: from a hundred years ago are pictures of the Three Mariners pub by fisher cottage row. As the sea advanced, so fishwives opened front and back doors, set down stepping stones, letting in and out the tide to flow across the earthen floor. Gone too are Easton and Eccles, Clare and Keswick, Newton and Shipden.

Yet to this coast came other migrants, people seeking other ways of living: the worker utopias of Bauhaus Bata and at Crittalls, creating shoes and windows, the Peculiar People and their tiny chapels, the low-impact groups at Othona, Old Hall and Assington. The moon once shone the same on every port and coastal place, even if they had no fish. On medieval maps, the ness at Easton protrudes to sea, the church of St Nicholas was the easternmost point of Britain. It was sheared away, and now Lowestoft holds the eastern mark.

This sea grows bolder, advances still.

———

There was cool air on the haven, and this was to be the hottest summer day.

The barge *Thistle* slipped away, took the lock, and descended down the river. It left behind the town of Gippeswyk burned by Olaf's flaming arrows on his way to raid the Maldon mint. The barge passed grain terminal and cement store, and slipped under span of concrete carriageway. The sky was blue and the river green. All was quiet, ringed jellyfish were floating by.

'There,' pointed the skipper, 'that's Bob Roberts' fine old barge, *The Cambria*.'

It had yellow masts, so was a Kentish boat, moored at Pinmill by the sloping hard. This was a day for barge revival, for in the Harwich harbour, where meets the rivers Stour and Orwell, there were many barges crossing in the onshore breeze. Wooden-hulled, concrete-hulled, red-ochre sails and crossing lines, tack and haul away. Njord was tolerant that day, and the barges surged, creaking at the strain of wind, ropes pulled and released, lee-board cranked up by capstan. Below deck there was sunbeam and dappled shadow on the polished wood. At first the barges seemed giants of the salt, beside yacht and dinghy, yet at this shore was a container port. The *Edme* fully rigged with white foresail and mizzen passed before a blue cargo ship. Cranes were plucking forty-foot containers piled high on deck, each filled with stuff we greatly need.

Two million, that's the count of containers coming to this port each year. Three thousand: that's the number of ships, and still the barge sailed on the power of wind alone. More than one degree: the amount the climate has already warmed.

Over here was shush of hull in water, the draw of wind past sail, over there the noise of civilisation.

All things are connected: wind as a future for the sea, the consumption economy, the growing climate crisis, the loss across the world of species. At this mouth of two rivers, at the weather edge of North Sea circle, you feel the earth is getting old, the sea tired, worn out by these pressures. Yet there was contentment that summer's day, for there are also plans to build a monument at Harwich to mark the place where two thousand Jewish *Kindertransport* children came ashore to safety in the last days of 1938, each clutching suitcase wrapped in string, a time of kindness for refugees. One was Hans Lichtenstein, and in *The Berlin Shadow*, his son and author Jonathan knelt on the platform at the ferry-train terminal, and kissed the concrete, the grit sticking to his lips.

'Why on earth did you do that?' queried his father.

Out on the water, nothing would make the sailing barge go faster. You settle in, watch for weather signs. The sun was low as the barge tied up at dock, and we just walked ashore, past eroding blocks of waterside flats.

Some years earlier, to these very estuaries, a wyrm did swim up the sweet river.

An egg had hatched in the Tower of London, it had been carried back from crusades by Richard Coeur de Lion, and the dragon escaped to swim down the Thames, north through sea, and inward to the Stour. In the valley, it ate sheep, put the land in chaos, and men bent bows and loosened arrows that sprang back from armoured plates. This wyrm chose a mere so deep, no one could find its bed, and it lay upon a hoard of gold. In a small waterside church, by black poplars loved by craftsman, on lime-washed walls above the north door, this wyrm is painted on the wall, beside Britain's oldest image of St Francis talking to the birds. Downstream, at the raising of two neighbouring churches, masons carved concrete heads, foliate men and lions on corbels and on the edging of the western doors. Upstream at Wormingford, it is said two dragons red and black came to duel upon the riverbanks, and in that church, in stained glass, is a green crocodile.

Dragons know much more than we do.

It was in this vale, some years before, that a lad was crowned king of the East Angles. The river meanders in this stretch, past the dragon's mere, yet the slopes are sharp and at the top is a stone chapel, thatched these days and the wooden slats drilled by nesting woodpeckers. The boy Edmund stood tall, this in the same year that six-year-old Alfred of Wessex was taken on a pilgrimage to Rome. He was a good king, wrote Ælfric in the passion of St Edmund, worshipped and humble, and 'To the poor and to all widows, he was charitable like a father.' His life would travel far, stitch itself upon the paths and ways, for the Danish army of Ivar the Boneless, son of Ragnar Loðbrok, had invaded the Anglo-Saxon heptarchy to seek revenge on Ælle for throwing his father in a pit of serpents. He pressed south and east, demanding payment and possessions. The East Angle bishop said to Edmund, 'Flee for these pirates will come and bind thee.'

The king would not renounce, and the army filled him full of arrows and threw his head in brambles of the forest.

The people of the sandy heath and heavy clay searched, heard a grey wolf calling, 'Here, here, here,' for the land was wild in those days, her paws protecting the king's head. Edmund was reburied and laid within a church twenty leagues away. His body did not decay, his neck healed and only a silken thread marked the cut. Over time, there came many St Edmund's pilgrim paths, worn deep in sunken lanes between the ancient oaks and hollies, leading to the Abbey, then crossing inland gap to the wet Fens further to the north.

People often wonder, what was it fetched the dragons to the vale and mere? How did they forge, the will of this lad to be a saint?

> What became of the horse? Of the young man?
> Where are the good times of the hall?
> … How that time has passed away.

[*The Wanderer*, The Exeter Book, c970]

Many a culture has a flood creation myth, so Merlin was right to be concerned.

The oldest written saga was found on tablets of clay, the *Epic of Gilgamesh* telling of cities of dust, and of the discontent of gods.

The prince Gilgamesh wished to tame the wilds, cut down cedar trees, so Enlil brought a flood. Perhaps his traders had learned how a wide dry land had been flooded by the sea; how ancient gods had been displeased, how so they wished we humans lived in different ways. Not many people get to name a country, and archaeologist Bryony Coles had an insight. There had been erratic finds, so curious none could place them, moorlog and flint found in fishnets, sunken forests at the coast, called Noah's Forests a century ago by geologist Clement Reid. 'Is it possible,' he asked, 'that thus originated source of stories of the deluge?'

By the end of the 1990s, the evidence was clear. The sea had risen after melting of the ice sheets, it drowned parkland and tunnel valley, took woods of birch and oak, displaced the grazers, turned freshwater marsh to salt and sea. Bryony called it *Doggerland*, after fish-famed Dogger Bank. That country had been dry, then drowned. People lived there, then were forced to move.

Long after the bones of the Pakefield giant were laid in soil, the last steppe people of Doggerland rowed to this shore. For until eight thousand years ago, nomadic hunter-gatherers roamed the prairies, searched for mammoth and giant elk, broad-browed auroch and great bison herds. On hunting hill and grassy plain, they camped at salty marsh and wide lagoon. At the still point of their world was Yggdrasil, the one tree that held up sky. Serpent circled distant sea, guarded all their ground. They shaped their land, sowed fruit and seed harboured from the wild, fished and fixed to spear barbs of antler bone. You can imagine, they could not hope for any better place.

Yet as eagles planed serene, there was a creeping shift, icebergs severed free, the waters rising up. They sensed a warp of salt and sea. The air was life, as it is today for people of the plains, a wealth of sun and rain. And while gannets screamed, a storm was beating at their border.

Now the waves rose fast, the height of you or me in half a hundred years.

So in that distant time, the people carried in and up their camps, dug up a hundred holy graves, buried bones once more. Still the surge poured in, league on league not letting up. They would have called on gods, on Oðinn by another name, on Thor and Ægir, desist and stop the sea. But they could not tame the tempest, all their shamans tried. One watery dawn, came a shocking sight. The sun-star rose from sea, later dipped into their western waves. Had they eaten fish forbidden, had a snake whispered from a tree, no one could recall. And so every hide of land and fire pit was drowned, each vale and fell seized by rising flood. They lashed boats of auroch-skin, flexed oars, lay their infants on the furs, and came upon the cliffs of higher land.

Did they meet a friendly king and queen; did these forest people rush down the beach and help the migrants from the brine?

What do you say when a whole landscape disappears, what words for sinking, when cultures go and sea village too? What hope is there, at all, when loved ones die?

Julia Blackburn wrote in *Time Song*, 'Oh I say casually, I'm writing about a country called Doggerland.'

Yet there was something else too, 'My husband died a few years ago; he has vanished yet he remains close.'

It had been dry and clear that spring, and now summer beat the land. We sat outside her Suffolk studio, up a hill four leagues from sea, ate lunch and walked the backcountry of the parish. There were promising signs of a new time, an incoming farmer had sowed wildflower strips for humblebees, dug fresh farm ponds, and golden barley rippled in the fields. In one wood pasture, ancient oaks were surrounded by rows of mown grass. 'The children liked to climb those trees,' said Julia. 'Yes,' I said, 'we have veterans like this in the valley, pollarded just so, perfect for climbing by the children.'

'Do you understand?' she wrote, 'I'm doing practice work here, trying to fill a hole, trying to find the songs that once were sung, that made us smile.'

And here was Doggerland itself: mammoth vertebrae, a stone axe, a round hip bone, on the shelves in front room and around the studio, every surface covered with objects of the old time.

I also have at home, on a window shelf, a flint axe-head, dredged up from Doggerland. It is grey-blue, flaked with serrated edge. The same fisherman, Eric Paisley then of Southwold town, also fetched from depths a piece of bog-oak. It is a dark wood heavy as iron. It could have been a piece of the rooftree Yggdrasil. These live beside a globe of golden amber, washed around the Øresund from Baltic.

These items grow old alongside us, unlike the dead who forever never age.

'What is your good life now?' I asked Julia.

It was the families of children, their hopes; it was simple food and plans for the next painting, the next book; it was the draw of porous world across the rolling fields; it was walking shore with friends. And we find we have some in common, as lifeways cross and intersect. The world grows a little smaller, friendlier. Chickens wander into the house, clucking. Julia had walked with one fossil shaman, he could spot them in the darkness, who said, 'I am interested in happiness,' and then he said to her, he thought it didn't matter what you did with your life, just so long as it made you happy.

'What about these past twenty years?' I asked archaeologist Vince Gaffney, whose deeper trawl nets have caught up bone and antler harpoon, charcoal from the fires that once were in the air.

'Well,' he said, 'We can peer through the yeasty sea, so our worldviews have slid sideways.' This very sea, that surrounds these islands, we know it once was dry. Just yesterday, it was. And what finds: thousands of bones, steppe fauna in the banks of west-facing Holland, tool and camp, woolly mammoth and rhino, many a wild horse fetlock. The Dutch fishers of the isle of Urk, long had weighted nets to trawl the sea floor. They also had a firm belief, the Bible's words were the highest authority. Up came ivory tusk as long as boat, stone skull, leg bone tall as man, and in the nets the fish were bruised.

The fishers were not threatened by these signs from deep, by this other design.

So they stabbed the bones with marlinspike, smashed them with an axe, threw them back into the sea in silence.

> Footprints need safe sediment,
> If they are to hold a memory,
> The creatures left nothing but bones,
> But the people left the remains of wooden posts,
> And hardly a trace of their passing.

[Julia Blackburn, *Time Songs* (4, 10, 17), 2019]

———

The Seafarer walked up from the sea, out of mist and ghouls of tarred net racks.

He had a gold earring, worn for long sight. He said, 'You know, this place was much more accepting in those days, when still there was the fishing.'

He had watched near four-score years of suns rising from this sea, he'd been a skipper for half a life. Fish big and small, came leaping from the sea. We sailed and steered, he said, to other ports and places, returned with tales, with fish laid out on ice below. We looked inward to the sandy sea, as did others, at every seaside port. We came in good faith, said the sailors, we will carry home a story, even as the water nymphs were poised below. We were sitting at the base of Lowestoft cliffs, where was once the Grit, the beach village at Britain's most eastern port. Yet today, no pebbled hut and corner pub, no smell of fish or sail loft, no women braiding nets. As we spoke, chattering sparrows crowded up, took crumbs from off his palm.

Keith Mayall was a deckie learner first, rose to skipper, sailed with men famed from here to Iceland.

Three years with Jumbo Fiske, six foot six and winner of the Prunier Trophy for the largest catch, the Scots called him Tiny. Those fish boys, they dressed in coloured suits on return to port, they were called the dockside dandies. I recalled those lads, walking through the town at night, each with gutting knife hidden up a sleeve. For in those eyes could be seen each man lost, each mother wondering with a watery glare, where exactly was her son, at the bottom of a sea.

'Well,' said Keith of the burnished face, 'we often stopped at Grimsby, walked with friends down Freeman Street, to the busy pubs. I went back. Oh Christ! Only ghosts.'

The Grit was renowned. Many a seaside town had a beach village such as this. The Grit was large, at the home of herring. The skippers kept logbooks, filled with secrets of the sea roads. They sketched each ground, each colour and the walls of chop. They named the banks of Doggerland. They read the signs, called judgement on the water, watched the sea turn, pulled up pail to taste the water green and clear. They searched for oil on surface, a milky tinge, sought guillemot and gannet diving down on shoal, also whale and porpoise chasing herring: blowers, shouted crew, they could smell the stenchy breath. They hated jellies, the cause of skin eruptions.

This was their life at sea: down below were silver fish, they could see at night the lines of phosphorescence.

These eastern ports now were weighted down with colder shadows.

Keith fished from Norway in the sixties, how hard it was, they thought the English had it easy. There were some men, grey and sick around the eyes, who did not care about return, from this sea of blessings. Yes crew outnumbered places, often at the dock, and once a deckie boy stabbed his gutting knife in mast, just stepped overboard. So put out something for the cat, there was much about sea crossings never spoken. Never whistle up a wind, never let a parson step on board, always pick the first good fish from out the net, gift it back to King of Herring. They frowned on any talk of cow or rabbit, and never-ever mentioned pig, a beast so sensitive to wind, it could whistle up a gale. Never sail on Friday, always fine to fish on Sunday. Let that rope go, let go! There was still the daily fight for dockside berth.

There comes a time, though, when there was no one left, none to wander on the sea roads.

'What were you searching for?' I asked: 'Well not fish,' just a doorway. 'That's why the Bethel

CHAPTER THREE

services were always filled by fishers and their families.'

All had gone, yet he had lived so long. Stare out on any piece of land and sea, and what spirits do you hear?

The fishers looked on lugger, schooner, packet ship, knew a storm could test both seam and skipper, a sail could rip from luff to lug, leave them stranded on a sandbank. For these beach men built the first lifeboat, two hundred years ago, swift-rigged for sail. They would go on to save fifteen hundred lives. The up-cliff cemetery, as in all villages by the sea, set slots aside for sailors, but these were claimed for boys and girls and mothers. As disaster loomed, when planks split and masts ripped, when waves were in not out, then to wreck rowed the beach men, the first hand claimed the ship for salvage. When the sailing barque, the *Erna*, broke ashore, bearing Norway timber, none would forget the sight. As the ship split apart, a thousand rats scuttled out of hiding, plunged into the sea to swim ashore. Some clung to spar and splintered wood, others perched on floating box and crate.

When the rats reached the beach, they formed up as one and ran together inland.

Alas fish bone was in the fishers' sinews. Men and women of the Grit faced outwards, east to sandy broth.

Twelve *skor* alley-ways long ago were scratched, from sandy flats to upper cliff, where business-man and burgher, far from reek of fish, lived in finest terraced row, lighthouse shining out to churning sea, over flinty hut and rotted horse-of-sea. So they slept, but with troubling dreams. We recalled, the sea defences then were less broken. This early morn the sun was bright, and here had been a lifeguard hut with flagpole, and we launched canoes to paddle down and up the coast. One summer, there had been a plague of greenfly. The air thrummed, hard to see more than a few metres through the insects. We cycled with makeshift masks, but still they burrowed into eyes and ears. The insects chose yellow and green cars on which to settle, and we brushed them into heaps, two to three feet deep.

Now all was silent, only waves gurgling.

My brother and I walked south toward the harbour, there was flash and chatter, a quarrelling flock of parakeets. What do these ring-necked migrants know that we do not? All else was closed, a harbour once thronged with drifter and herring cask, market bell and shouting men, women down from Fife gutting at the barrels. Small businesses seemed stranded. We walked by the lead-en mirror of the harbour. It felt like a whole day had passed, yet it was only breakfast time. There were a hundred Saturdays of memory, up the High Street, past dark recess of empty shop, places worked all day to buy a music album made of wax.

At the theatre, we sat outside with coffee, watching slow advance of shadows.

We strode the scores, down and up, those dozen narrow lanes scored in cliff by feet and cart and mule. Spurgeon's Score, name of our paternal grandmother; Maltsters Score, tight entrance, a knock on the head and you're in the King's Navy for life. Brick crinkle-crankle walls and an old red rose wonderful with perfume. Wilde's Score, where lived the merchant who set up the town's first school, the only way up for fisher girls and boys; Rant Score, where came Cromwell in 1653; Martin's now Gowing's, where came cleric John Wesley to preach in 1764, writing 'A wilder congregation I have never seen.' George Borrow walked and wrote from here, Matthew Arnold too. We descended Lighthouse Score through the Sparrow's Nest, and came to marine museum with hope.

But they had not found the *Boy John* model drifter, crafted for our father by his father. It must have been thrown away. They later sent a photo, it had been burned in that museum fire.

On the road outside, there were poppies growing in the gutter. The net racks on the denes were tarred and rabbits scuttled in the tussocks. The pebbled homes of Grit were gone.

> In ruin, the site has perished,
> Broken up in heaps, where formerly many a person,
> Gracious and gold-bright, clad in radiance,
> Looked on treasure, on silver on knowing jewels,…
> On the bright city.

[*The Ruin*, The Exeter Book, c970]

They were pilgrims, each seafarer and wayfarer, crossing over ancient sea roads.

They walked up to isolated church, in Iceland village, on Faroe shore, and sought a peace, for on a ship was endless noise, wind in stays, the constant growls of wave.

Yet they could find a cloud of unknowing, it seemed to some, this was why they crossed the sea, why they wandered far in search of fish. The Peddars Way courses north from end of St Edmunds Way, one of half a thousand pilgrim routes that thread the land. It was wet and we went out, took our places on the straight path. It was cold, by the wintry fields, and rain fell steadily. To the west were the Fens, once the size of inland sea, to the east the pilgrim's holy halt at Walsingham, where came every later king to pray. Henry VIII paused at hallowed well, then declared all pilgrimages were illegal. How wasteful, he said, to be walking when you should be working.

The vast Fens were once a common wetland, then drained. Eight rivers flowed in, and out northward to the sea. On islands were established monastery and cathedral, to tower over country. There was a saint called Guthlac, son of Tette and Penwalh, he fought with the king of Mercia, became a monk at the double-monastery of Repton. He chose to live as hermit on the isle of Croyland. He built a marsh hut at the end of wetroad, wore garments made of skins, ate as fen people did, suffered ague fever as they did. Yet he soon was famed, providing water refuge for a future king called Æthelbald.

This was at the time before the Vikings sailed longships to Britain's shore, when another king was also saved by such a waterland. Alfred of Wessex had retreated to the isle of Æthelney, deep in the Levels of *Sumersaete*, the summer country. He escaped the army of Ivarr's brothers Ubba and Halfdan, burned some cakes, then united all of England. The interior life can be a place of the wild, a blessed garden, but Guthlac was besieged by thoughts, like the desert fathers in their oases, the noisy chatter of the demons.

These fiends were 'terrible in shape, with great hands, long necks, fierce eyes, and… a mighty shrieking that filled the whole space between earth and heaven.'

The cult of Guthlac grew up after his death, his body when found shone with light. At that time, the commoners of the Fens travelled by punt, walked on stilts, lived by fishing, cutting willows, farming geese and hunting wildfowl. Aside from demons, it was a world of neon kingfisher, flashing over streams, blue dragonfly and rust-red hawker, rising mayflies sparkling in the sun, an otter splash, a beaver slap.

Alas all was not well, for there was devised a national plan to drain the wetlands dry.

Landowners learned drainage skills from visits to the Flanders' lowlands, soon grasped that unproductive wetlands could be taken into farms for crop and cattle. In the 1620s, Dutch engineers led by Cornelius Vermuyden were commissioned. Two memes emerged to push along this drainage plan: call the land a worthless wilderness, call the people backward. So the Fens were 'a wilderness of bog, pool, and reed shoal, a vast morass, with only a few islands of solid earth;' and people a 'barbarous sort of lazy and beggarly people.'

The commons, wrote Adam Moore in his 1653 *Bread for the Poor* treatise, were 'pest-houses of disease… hither come the poor, the blinde, lame, tired and scabbed.' Knighted Vermuyden called the vowed land *summer ground*, so he dug and drained across the reigns of kings and past the Civil War.

This was a low point, but not the lowest.

Works were spoiled by the Fen people, and commissioners reported 'Outbursts of indignation and disturbances of lewd persons.' They burned the ricks, opened floodgates, drowned again the land. Riot and discontent flowed back and forth for sixty years. Dark as this was, now were launched two legal floods, 4,500 Enclosure Acts signed by Parliament, and the one Waltham Black Act of 1723. This *Black Act* created fifty capital offences for those who took from forest, waste, marsh or clearing, for anyone found with their face black or who might 'appear in any forest, close, park or in any warren, or on any high road, heath, common or down.' Calling these wastelands was a term to last for centuries, for the Empire practised on its people, then exported measures to more than sixty countries overseas.

And so the beached Trinity Bridge still stands at Crowland, three stairways crossing up and over the surfaced high street, dry where once had been a river clear and full of fish.

Mist wrapped the rolling hills, winds blew over wintry fields, over hedges stooped and bent, months to pass before the blackthorn blossom brightens land in spring.

The fields were wide and trees few. A crowd of speckled starlings tumbled, a rushing river of wings. At Ringstead church high above a hamlet, there were three interlaced fish in a circle, baring teeth, on floor bronze slabs, stitched on kneelers too. The church was dry, there was on the wall a lion with wings, an eagle haloed. When we walk the path, on such a way, the affairs of earthly world seem distant. A thousand geese rose in echelons against the clearing sky, pink-foots down from Arctic, calling down to the land, all things shall be renewed.

Corvids clamoured in the village pines, and beneath was a sign displaying Richard Gillard's Servant Song: 'We are here to help each other / Walk the miles and bear the load.'

Well, there had been rivers of salt tears, and new efforts to rewet the fens, the wilding of Wicken Fen. It turned out the Fens were a paradise after all. But people still shall weep, for enclosures still are underway, in unroofing of the rainforests, burned for soy and corn, in the hiss of rigs that drill the Arctic. A man was on the pilgrim way, moving his mouth soundlessly, and then spoke, 'I am lost.'

At the wide shore, the rain gave way and mist clung to the cold marsh. A low sun shone on the wild dunes, on the distant foam of waves of Ægir's daughters, he the spearman with net and trident, devourer of sailors lost at sea. The gods are gods, they never change. The worst insult of one village on this coast, 'bitefinger' they said through clenched teeth, at those who chewed the fingers off the drowned to pull off rings. A river on the slacks took on the colour of the sky. This was not a rugged shore that could tear the skin from off a swimming sailor, break each bone on jagged reef. It was near the sandy place where had been found at low tide fifty-five oaks set in a seahenge circle.

Yet winters can be bleak beside this bitter brine.

Gold, it is said, gets in people's eyes and causes blindness.

The world began with flood, and could end with fire. We turned west toward Hunstanton, up on cliffs of red-white banded chalk. Waves rushed at the shore, over wreck of trawler *Sheraton*. A paraglider leapt from the cliff, oh what would the old gods say, and oystercatchers thronged amongst the seaweed on the fallen chalk. This whole hoop of shallow Wash is the rare stretch of eastern shore where the sun sets in the sea. Come let us hope, for the level sea lies calm. On the west side was the Lincoln shore, and a day's sail north the fish port founded by a Danish longship captain whose name was Grim.

Spring should bring a balmy breeze, down this shore, and milder sunshine, but alas too a step toward a hotter world.

None yet knew, nor even guessed, that an old world was about to end. Gerard Manley Hopkins sliced the world sideways in 'God's Grandeur':

> Generations have trod, have trod, have trod;
> And all is seared with trade; bleared and smeared with toil.

HERRING FOR THE GRIT CITY

This saga happens at the easternmost point of Britain, beginning in the early twentieth century. An old skipper Ned and his friend Waxy Jack the cobbler meet on the cliff tops each morning, where they stare at the empty sea. Below too is the emptied site of the once-thriving Grit, the city of the fishers. The boy Edward grew up in a pebble house with his grandmother, learned to paint boats, sail, and then to skipper drifters. They fight U-boats in the Fourteen War, and soon he comes to know every sea road of the North Sea, each swatchway and every fish ground. Joskins men from inland farms of clay walk each autumn to crew the drifters. It took a tide to pull a bursting net. And then one day the fish were gone.

It always ends like this, the slender scores,
Curled down the cliff, past brick and flinty wall,
No more a famed fish town, yet for years,
The fearless skipper, Ned had faced the waves,
Now he stared to empty sea, a pipe held in his hands,
How the sea had taken, all the fish and all his friends,
Yet at morning under blossoms, how charming it could be,
Even when the bells, were pealing for the dead.

For a hundred years or more, he might have thought,
We have fished this shore, set the fairest sail,
And ploughed the waves, put out the net,
And pulled in crans of silver, such glittered ocean spate,
'It's herring boys, herring,' bawled lads in northern ports,
Yet at the midnight hour, against the arch of stars,
Even sparrows would no longer dwell, in wreckage of the village,
Oh my soul he thought again, we and fish have fled the sea.

Now in declining years, Ned rarely slept past dawn,
So well before the appointed hour, he sat by sighing cherries,
That pitched the perfect breeze, to sing upon this cliff top,
He watched below and far away, as white horses traced,
Lines on empty blue, nothing else was on the water,
Not a handsome sail, where once he could recall,
Barge and smack had tacked, on sea roads north and south,
Where once the herring hordes, were warriors in their havens.

Waxy Jack the old cobbler, walked up the path with care,
Sat beside his friend, he had crewed the winter drifters,
And was used to fitting leather, around the feet of many people,
So he became a preacher, even as his eyes were dimmed,
It paid to study fish, Ned had always said,
They were like each fruit and herb, they had their seasons,
He had gained prestige one year, the fabled Prunier Trophy,
Awarded to his ship, for the largest haul of herring.

The two men met, each morning on these cliffs,
Lit their pipes, listened to the wind and birdsong,
For they'd survived, when much around them,
Had disappeared and died, yet they shared a common life,
Now Ned pointed, and described how boys and girls were running,
In white vests and shorts, on the denes below,
Where once nearby had been, their vibrant village of the Grit,
On the breeze came drifting sounds, they heard the teachers shouting.

If Ned and Jack had been inclined, to tell a tale,
At home they might have started, for Ned had never known his mother,
His father died in Fourteen War, and Ned could never visit,

The ranks of marble gravestones, on a distant Vimy field,
His Gran had died of flu, his best friend Albert,
Was bosun on the *Dhoon*, wrecked and rescued up at Iceland,
Each day at least, he could pause at the grave,
Of his lovely Maggie the gutting girl, lying silent in the soil.

When Edward woke on straw, four-score years before,
It was to aching emptiness, the torrents long since,
Coursed from roof, and so he coughed,
Could taste the sulphured silence, and down below,
A door hinge creaked, the dull metallic clink of pot on stove,
He wiped cold dew from tiny window, saw the wall of fog beyond,
At last he heard the voice below, 'come you down boy,
Breakfast's ready, I believe it's going ter blow.'

The day before, they'd raced the Rant Score gang,
In rain came rarest luck, a barrel rolled and split,
He and skinny Albert, scooped up the salty herring,
Fled the briny wharf, laughs upon their freckled faces,
Down back lanes they peddled, the fish to wives a ha'penny each,
From his hand he poured, a tanner's worth of coins to Gran,
Now he chewed on bread and peas, picked flesh from off a kipper,
She ruffled up his hair, bid him wait a little more.

The eastern air gained light, the sea fog thinning,
They stood at open door, watched longshore men prepare,
For each Beach Cooperative, was making ready for the storm,
They would take a morning sip, at Sailor's Return or maybe Rising Sun,
She nodded at the sound, of muffled clog and shuffling foot,
Now came the clap on flinty cobble, and out of fog appeared,
A pale man in a coat of serge, his piercing eyes blue-bright,
'Well Edward, are you coming boy, bring your brushes too.'

The thin man Abraham, clasped his mother's arms and crinkled eyes,
Limped with boy inside the fog, across the marram hills,
This boy was yet too young to row, to yell for place aboard,
So they painted planks, his father's hack since his foot was broken,
The beach men built their lifeboats, swift-rigged for sail,

And to each wreck they rowed, the first hand claimed the goods,
And each wet grip, grasped with courage men and women,
Their other contest, was for the silver herring.

Fish bone filled their sinews, put another way,
There was no other choice, no way up the scores,
So the daring men and women, faced east to sandy broth,
The dozen *skor* alley-ways, long ago were notched,
From sandy beach to upper cliff, where businessman,
And resident of town, lived far from fishy reek,
In finest terraced row, by lighthouse shining on the yeasty sea,
Far below they knew, were fleas and bugs in every flinty hut.

Men supposed on land, a kind of savage culture,
Lived in pebble-built, and pitch-lined cottage,
With chimneys tall to draw in air, a corner pub by Bethel church,
Smoke house for the herring, rope shed over shop,
Net racks lined the denes, purple with the wretched pea,
You may also think, in splendid isolation,
They knew little of the world, yet the Grit looked out instead of in,
The good winds blew them on, to many distant ports.

Out on Dogger Bank, past Shetland cliff and frothy shore,
Line and net out for the cod, they shared a joke at Arctic harbour-side,
They yarned and carried back, the songs and tales of fish,
This is how they knew, each sandy bank,
Each fishy ground, how they tasted other places,
It seemed to make this edge of land, more kindly round the northern sea,
Than those inland, who lived so far from salt,
Yet they daily lived with loss, and every era one day comes to close.

The painter's boy learned quickly, took on calling as a skipper,
Ned was tempered, skin burnished bronze by icy squall,
His right hand was a finger short, he had scars on iron forearms,
He listened to the fish, the many layers of grounds,
From every craggy seabed, each crossing current,
The tidal flow and surface chop, the air above,
His crew set nets on leagues of rope, their drifting dandies calm,
On the water roof and under stars, they waited for the corks to drop.

When the nets had filled, now was six hours pulling,
Balmskins shone by morning light, sun glittered on the mirrored sea,
But market grief they knew, might greet the best of harvest,
Then hollow slate in shop, the children hungry once again,
For some it meant the poorhouse, breaking rock for seawall,
The harbour could be full of ships, the insistent ring of market bell,
By this labour, did they bear those oily fish,
By their rulebooks, did the auction buyers work.

Skipper Ned kept a moleskin logbook, his secrets of the sea roads,
A sandbank dry at certain ebb, might smash a keel,
Fast current off a swatchway, always clutching,
He sketched each ground, its colour in the walls of chop,
Skippers shared their terms, for the steppe and hills of Doggerland,
Gabbard and the Galloper, Skate Hole and the Sandiette,
Brown Ridge and Kentish Knock, Smith's Knoll and Silver Pit,
Fast along the Gut and Wallet, slow ahead in New and Middle Rough.

Chaos came upon their world, what was it for,
This war that sent the men, to fight the other men,
Who had last year, bought their herring,
What was it for, wondered Ned and crew,
As they sailed their smack, on the guard not now for storm,
But for breaching submarine, whose guns would point,
Upon the smacks, whose commanders ordered,
Put a bomb in locker, you can row the lifeboat back to shore.

The Grit men fished for food, and fired the guns,
Alas this made them soldiers, in the eyes of enemy,
Ned and Albert had the luck, not to be aboard,
The smack *Ethel & Millie*, when all the crew,
Were forced to stand, on foredeck of a submarine,
As it sunk to join, the herring in the depths,
It was all so nice and easy, said the fishers,
Till we were ruined, in the icy brine of home.

Ned was skipper on the *G&E*, a swift and drafted smack,
Albert was now in charge, of homing pigeons on the deck,
Yet this day, the messengers were not required,
For as a boat emerged, they fired the thirteen pounder,
And hit the conning tower, soon oil was slick upon waves,
A fast P-boat came rushing out from shore, frothing at its bows,
'Oh we've sunk him,' yelled skipper Ned,
'Give three cheers for these boys,' laughed the captain to his crew.

Well the written records say, one hundred men,
From just one village, on the claggy clays,
Walked east each year, to search for winter work,
They had trudged the furrow, followed heavy horse,
And now sought a wooden cell, on top of salty main,
They made the crossing, these half-half joskins,
Had strength to pull, one league of sodden warp,
The smacks were polished, and skippers needed muscle of the field.

They took the path, the dewy ground to gate of port,
Thick mist lay over marsh, grey was on the many-coloured land,
They knew the top of ocean, never was as safe as soil,
When the boat brass gleamed, and lattice nets were shot away,
A snaking rope might grip a leg, that man was going down,
Oilskins chaffed at neck and wrist, the salty Dogger itch,
The stinging jellies, fish bones lancing through their fingers,
If a skipper's cabin-drunk, all would wish they'd stayed on land.

At the port, they saw the waiting ships,
The herring girls and auctioneer, the preacher at the Bethel,
There seemed no fisher over fifty, no fingers left to work,
Yet still the fish rose nightly, from the seabed to the net,
Boats were dense in harbour, coal piled for modern furnace,
Some joskins might not find, the winter work on salt and sweat,
Yet Ned was always waiting, for Jack and other men,
For these lads were his best crew, for the scuffly sea above an older land.

At shore were also stationed, beatster girls and women,
Ready for the nets, they mended norsel and the oddie,
Their arms were skinned by creosote, faces bleeding raw,
Life was worst with jellyfish, dried as pepper on the net,
From spring to winter, beside these ports,
Herring shoaled while nomad fish girls, travelled south for work,
They flashed their razor gutting knifes, they could slice a fish so fast,
Even as the salt, ground into wounds on hands.

And when the season stopped, balmy breezes on the shore,
The men dressed up, for drink and night parade,
Yet as spring stole the winter storms, and fish swam north,
The men walked west from coast, turned to barleycorn again,
They readied for the sowing cycle, watched sky for migrant swallow,
Faced the oldest enemy, solid clay below,
Later they will later solemn say, we cut the corn today,
A verdict on the soil, before they crossed again for fish.

Ahoy again, it took a tide to pull a bursting net,
It took three-score years, to empty herring from the sea,
After second war, there was not one herring left,
Alas too the Grit collapsed, evacuated at the war,
The army took the cobbled streets, a practice ground for fighting,
This was a clearance of their village, of their fish grounds too,
Now anchors rusted on the denes, net racks rotted,
Thistle grew and sandy grass, was good for only rabbit.

Ned lived in compact cottage, by Herring Fishery Score,
And for years had strode, these long steep climbs,
Yet he now was thin, gaunt as a dragonfly,
And put out his arm, and Jack gripped on tight.
Jack's eyes had long before, lost most of sight,
Now they walked, slowly past the lighthouse,
They took the path, crunching on the gravel,
Down through gardens, for their morning cup of tea.

BARGE REQUIEM

This saga happens on the sea and at the shores of wind, in the late 1940s. The last coasting bargemen felt forced to shiver. Half a thousand barges sailed the roads, carrying coal and corn, cement and straw. Captain Jack lived his life below the sail, yet awaits one last trip in the marsh pub. The sea has riddles, the brine is devious, but no one could sail faster than a bargeman. His daughter Thora buys a cottage on the Nore at Whitstable. She joins him and the mate, they carry barley from Poole to Snape Maltings, run to Keadby on the Humber for coal, are almost sunk by a gale on Holland's shore. They offload at the black and bleak London River docks, and race a famous barge at dawn on the estuary. At night, a parting line of phosphorescence streams behind this last questing barge.

Beneath a summer sky, the last coasting bargemen,
Felt forced to shiver, for they could see that dark advanced,
It seemed the days of sail, would shortly cease,
An abandoned barge in creek, another bracing seawall hole,
A skeleton of timber ribs, swamped by banks of lavender,
In time each corpse would rot, and by the salty tide,
Each skipper and his mate, would then be stranded on the beach,
Oh how they wished, they still could race the sea roads.

Standing tall at transom stern, a wind-burnt captain,
Would cradle smouldering pipe, look to moonway under stars,
Three-score years on wood, a ceaseless search for wind,
What quiet men were these, the crew of sighing barge,
Often deep in peace, twenty leagues from buoy-light beaming,
By help of wind and spritsail rig, they hauled two hundred tonnes of coal,
A load of wheat or block cement, linseed sacks or sugar,
Many a working day, they could be wet to waist with sea.

Captain Jack began as bargeboy, lived his life below the sail,
Schooled by tidal river, sensing every weather sign,
He had a rolling pace on land, the long eyes of a waterman,
His final ship was the *Cambria*, built at shipyard on the marsh,
Drawing single salty fathom, it had five thousand red square feet of sail,
By mizzen main and topsail, shroud and topping lift,
By flying jib and job, blocks run up the ropes,
You could never beat, a bargeman in a tideway.

And sure enough, all ships relied on wind,
On breeze and puff, a gusty gale or simple zephyr,
A blow that howled with rage, causing hearts to flutter,
A sough that murmured, over moonlit water,
Each sea has riddles, this brine was devious,
It had fast-flowing rivers, currents changing hour by tide,
Many were the white-capped seas, and wicked waves awaiting,
And at the lowest ebb, sandbanks rose as driest land.

Not long before, as battles over land began,
A thousand barges hummed, up and down the London River,
Each shore was barbed with wire, booms were set at sea,
A skipper and his mate might set sail, half a loaf between them,
Their hammocks slung, on hooks between the shrouds,
There were no lights at sea, they sailed by memory alone,
Through shoals of sand, in dark they dared not come too close,
Yet a true sailorman never hurried, he let the vessel do the heft.

When war ordeals were done, all on land had changed,
Under calm and cleanest air, a barge might still strain her seams,
The heavy canvas sails, snapping in the breeze,
But now Jack and Blondie Bill, took her up the creek to Oare,
Past the Ferry Inn, nestled under green hillside,
Where gull and lark, looked down upon the olive marsh,
At the bustling quay, they chanced upon old friends,
Arranged with local skipper, to help them off the mire at dawn.

Unpaid at Yantlet Creek, they waited in the candlelight,
Watched through fearsome winter, saltings deep in frozen snow,
The people of the marsh, had to climb from upper cottage windows,
Yet summer heat would bring, one closing call from London agent,
Now came a visit to the barge, from his daughter Thora,
She had married in a local church, a naval man of middle rank,
Stationed now at London's Arch, so they now were searching,
For a seaward cottage, close to trains from shore to city.

They collected keys, walked beyond the tarred fish-sheds,
Past sailing lofts, and opened door in peeling weatherboard,
Bombs had broken every window, chairs were swathed against the mice,
The basement had been emptied, and at the top of tide,
They saw the water come inside, cried Thora,
'It is perfect, look at views of bay and oyster beds,'
There were rolling waves, small boats jumping on their moorings,
'Now the war is over, we should be safe to start a family.'

Jack looked out and said, 'I remember steering a powder barge,
Past this very house, as bombers flew above,
We grew two feet of weed, the gear all rotted over winter,
One week on another off, and only sperm whale oil,
Allowed for lighting, all naked lights forbidden,
We had to poach ashore, cooked rabbit stew with wild pears,'
So now her father smiled, even as his trade was fading,
Perhaps he now could find, a way to help on land.

So at Herne Bay, at mouth of London River,
There will come a time for grief, so Jack said to Thora,
'In the daylight hours, I'll help you with the house,
There is much to do, to make it watertight,

If I die too soon, I'd like you then to lay,
My melodeon in coffin, and bury me in solid soil,
You buy the house, and why not crew our final trip,
You can steer the *Cambria*, up and down the tides.'

Skipper Jack and Bill, barging made them lean,
Were down at Poole with Thora, loading up with golden barley,
They edged across the Brownsea bar, long ago a Viking post,
A sea breeze bloomed, two lee-deck seams were under water,
They raced the boats from Hastings, approached the tidal switch,
And in Rye Bay came about, for Norman fishers out from Caen,
Who swung across a bucket full of scallops, their thanks for news of route,
Now the ebb was going north, so they sped into the northern sea.

This sea was often not a sea, sandbanks climbing every tide,
And a careless barge could strand, shudder stem to stern,
Broken-backed in centre of the sea, wind screaming in the rigging,
In pitch dark, crews had drowned on rising underworld,
Jack had in his mind, this map of every swatchway,
Each gut and course, more like steering on a creek,
So they safely sailed the Maplins, its depth at flood of half a fathom,
There were grey seals basking, on the Barrow Sands.

They put ashore on northern Dengie, by the ruined Saxon chapel,
At the tarred cottage on the seawall, and called for old friend Walter,
The final fowler of the wild, a quiet man without a fear,
Jack swapped out a sack of barley, took aboard two brace of duck,
All four sat in gloaming, Thora shared her naval cigarettes,
The water now was calm, an eastern moonway on the sea,
Five years hence one bitter night, a howling hurricane will strike,
Walter will have to race with son inland, as all the sea walls burst.

Thora took the wheel at dawn, waited at the bar of River Ore,
A feisty reach on ebb, so on flood at Shingle Street,
They dashed upstream, where the river changes name to Alde,
Turned to port past Iken church, and moored at Snape,
It took a day and night, to unload the barley for the mash,

In the Plough and Sail, ale was sipped from wartime jam jars,
So next to Keadby on the Humber, to fetch the coal for gasworks,
They travelled back to salt, and the good clean air of eastern coast.

The sails spread taut, they coasted northward,
Passed fishing villages, that once were havens,
The sun set over land, where were stabled shire horses,
And the morning's whetted scythe, was propped against a wall,
They skirted Grimsby, saw trawler stacks in dock,
Sailed leagues inland past ports, to railhead on the Trent,
Each coal truck tipped ten tons, trimmers scrambled down below,
At the jetty pub they ate, and joined in songs of mariner and railwayman.

The hamlet's task was trade, so the heavy barge sailed next day,
Anchored off the shore at Hull, waiting for the flood's last hours,
While Jack and Thora rowed, hard ashore for stores,
The wind had backed, west to south-west squally,
There were distant signs, darker weather causing frowns,
Thora cast off, and away to southward,
Was a rainbow flash of troubled colour, and ahead was rising up,
A tall black thundercloud, beneath was a wall of angry water.

The three were shouting now, and reefed the sails so fast,
But the brutal wind and rain, slammed into barge,
And over went the *Cambria*, her hatches under water,
Both Jack and Bill, bent their bones,
Thora at the wheel was pulling hard, they ran before the wind,
The wind was horde of devils, and another squall attacked,
Shouted Bill the mate, 'Blinking dark isn't it?'
Referring to their prospects, perhaps this post-war epoch too.

The *Cambria* staggered in the wind, rain drummed on wood,
And away she went, racing now at nine knot speed,
Far from sea road south, with her weighty haul of coal,
They hurtled hard, chased by wretched wind to Holland,
The barge was surging, sending spume across the hatches,
The three were sodden, watched the coast advance,
Beyond the white caps, the beach grew sharper fast,
No one dared to hope, this storm would peter out by shore.

In days gone by, wreckers might have gathered,
On the beach, awaiting spillage from a broken barge,
As it stranded in the waves, now they were so close,
Their limbs still shaking, frozen stiff by effort,
They could see quite clearly, blossoms on the dunes,
Banks of blue sea holly, clumps of white seakale,
But alas for any waiting company, the wind blew out,
The clouds rolled by, and sea and sky turned blue.

The brine set calm, Jack and Bill and Thora hooted,
There were gentle ripples on the swell, a north-west breeze commenced,
They set the course again for London, it would take two added days,
In the galley Bill fried sliced potato, this was now a cheery tale,
A hundred extra leagues to sail, could they make the Surrey docks for dinner,
Thora pumped at salty bilge, slopping in the coal,
And then in bow-wave of the barge, arching in and out,
A pod of dolphins dashed, grinning at the crew.

It was filthy black and bleak, the dark London River,
None of beauty of the open water, though a curlew called on flats,
Oil pooled on water, there was smoke and smog above,
And chaos at the docks, the hubbub hard to bear,
Rattling donkey engines, lighter men unloading coal,
They fled the river clutches, and there at estuary mouth,
Was moored the *Will Everard*, rival barge to *Cambria*,
Whispered Jack, 'Put on hatches, we might just race her.'

At the quiet of morning tide, Jack took the wheel and crept away,
But the *Will* was going too, and now it started,
Low sun twinkled on the sea, they tacked together,
One seized the wind, the other spoiled,
From above the circling gulls, saw the barges charge at one another,
Each skipper still as rock, playing bluff and double,
Neither gave a quarter, glaring straight ahead,
Taking in the wind, every wrinkle on the water.

The *Will* bore away, pouring under lee by inches,
The battle raged, tack for tack,
Neither gained advantage, until a shout of glory from the bow,
Bill was jumping, up and down and waving arms,
'She's aground, she's on the Shoebury,
She's up a field, stuck on bloody Essex,'
What a taste of pleasure, what a racing win,
This story that could grow with telling, in the ports along the coast.

They cruised up the Colne, deafened by the noise,
Of shipyards on the marsh, and beyond the facing villages,
Children skipped along the seawall, so Thora waved and shouted back,
The harvest now was in, so a mill at Kent,
Was cooking straw to mash, for the country had no wood for paper,
The final journey of this barge, was to carry fifty tonnes of straw,
At the port the three lay back, lazed beneath the cloudless sky,
As men from fields and farm, worked their stacking hooks.

They waited for the final waggon, half an eye for wispy smoke,
For straw's internal heat could blaze, and burn a barge to hulk,
Creeping down the Swin that eve, they found the edge,
Of sandbanks with a lead, standing on the stack of straw,
In shallow channel, there was not the room for slightest error,
Ahead they saw was moored, a giant naval battleship,
And a solemn sailor's face, poked out of porthole high above,
He hailed the stackie barge, with a long and lowing moo.

They quietly sailed that night, left a parting line of phosphorescence,
And moored on sandbank, listening to the roar,
Of wind in trees ashore, stepping down to solid land,
It was their final view, of stars from out at sea,
At dawn they now could hear, larks singing from the coast,
And viewed on eastern skyline, the copper flood of light,
It was their closing requiem, so Thora steered from sea to creek,
Jack and Bill were at the stern, staring at the passing water.

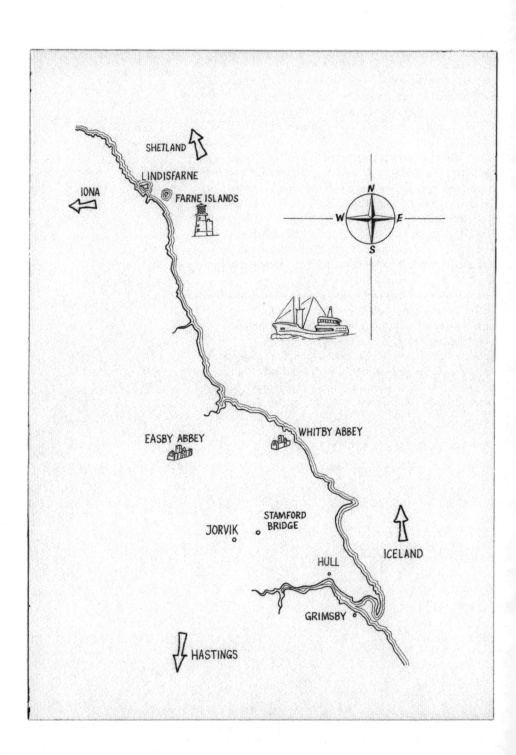

CHAPTER FOUR

THE NORTH LANDS

Lindisfarne castle and harbour

All was wreck. All was ruin.

The ship roads had been abandoned, the docks had crumbled.

Deepwater ports had been felled, once fine orchards that would never bloom again. Long ago, soon after the sky and earth became separated, the hopes of fishermen were simple. Catch fish, sleep deep, wake to watch the sun, climbing from the sea.

One port, Hull, grew on the trade of corn and cloth, spice and iron. The first dock was built in the 1770s, then more in 1800s, creating harbour water always full behind the gates. Whalers sailed, then deepwater trawlers, migrants came too, thousands from Russia and Scandinavia by steamship, taking trains to Liverpool and transit onward to Americas. By the 1960s, Hull had one hundred and forty distant water ships, Grimsby eighty-four, Aberdeen and Lowestoft one each. On shore were processor and bobber, engineer and rigger, merchant and the dock police, painter and the press-gang runners.

The other port, you might recall twelve hundred years before, had been named as village on the marsh. Grim's crew in morning calm had rowed ashore, the sailors chanting at the oar. Now rail tracks were in, but the trucks were empty. So investors built a harbour, hewed it from the saltings. As striking as Siena was raised a terracotta tower, inside the minaret a salty column to drive the gates to lock. Sure enough the coastal parish split, top town on the inland hill, and down by dock all the back-to-backs of Freeman Street. Both districts grew on the silver scales of fish, the gaping cod and saithe and ling.

I walked through Grimsby's docks one grey autumn day. The old commons were fenced, and permission had to be pursued at barrier.

'Why do you want to walk? You mustn't take any pictures.'

There was the old ice factory, and pontoon famed in every other port. It was a city where three thousand people worked, fetching in a thousand tonnes of fish a day, sending out loaded trains to cities of the north. Some called it Dodge City, there was thief and barter, secret-marketeer, customs crew all dressed in black.

A car screeched to a halt, and a man leapt out: 'We have been watching you on our CCTV,' he warned. There was lettering in French on broken walls of brick, it was a place that looked enough like war-torn Dunkerque, and so here the recent film was shot.

In the docks there was one last small business. Alfred Enderby had been smoking fish for a century. The radio clattered in the office, the floor was sluiced with seawater. Haddock and cod were being washed and hung on metal speets, placed in the six tall chimneys black with tar and resin. To start the smoking, the men tipped into pine shavings a teaspoon of smouldering ash. Tomorrow out will come these Grimsby fish, all now sourced from Iceland. They seemed the last ones left.

The foreman nodded, said they were embarrassed by how the port looks now.

There was one last factory business. I trailed to the tenth floor of Young's, long ago shrimpers down at Leigh-on-Sea in Essex. Mike Mitchell was author of *Hope Street*, a tale about this fish and factory life, and we gazed down upon the port. On the inside were the factory buildings, and people far below were dressed in white. The company under Carl Ross developed the first factory ship with freezing machines in the 1960s, all its ships were branded with the Ross name. Now Mike nodded, all the fish were caught at Iceland, packed in containers and travel to this port by train.

There was one last trawler fishing out of Hull, skippered by Charlie Waddy once of the urban village called Hessle Road. The *Kirkella* is eighty metres long, bringing home each trip eight hundred tonnes of frozen fillet fish. I called Charlie on the socials, they were in the Barents Sea. 'We are sailing toward a fine sunset,' he said, 'The crew have just fixed up a barbecue and jacuzzi on the deck.'

So, on the western rim of this shallow hoop of sea, I stood aboard a Grimsby ship with the son of Sargon's mate, Syd Wakwerit, a trawlerman himself and in declining years.

'The sea is a different world, anything can happen, everyone helps. But father didn't talk about the *Sargon* rescue, never talked about the war.'

His father went back to sea, yes like the other men saved from icy Patreksfjördur, but retired to take on lonesome duties on a lightship, safely anchored to a sandbank. Now the fishing long was over, and Syd missed the tossing of the sea, the many miseries of chasing cod. He went down-dock one open day to look again.

He sighed, 'It just made me cry.'

> I have spent winters on the ice-chilled sea, on exile's roads,
> With friends and kinsmen, taken away from me.

[*The Seafarer*, The Exeter Book, c970]

The lands north of the Humber River and estuary were once the largest kingdom of the Anglo-Saxon heptarchy. It became a source of saints, famed monastery and holy isle, inland pilgrim roads and a growing draw for wealth. It was a place where a boy with long face and green eyes opened up a window on a distant future, he said the air would be heated and the seas swell up once again.

This is the thing. There once were many wyrms.

Someone had to shield the buried treasure, the brooch and bracteate, the plate and clasping arm ring, all manner of gold and silver coin. Someone had to look after the wisdom gathered cross the ages, and remind people how best to live. After sarsens had been raised and bones entombed in water, so smiths learned to smelt iron from rock, and blend copper into veins of tin. Then the land was brimmed with beasts, and one day Vortigern the King called his masons, for none could stop his tallest tower from sinking into soil. The rule of Rome had fled, half a hundred years before.

These magi bade him send for a tall boy with no father, and then kill him so that brick and mortar could be sprinkled with his blood.

Messengers found a lad playing by the gates of distant town, he was named Merlin and his mother was a nun. The governor commanded both be sent for sacrifice, yet the boy was bold and he had a way with words.

The future magus Merlin explained a pond would be found beneath the tower, broad and deep as any, and when it was drained, they would find two hollow stones, and inside each curled asleep would be an ancient armoured dragon. This was the first of many prophecies of this boy Merlin. The king sat on the bank and was first to hear a bellow, as each dragon started breathing fire. One was red, the other white, and they clashed as they flew, fire falling from the sky. As they soared, the king called upon the boy, for he wanted those wild dragons back so he could beat his Saxon foes.

It is said that Merlin was later counsel for grey-haired Arthur, and it was he, the man with magic in his staff, who spoke plainly to the king.

He would later discard all soft possessions, seek the sweetest apple tree growing in a glade, and ride a well-horned stag, his prophecies slowly spreading cross the realm. This was why, in later years, the old folks used to say, leave things as they are, don't disturb the creatures of the natural world. For Merlin knew that a dragon's breath caused forgetfulness in people, who would go on wanting gold, and add to burning of the air. And Merlin garbed all in green told Vortigern, cities would be destroyed by rising seas and summer heat, and wild animals enjoy a peace one day. People would bewail how they felt so punished, as populations fell and town walls tumbled down. Drought would strike at harvest, and bitter vines would come, he said, and dragons fight the people and ancient oaks burn, in every forest grove.

Merlin prophesised the seas would bubble up, one day the rivers boil, and floods from the River Thames would surround the London city.

Merlin spoke:
> Beasts shall roar revenge,
> And come hunting through the empty streets;
> Blow after blow, the earth will suffer,
> And then the people too.

[Geoffrey of Monmouth, *History of the Kings of Britain*, c1136]

In later years, Merlin's descendants were called cunning women and men, they were shamans who could heal, speak the language of animals, work magic high and low.

From village to village walked Ellen Haywood, Ursula Kemp, James Murrell, Old George Pickingill, Pigtail Bridger, Eric Maple the last to die in the 1960s. Cunning Murrell was a shoemaker, he knew how to shape the leather round the tiny feet of children. They each had books at home, wrote scripts to open doors, knew how to bake a magic gooseberry pie, above all perhaps they offered hope. So the King Vortigern quavered, and said those prophecies seemed fanciful to him. He could not believe it could ever get so bad. And no one was wholly sure, did Merlin later live in woods, was he depicted by the bards and sculptors as a green man with oak leaves sprouting from his mouth?

Well now, numberless years passed after Vortigern, and scores of kings and queens sat stiff on thrones. Then it came to pass there were three good Anglo-Saxon kings of Northumberland.

Edwin kept such good peace, and so a woman with her newborn child could walk from sea to sea in safety. He was the first to convert to the new ethic flowing over the narrow neck of hills from the western isle of Iona. Edwin built a hall of planks a handspan thick, great enough to hold three hundred people. It was as famed as Hrothgar's Heorot, across the sea at Lejre. Oswald was his successor in 634 CE, and he gave alms to the poor, ordered silver plate be broken up to care for travellers. It was he who sent for a missionary from Iona, come to set up monastery on his isle of Lindisfarne. Oswiu was his brother, and it was in his reign of thirty years that the land began to reveal the saints.

A princess was born in Bamburgh castle by the sea. High on sandstone rock, she gazed from royal citadel, north across the inlet to the isle of Lindisfarne.

It was a stretch offshore, by fleet and sandy spit, and safely at the harbour were fishers' huts of straw. Castle isles are mountain-tops, often wreathed in autumn mist. Yet on the clearest morn, the monks could watch the rise of sun from sea. It was a place of dune, marshy slack and sapphire flowers, overhead from silvered gulf were mewing gull and gannet, winter flocks of dunlin, the burbling eider broods of spring. Inland came the bleat of lamb, and from the shore the laughing women gutting fish. And to this isle were drawn pilgrims walking over wetroad.

The girl was called Hildr, as a child she raised stranded creatures found by servants, a fox with fractured leg, an eider duck with broken wing she adopted as a pet. She dripped honey into the mouth of an injured bat, and held out seeds to feed the castle's flock of sparrows. Yet as she grew, relatives began to mutter, would she consent to early marriage, to forge alliance with a nearby king. Now Merlin all those years before had believed a fair girl with soft eyes would forge a path, would dry up the poisoned spring, wake the forest spirit, ensure the ewes of whitest wool would birth two lambs apiece.

Like her hedgehogs, at their home in castle garden, their spines weighed down with apples, this princess would attract those of grand pavilions, and draw white herons from afar to find an inner road to heaven. This Hildr was a drover, she soon was influential.

She was baptised at thirteen in York minster, and chose a monastic life at the age of thirty-three. She built an abbey both for men and women, and became the Whitby abbess, the leader of the diplomatic ways. So from the east cliff, high above the fisher cottages, she sent an offer to Iona and to Rome. Come south and north for a synod, we should decide how to set the Eaostre dates, how our monks should wear a tonsure, how we might be more cohesive with a single set of rules. Oswiu the King had placed his daughter Aelflaed into Hildr's care, who had taught how the courts of kings, when at their best, would listen to the voiceless and would be wise in all decisions.

Hildr now would try to weave a truce, for the Christian way had stumbled. There were fewer river rites, and many now were switching back to grateful older gods.

Late one summer's day, two moons from equinox, two parties could be seen on the steep path to the monastery. Sunshine streamed through doors, just as the saints desired. First came the Ionians, led by Colman and his monks, then Wilfrid with the Canterbury crew, prepared to speak to Rome's position. Hildr greeted all at doors to double house, the cooks had gathered herbs and every finest vegetable. Yet at the mead tables, they felt the tension in the air. That evening at the benches in the spacious hall, Hildr mixed the seating, let the parties talk of weather, of local customs for their dishes, of the marriage plans for daughters and their sons, of anything at all except their chief business.

At the table lit by fire, sat Oswiu and his wife Rieinmelt, it was he who gave to Hildr these ten hides of land for her monastery, and he too had studied under Aidan on their holy isle of Lindisfarne.

When the guests had eaten, a contented murmur filled the hall. Hildr nodded to the king. She was not tall, yet had a presence, her brown plaits framed a flat face with flashing eyes. She scanned the crowd, 'Let me say how we came to sit, side by side in this hall, where sparrows fly for life, to disappear at nightfall far beyond our sight.'

CHAPTER FOUR

The assembled folk settled in, filled their flagons once again.

'Long ago well-read bards learned from annals, and told how people, those who gathered goods in the growing cities, would feel discontent. And history tells, there was a way to halt the opening gap between the rich and poor.'

'So the desert fathers gathered up their strength for words and feats, for in the bible psalms, it was our Lord who told them how to live. Yet day gives way to night and houses fade, and so some men and women simply walked outside the gates, took the path to wilds and set up lives much slower. They soon enticed admirers by this silent opposition. So in every desert, amongst the heat and dust, there was a silent place of palm and giant reed, where water trickled over stones, fish flitting in the shadows. In groves of birdsong, they created circled worlds. Let us keep in mind, an oasis is an isle, a place in wilds to calm the inner torment. From here in Whitby we can see the whole horizon hoop, and on oceans wide, there are many magic isles. As in every desert, these oases offered paradise between the sea and sky, a closer step to heaven.'

'So we set up the monastery, promoted better ways of living, laid out the land for a hospital, offered poor relief and food from gardens.'

Oswiu said, on behalf of all the bishops, 'This is a graphic tale, it will surely comfort all. Let us pass around the harp, pause awhile for song.' And Hildr checked for food and drink on every table, servants from the kitchen stoked the fire with logs.

Outside the sun had set inland, and in the dusk she continued.

'On illustrious Iona, Oswald was baptised in a barrel. The first Iona teacher to come, you may recall, by ship and over donkey trail was angry Cormán. And soon the people flung at him fish and rotted bones. His weight of words was harsh, people said he never heeded any of their hopes. So grey-haired Aidan sailed instead, a monk who liked to walk and listen to the fisher people, he felt they deserved an understanding of their daily dangers. So Aidan drew up plans for the monastery, and Lindisfarne became the seat of learning. It has created work on the isle for cook and local cleaner, for miller and the mason, for butcher and shoemaker, glazier and garden-doctor. And then ten years ago, Aidan sent Cedd south to build St Peter's chapel, a rock on the east-most Saxon shore. We all share a hope, long will stand that marshy church.'

'I have to speak of our highest holy man, how at Lindisfarne Cuthbert left to live on smaller isles. Yet it seems to me that phase for flight to isles has passed. For we must take the word to all the waiting people. You know how Cuthbert took to rocky keys of Farne, where from off the crag, the shore folk gathered birds and eggs. He built a home of stone, a roof of straw, coaxed a spring to come from solid rock. He sent for barley seeds for soil, all this in view of busy markets at the castles on the coast. Yet ravens swooped, so he sternly spoke and the birds bowed low, outspread their wings and returned with gifts of pig fat for his boots. He banned the killing of the eider duck, but his solitude was wrecked, as word spread fast and people sailed to beg for miracles. Yet he was patient, showing how to brush aside their demons. So you can tell, how our two traditions began together in the desert, brought north by brave monks. How we have created isles in seas of older gods.'

'Yet our God is discontent, for we have let divisions divert us from our mission. Let us now walk outside, for tonight the moon is full, and will have risen over water.'

And so the assembled parties stood together on the cliff top, stunned to silence by the moon way, a silver path upon the sea.

All week Hildr held the ring, Colman and Wilfrid set out their cases, yet it soon was clear, Wilfrid was the most convincing, and King Oswiu agreed. So it was decided, free-standing stone high-crosses should become a tradition, the rock on which to build this new united church. Crosses soon appeared in every market square of Britain, a rough-hewn focal point to be seen from far and near. Some were painted with bright colours, others carved with vine-scrolls interlaced, at Ruthwell, Easby and Gosforth, with images of Christ and gripping beasts.

Bishop Biscop took the moniker of Benedict, and founded river monasteries at Monkwearmouth and at Jarrow. He raised stone walls, invited Frankish craftsmen to install the window glass, the first in all the land. And now six hundred monks could copy out and decorate great bibles, and they were led in time by another saint, Bede the writer. He revived the *anno domini* of Dionysius, he showed how day length changed, how the moon pulled and pushed the tides. It was the start of three hundred years and more of finest Anglo-Saxon age.

Yet it seemed to many people that respect for hare and running stag, for the geese and stork that returned with faith each year, for giant oak and silent harrier, it seemed it had become too easy to forget importance of the wilds.

As Merlin said it would, dawning on the people far too late.

> *Praise no day until evening,*
> *No blade until tested,*
> *No ice until you cross it.*
> [Sæmundr Sigfússon, *Hávamál, Sayings of the High One, Poetic Edda*, c1290]

Late summer rain fell, it was grey and cool.

There were thick clouds on the Cheviots and ahead lay the line of posts marking this wetroad and the pilgrim route.

Many a pilgrim walks the two leagues barefoot, across the sediment and stone. The holy isle is cut off from land for five hours, and there were refuges to the south of road, enclosed platforms high on stilts, a ladder up from mud. Each year, it seemed, a modern pilgrim is beaten by the tide, their cars disappearing as the bay fills with glassy sea. On the far side of the bay was Bamburgh castle, Oswiu's home on promontory, and beyond to south were the ruins of Dunstanburgh. This isle was the brightest light of Anglo-Saxon age, with Iona the greatest Christian centres north of Rome. Here too began the Viking raids on Britain and the Irish isles, an armed longship up against the monks of undefended monastery.

Lindisfarne is a small isle, and we walked the shore anticlockwise. The fishing village looks inward to the bay, and at the first shop was a box of plastic Viking swords and helmets. There were small tough trees of ash and sycamore on the isle.

At the museum were reminders of the glory of those days, the golden Lindisfarne Gospels, pillars painted white and overlaid with pigments of purple and black, red and green. These stone pillars and crosses had stood tall in landscapes, pointing to the sky. The Priory took a beating from Henry VIII, the king who raided his own country's commons for land and gold. The ruined walls and arches were red sandstone, brought south from Edinburgh just seventy leagues away. In a field was a dig, trenches cleared of grass, the search continuing for the first wooden monastery. From the seawall was a view of inward racing tide, and out to sea the twenty isles of Farne, their wrecking skerries and the red-and-white banded lighthouse.

In the bay was St Cuthbert's isle, fifty oar strokes from the shore, where the abbot of the monastery first retreated to live as hermit, before sailing for greater seclusion on the Farnes.

There were seals in the sea, and on the far side fishing boats were moored by the castle on the crag. Upturned half-boats had been converted to fisher sheds, planks tarred and paint flaking, outside a flotsam of marine goods, plastic chair and lobster creel, rope and net. Swallows were flitting through a door eroded by rot and salt. Small children skipped stones, their mother watching from the shore. The sky was low, the sea air wet. Etched on slate were records of all the lives saved by lifeboats, *The Gertrude* was the last.

Inland from castle was the walled garden designed by Gertrude Jekyll one hundred years ago. Sheep grazed outside the iron-gate, inside were sweet pea and aster, tall fennel and black hollyhock. There was every saturated colour, and a seat at each corner for contemplation. The route turned past shore of rounded stone and pebble, then to high dune and wet slack. Northern gales could beat upon this shore, and yet the monastery and village were safe inside. In the sheepy meadows were lapwing and curlew, and in the wetlands an invasive pigmyweed, spines that caught on sock and boot.

In the yard of coffee shop were half a hundred sparrows, their seedy chatter filled the space between the floor of flagstone and the sky. On the wall was a stone model of a hawk, quite ignored. The bay was full of sky, white bubbling clouds above the inland hills.

This was a coast of castles, yet they could not protect the shipping as tide and current dashed. From high inside Bamburgh castle, all seemed silent. The blue sky and silent waters, the wide golden beach, horses on a gallop, children playing in the sand. There were two white sails out upon the sea. This day all was quiet down below, a quiet lapping of the sea on the sand, the water crystal clear. Sandbars and swales were revealed as the water ebbed north. A white crest, pure in morning light, ripples splashing. On the shore was a fossil of a fish in stone, vertebrae and bone crushed here in sediment so long ago. On the sandy cliff was a line of half a hundred nests, and sand martins swooped and stalled at entrances, then fell out and flashed away. The swifts by now had gone, the puffins too. There were eider on the sea, and a huddle of cormorants on a sandbank.

At Seahouses, once called North Sunderland, was the harbour gate to isle of Farne.

A sea-angler sat in his car, the engine running, staring at the rod cast over high stone wall. The coast was dune and castle, dune again and fishing hamlet, dune again. At Beadnell were lime kilns on the quay, children leaping from the jetty. This late summer day, the beach had drawn a crowd from the city, and people seemed happy just to sit and stare at nothing, a kind of silence from the jostle, children rushing up with spade and bucket. A few kilometres from the village all again was silence, the shore empty and river flowing out to sea by protected colony of terns. The sun shone on everyone alike.

> *Listen!*
> *A dream came to me,*
> *It seemed I saw the Tree itself,*
> *Borne on the air, light wound around it,*
> *A beam of brightest wood, a beacon clad,*
> *In overlapping gold, glancing gems.*
>
> [*Dream of the Rood*, The Exeter Book, c970]

The rain fell again, on everyone in the upper fells and moors.

It was the land of abbeys, once heart of the Northumberland kingdom, then razed by Tudor king. One summer day, a monsoon came, a once-in-a-century storm by the pre-climate crisis currency. Five inches of intense rain fell in two hours in upper Swaledale and Wensleydale. Surface water dashed over sheep meadow, down gill, through hamlet streets, carried away one tonne bales from farmyards. Village greens became tidal, roadways slipped, landslides took away paths, farmers would find dead sheep in trees. The tea colour of moorland waters had gone, all was turbid soil and raging river. We came on foot, walked along the Ure and over tops to Swale. The Grinton moor bridge was gone, five hundred years and now a ruin. In the streets of Reeth stone walls were down, and tidal mats of grass and straw were gathered up in hedges.

At Nun Cote Nook farmhouse, one thousand feet up above the plains, we sat in the farm café in a walled garden, watching white clouds race across a breezy sky. In the farm kitchen, every ceiling beam was decorated with winning rosettes, for the North Country Cheviots and Texels, for the Blue and Limousin cattle. When Gawain rode in these very dales, searching for the Green Knight,

> *Wild was the weather the world awoke to,*
> *Bitterly the clouds cast cold on the earth,*
> *Bleakly the snow blocked, and beasts were frozen,*
> *Driving great drifts, deep in the dales.*
>
> [*Sir Gawain and the Green Knight*, c1300s]

Forty years and more before, as students we brought young children from the ancient Viking capital for days out on these moors. Some had never walked on uneven ground, yet whether the land was frozen white or warm they ran and rolled and laughed under freedom of the skies.

Years before I had also walked with a friend, their farm family had moved away from marshy east, and we came upon a grand house in a forest clearing. All the windows were nailed with plywood, and roses had grown thorns and gone long. The sun shone that day too, yet all the formal gardens were a sea of rabbits. Their eyes were weeping, many gasped for breath. They sat still, and it seemed they could do nothing but wait.

We walked up from Middleham, town of racing stables. Early morning the streets resounded to the rhythmic drum of horse hooves as they walked up to gallops on the moor. The castle was a ruin, home to Richard III, the last English king to die in battle. There was a glade of giant limes and down on the banks of the Ure was location for the country's first cricket match at the time of Queen Anne. Over time, it grew to be a way to increase the togetherness across communities. Nearby was the Cistercian Abbey Jervaulx, famed for four hundred years at northern edge of art and culture centred on Citeaux in Burgundy. It was one of eighty-seven Cistercian abbeys sacked by Henry VIII's troops, the white monks and nuns dispersed by the country's own soldiers. In the pub at the Ure crossing, an extinct red squirrel was in a glass box on the mantelpiece.

At Spennithorne church was a twelve-foot Celtic cross, the pillar of interlaced vine and grapes, and there were green men on the corbel ends. In stained glass was St George with blue wings, and there was a green dragon grinning at his feet, in a stone as Merlin had predicted. The way worked up river through Wensleydale, and at the flights of falls at Aysgarth the tea-water river was roaring, white-water brown-water, leaping over limestone pavement.

The riverside church of St Andrew, with the largest graveyard in the country, houses Jervaulx rood screen, smuggled there by fleeing monks. This was a celebration of wildness, a golden frieze of animals on purple screen. There was winged dragon and unicorn, antelope with horns entangled in a thorn, running fox and elephant with castle on its back. Here was the dragon those monks had needed, a beast with fire enough to hoard the treasure.

But perhaps this was nature so wild and ferocious it could untame the mind. At the time, who of local hamlet and village had ever seen such gold, such expanse of colour, even here just sixty leagues from coastal seats of Jarrow and Whitby?

At Castle Bolton in the shadow of the keep, where Mary Queen of Scots was held in prison, was a 1300s church named after Oswald, and down on the Swale banks was another for St Andrew. The streets of Grinton were blocked by debris, the road still closed. The church had a leper's squint, a square hole for distanced infectious parishioners to watch the service from outside. And in stained glass again, George wore silver armour with a purple cape, and stood by a long-necked dragon breathing orange fire. On the far side, east of Reeth at halfway marker for the coast-to-coast path, was Marrick Priory, a Benedictine nunnery with Saxon carvings in the chapel. The paved route to the lead mines and moor tops was up the Nun's Causeway through steep woods.

You can see how the king turned these abbeys and their lands to create an income for the crown.

The sixteen nuns were evicted in 1539, the site leased to local landowner, who bought low and sold high, and then resold again. There had been seventeen prioresses at Marrick from Agnes to Christobel, and they raised crop and stock, gave away to poor, offered lodging to passing travellers. Written in their articles were instructions to be affable and kind, and treat all as equals.

St Teresa of Ávila wrote, 'On arriving, the soul begins to lose desire for earthly things. Those of us who are on the earth, it seems to me, rarely understand where this satisfaction lies.'

On the lower Swale, the river cut through the ravine at Richmond, then widened at the Easby shallows. There were a thousand rooks and jackdaws calling, and swallows dashing over glittering river. It was here, at Asebi records Bede, that river baptisms were conducted for King Edwin's court. The monks wore robes of white, and worked for the local community. No doubt they would later have known of the Cistercian abbess Hildegard of Bingen, who became a religious, moral and political leader across the continent in the 1100s. She was writer and composer, humanist and herbalist, writing of *viriditas*, the green vigour, at the heart of life and nature. Earth, she wrote, was 'a paradise, a pleasant place, flourishing with fresh greenness of flowers and herbs and the delights of all spices, filled with exquisite perfumes, adorned for the joys of the blessed.'

The Cistercian success seemed, in part, to come from a focus on simplicity, on the time for contemplation, and on the close connections made with local community.

Yew bushes sprouted from the high walls of ruined refectory and library of the abbey. At St Agatha's church beside the abbey site was found the free-standing sandstone cross of Easby. It was carved ten years after Viking attack on Lindisfarne, the surviving fragment depicting Christ on throne, angels and apostle figures, a pecking bird, and on the rear side a vine scroll with gripping beasts, serpent and dragon in a forest. On the walls of St Agatha's were paintings, the labours of the months, digging and ploughing, cutting hedge and sowing seed. These alone date four hundred years after the cross, and three hundred before the raiding of the abbey, when the crown took the land and let it to the lord housed up at Bolton Castle.

Yet it did not all go smoothly here for Henry the King, for the uprising of 1536 grew great in Richmond.

The Pilgrimage of Grace commenced when vicar and shoemaker at Cistercian abbey of Louth Park brought forty thousand people to march on Lincoln. Henry sent his army under the Duke of Suffolk, and the leaders were hanged. But now was provoked the revolt across all the north lands. Henry then instructed the Duke of Norfolk, he should, 'Repair to St Agatha and other such places as have made resistance… and without pity cause the monks to be hanged without further delay.'

By mid-1537, more than two hundred abbots, monks, lords and knights had been hanged or burned at the stake. At Whitby, the last abbot was forced out by Cardinal Wolsey in 1539, the roof stripped, the bells and all other valuables removed.

> Sing as travellers on the road, but keep on walking,
> Relieve your toil by singing,
> Sing, but keep on walking.
>
> St Augustine [Sermon 256]

CHAPTER FOUR

The rivers Ure and Swale merge at Myton, join the Nidd at Monkton and then take on a new name. The Ouse flows south through Jorvik, the Viking capital of the north lands, and by now has gathered water from ten thousand square kilometres of moor and dale. This city always floods, even with the new defences. Still the river journeys south and merges with the Derwent, the river bridged at Stamford battle site where King Harold won his only victory. Had he been defeated, Harald Hardrada the Norse Viking would have fought William the great grandson of Rollo the Viking for the English crown. After sailing up the Humber and the Ouse, Harald's pavilion was impressive. And around the tent was now assembled, all the shining force to take the country crown.

Harald crushed the first English army, the dead piled so thickly, it was said the Norse could cross the swamp dry-shod. Days later the weather broke, the sky bright, and the armies of Harald and English Harold's brother Tostig went ashore but left behind on longships all their armour.

They carried shield and sword, and the trumpets sounded, for now Harald expected to be crowned in York. Yet on the horizon was seen a cloud of dust, a gleam from shields, sun shining on white coats of mail. The closer came the army, the greater it grew, and the glittering weapons sparkled, as if a field of broken ice. This was Harold's elite force reinforced by local fyrds called up as he marched north. So the armies drew up, and Norse Harald took to his glossy horse, black with a white blaze, he in blue tunic and golden helm. But while inspecting his troops, the horse stumbled. The king jumped to his feet laughing, a fall is fortune on the way, he said. But there was ghastly loss at this Battle of Stamford Bridge, Harald was struck in the throat by an arrow, this his death wound.

Many of the English force were felled, yet almost all the Norse were killed. Of that vast invasion force, a fleet of only twenty ships sailed away from carnage. Little did English Harold know, his army now much reduced, he had nineteen days left to live.

The River Ouse flows east and changes its name to the Humber. On the north shore lies Hull, on the south is Grimsby. And now age embitters many once associated with the fishing.

'An awkward lot,' said the Great Grimsby Member of Parliament of his fishermen. 'Always drunk.' Fishers drank to forget the life of sea, then could not wait to sail again. Syd Wakwerit was a fifteen-year-old deckie learner when *Roderigo* and *Lorella* went down. He stood at the bridge door listening to the radio calls. Thirteen years later, he was on the *Kingston Peridot* out of Hull when the cook took ill. The skipper put the two of them ashore at Isafjördur to walk to wooden hospital. Two days later, the *Peridot* had sunk in the fiercest storm known, one of Hull's triple trawler disaster. This was the daily fear that united families across the river, just please escape the clutches of Ægir, Ran and all their daughters.

At home, dead drunk, wives might wipe bacon fat around a husband's lips, yes you've eaten, they'd say, when he finally woke. On board, mistakes were inevitable. The hours were attritional, it was a sign of weakness if you needed sleep.

Hull's *King Edgar* went down in Dyrafjördur, the compass thrown overboard by a drunken deckhand, the skipper trying to steer by marks on land. The *Lord Lyon of Grimsby* was lost, the *Sando* saw a mast in the Iceland skerries, there was no sign of any crew. *The Oðinn* saved twenty crew of Grimsby's stranded *Northern Spray*. The *Langanes* of Grimsby was stranded on rocks fifty yards from shore, the Hull trawler *Bunsen* sent out a lifeboat, but it capsized and the mate was drowned. It was *Langanes* trimmer Albert Howard's fourth shipwreck, but this one he did not survive. That same winter, the *Jeria* of Grimsby was lost with fourteen crew, the *Edgar Wallace* of Hull gone with fifteen men. The *Ross Kenilworth* foundered, seventeen men saved by coastguard *Thor*. The *Macleay* was stranded when a drunken skipper ordered out the trawl when the vessel was inside Iceland waters, the wireless operator swam ashore with line, and all the crew were saved by shore party operating breeches buoy. The skipper was suspended, the radio-man awarded a silver cigarette case.

The Grimsby MP's office was high in House of Commons attic, small and cramped. Soon would come retirement, after forty years of fighting.

Austin Mitchell granted, it was his predecessor who as minister botched the cod war, letting Iceland win the parley. Britain wanted a quota of one hundred and twenty thousand tonnes, Iceland offered sixty. The government preferred to fight and went to war, sending in the Navy. 'Those gunboats made us look silly,' he said, 'they cut the warps and the trawlers lost their gear. Britain ended up with no quota.' Austin Mitchell sought a guarantee of payment, for every year of fishing service, yet these hopes again were dashed, the owners changed their operations. He helped Dolly Hardy lead the British Fishermen's Association to create a charter to guarantee £1,000 payments for every year of service. It was brushed aside by the minister and owners.

'The bastards,' he said, 'the bastards just bought land and pubs and businesses.' He went to Iceland to talk, and said, 'You've given us areas with no fish.'

'Yes,' they said, 'you're right.' The division bell rang and he looked up at the screen and remained seated.

The Hull MP was once a Secretary of State, so Alan Johnson had a corner office full in view of golden clock, Big Ben gleaming in the winter sunlight.

When Iceland won the cod wars, the trawler owners shrugged and seized the compensation. The crews were causal workers, for them no severance pay, no pension at retirement. He campaigned for years, and it was correct to say, there were some cases won in court, for lesser reparation. But promised settlements in the year 2000 dragged on a dozen years. Surely none in government were trying to let the time just toil along. Well-deserving fishers died of old age, secluded in their homes and digs. When he sought a change in law, a party colleague in the cabinet, a minister on his own side, flatly turned it down. 'Come on,' she said, 'The economy grows by competition.' The division bell again was ringing, so the lifts filled with voting men, descending to the secret path beneath the busy London streets.

Jim Williams was in his mid-nineties, served a life on ships, often in the hostile cold, spray freezing as it hit the metal superstructure. Such a life brings many tales, stories to swing the lamp, to laugh a little at every kind of adversity. But then he asked, was it worth it? 'I missed all the key moments of my children growing up.'

With Charlie Waddy, the last fish skipper in Hull, he led a group around the *Arctic Corsair*, moored at the River Hull. Jim had been a mate on this ship, had also been due to sign on with the *Sargon* on its final trip, just before his marriage. He held a pen in hand, then saw his uncle's name on the crew list and switched to her sister ship. Only five men survived that saga's ending in Iceland's Westfjords. By the *Corsair*'s time, one man had to hold a medical certificate, safety had advanced as a result of women's cries in Hull. Just last year, said Charlie, a young lad lost three fingers, they were up at east Greenland's grounds. He stitched him up. As we stood, we heard a ghastly noise and laughter, and a rattle of footsteps danced a jig. Everyone froze, then opened doors, all the corridors were empty.

Of course, and why not, it was drowned Ronnie, the ship ghost. We ate in a nearby café with Anita, Charlie's wife, revisited fishing life of Hessle Road.

'Never look back,' said Charlie, 'Iceland looks after us better than any UK ship owner.'

The glass case was crammed with silver gifts and shields, and the marble staircase echoed to a measured rigid step. One display contained faded flags from distant docks. Crews had travelled far, while land-locked men and women rarely even crossed the river. 'I could always tell when father was home,' remembered an old fisherman thinned by age, there was the smell of creosote and salt. He always brought two bars of chocolate and a bottle of cod-liver oil. But as the town struggled, the stigma of poverty, the low-achievement, so the fishing slipped away. Each mayor held office for a year in the wood-walled parlour, where panels were carved with fish and fruit, and portraits stained by candle smoke and cigarettes.

Mayor Mary Glew pointed, 'Let us warm ourselves by the fire.'

She rested the golden chain on her lap, and tea was served in china cups. The fishers spoke of Hessle Road, the distant way of life, and then we walked through the moot hall, and stood under the stained-glass window bright with heroes. Yet the same city filled St Andrew's Dock with rubble and made a soulless car park by the windy estuary.

Where bobbers' clogs clumped on cobbles, and auctioneers called, and men signed on for distant trips, where those ghosts walked now were retail outlets, for sofas and for pet-food. Waves were whipped by breeze, and the salmon sun set in the western haze beyond the long suspension bridge. Factories on the far side were belching smoke and fume, and container ships formed a queue, and fondly had said the mayor, 'We could win the competition, we will be a Culture City.' Might this bring the money for a fishers' monument, some way to recognise six thousand men who long ago were drowned?

But perhaps some would rather see concrete than celebrate the reek of fish, the distant days of silver scale.

I will never believe,
That earthly wealth stands,
Eternal for us all.

[*The Seafarer*, The Exeter Book, c970]

—————————

Slavery reform began in Hull with the merchant Wilberforce. But fishing out of Grimsby brought back domestic slaving just forty years later. It was the worst of times, it was the best for local economic growth.

This was the era when restless orphans sat on wooden benches sewing sacks. They slept on bales of straw, hoped for broth, stacked the corn, fed the stamping shire, in autumn picked potatoes, and at every other hour they hammered stone, each slice of childhood crushed. And sure enough, these abandoned children often smarted at the hand, suffered from the slipper. Their escape, they guessed, would come from growing old.

'Boys pack your bags,' might have bustled a beaming matron. 'Boys you are the blessed, you're going on the boats.'

Two hundred and fifty years before, in the Elizabethan age of muskets, Parliament declared a Poor Law, the destitute should take a trade. But not for pay, so preventing parish costs. This law skirted school, sent many straight to workhouse. The new 1834 Poor Law made criminals of those with no work, broke up families and put adult and child to work for only food. Between 1830s and 1914, one in ten of Britain's people were locked inside a workhouse. It helped the economy grow fast on zero wages. Though Wilberforce had led reform, now slaving sneaked in once again. So was slipped inside the Merchant Shipping Act of 1872 a crafty labour law.

A rising clamour came, the roar of engine iron across the isles. Awl and axe were cast aside, rail fast moved the freight, soon in the mills were captured children secured to every stall. And the sky was filled with soot, but how would owners feed the factory workforce? So the play for fish grew fast, in an era still of sail and gust. The landed men possessed the boat, supplied the coal, sold the salt and tanning cutch to skippers of their smacks. They owned the track and railway engine, they stocked the shop where sailors bought their tack, clothes and bedding for the sea. Yet a piece was missing, where to get the men to work the smacks. Migrant crews came north, and Grimsby accent took on drawl of Devon dock and Suffolk shore, and cockney from the Barking Creek.

And so on sea was legalised a new apprentice system. It was a scheme to seize the orphaned kids from every wretched slum.

The boys who escaped from the cold orphanages, away from breaking stone, they savoured at first this freedom, this voyage on a rattling train. They had seats apiece, and chattered in excitement. Soon was glimpse of sea, so much light in sky. No doubt the lads thought this was at first a fine adventure, for never had they seen ships fill a port, such boxes full of fish. Yet they shortly wished for workhouse once again. From over hill and vale, from secluded lane, each orphanage and charity traded boys to ships. And in the city streets, press gangs captured others, the police

CHAPTER FOUR

told mothers, you have to pay for their release. Boys for three decades and more would have to bend their backs.

As steaming trains drew up, ship owners paced the platform, and lads were snatched from carriage to the busy dock.

Many thousand sons were sent from prying sight, they crewed the smacks at sea for weeks at a time. Each fleet supplied a flying cutter that raced to dock when full, and soon they learned that this Merchant Act contained a secret clause. If a boy refused to sail, leapt ashore as ship was leaving dock, then he became a fugitive, a breaker of the law. Thus it was that new police were salaried to keep the peace. And before the magistrate, each skipper claimed those lads were idle, it was they who were placed in an awkward situation when certain boys refused to work. One lad walked the rural lanes, only grass for his daily pillow, seventy leagues to Nottingham, luckily his father fetched him back. 'This is how you make your way in life, they know best, you will now continue your education on the sea.'

And true, some crew did treat the boys as sons.

Fleeting was a wonder, up to fifty smacks on fishing bank. Yet a ballast shift, a hatch uncovered in a storm, some weakness in a wooden plank, no inquiry ever seemed to care. Fingers could be gashed, torn by rope. A boy falls from the rigging, another sinks fast, never seen again.

Just thirteen years of age, Jacob Kesler was beaten badly, kicked overboard, the skipper drilled the crew to silence. William Papper was murdered too, starved and hit with iron shovel, this the only skipper found guilty at a trial. In one decade alone, two thousand men and boys were drowned. Pressure grew in hearts of boys, so plans were whispered. One led a jump off, passed word around the dock, and one breezy day at six bells, as sun was rising from the sea, all the boys leapt from smacks. They marched to Riby Square, where, years later, these very boys as men would gather once again to call for equal pay. But now the constables were quick, rounding up the striking children.

Oh to hell with fleeting, far above the Dogger Bank, they had faced weeks of thirst and sorrow.

Could life ever be more grim, those ugly days of terror? Would there ever come a cheerful turn of tale? The magistrates of town, high on business acumen, sent five hundred boys to Lincoln, chained them in the street. Did any adult visit them, did any skipper feel concern?

The castle was converted, the jail perched high on the hill. The walls were stone, the cold and wet were constant, each cell designed to separate each guilty convict. There was a wise regime to isolate the boys, even in the chapel there were separate stalls for prisoners. Here was robber of the highway, murderer and thief, here were children young as eight. Yet the boys called it Lincoln College, it was so much better than a smack.

Time slipped by, it was the second summer of the century, and fishers joined the call to act together. Each man raised a hand to strike for better treatment. So the owners chained each ship and locked up the dock.

History said the Riot Act, signed to law by long-dead monarch, was helpful to authorities. It allowed them to declare illegal any group of twelve, and then with force to quell discord. Local men and boys carried food parcels to families with children. Gangs of fishers walked to friendly farms, they picked potatoes from the fields, yet as the strike was going on, the fishers and their wives at other ports seemed quite content, to carry on their search for cod. The royal court sent four hundred constables, half were mounted high on steeds, and another hundred soldiers skilled at war in colonies. Three troopships also anchored, outside the port, it was a useful practice against their citizens for the coming war.

Drums pounded and the people cried. But by the end of fourteen weeks, all was silent in the town. Now their bleeding feet caused the strand to redden, for the shoes of leather had split, and none could pay the cobbler to make repairs. At the church beside the dock, an anxious holy man wrung his hands, for his role in all of this was to preach that heaven waited. We promised to stay together, said the fishers. Yet their hopes were crushed by weight of hunger. As winter's breath came on the wind, the owners agreed to change the fleeting system, but would not budge on how proceeds of fish should be shared by crews. Snow fell out of season, but they were not pained, for the costs of fishing were simply set another way.

Not long before in London, a reporter had filed a copy. 'Those apprentices,' he said, 'were fine little fellows, each a slave with a hero in him, like Spartacus of yore.'

Now no music played, no dancers danced. None gathered for some wine and song, they could only hear the outcry. They would have to wait for thirteen years to pass, before the labour system broke. It seemed the trenches offered better future for the fishers and their fellows. Yet they missed the pitching, the freedom of the breakers, the open life at sea.

In later years, Rita Clark worked in a pontoon dock café for forty years, feeding four hundred workers every day: 'I loved working down the dock, and I miss all my boys. I have been lucky to have such wonderful times.'

Norman Ridley was on the pontoon for half a century, and said, 'I miss the buzz of the fish dock. If anyone was ill or in trouble, then someone would organise a whip-round to support them.'

The boat grumbled in the stone harbour, surged out to shining sea. It steered north-east from Seahouses, a well-trodden sea road for the lifeboat stationed on the wall. The rocky isles of Farne channel the racing daily tides, home to six thousand seals and one hundred thousand seabirds.

The boat motored past the wrecking rock of Harcar, where lay the ruin of iron ship *Forfarshire*. As water slapped at wood, we saw the seals resting on the rocks, the guano on the cliffs, the water crystal clear. On Inner Farne was Cuthbert's chapel, built seven hundred years ago over his well of clear water. We sat in silence in the stony chapel, where three saints of Lindisfarne stood tall in coloured glass. One Arctic tern ringed on the Farnes flew to Australia, just three months after fledging.

Despite the lighthouse, hundreds of ships, it is said, have been stranded on these isles.

William Darling married Thomasin, her father was the Bamburgh castle gardener, and they came to choose a sky-name for their seventh child. Grace kept eider duck as pets, puffins wandered through the home. They farmed the rocky isle, raising sheep and rabbit, from the scanty soil persuading up the cabbage.

Grace was schooled by William, sitting high by bright acetylene that shone at rising moon. They could row a clinkered coble, in and out of currents that streamed through basalt columns. One day, a hundred leagues north, on the black cloudy river at Dundee, ship-designers had declared that iron could float. They put in boilers fuelled by coal, piped steam to drive the paddles, and from that whaling city an iron ship so well furbished soon would churn the sea from Tay to Humber back and forth. But the *Forfarshire* sailed only once with passengers. They left Hull with faulty boiler, and so it took three hours to pull past Spurn's long sandy spit. She shuddered north, passed outside the Farnes, then all the boilers failed.

A new storm struck, the steamship wallowed south. On land the wind ripped the slate from roofs, it shattered glass. Water struck the brigg and ness, each wave exploded, casting sea high upon the light. The ship stranded on the skerries. It had snapped, the aft piece sank, taking down to salt all those in the cabins.

Dreams are bad in storms like those, so Grace gazed from the tiny window into gloaming light of dawn. She had watched these isles for twenty-three years, and saw a piece of ship was on the Harcar rock. She shouted down to William, and through salt and spray they peered to see figures standing on the seething water, clinging to the rock. Thomasin begged them stay, yet Grace was strong, and each life brings such a moment.

They launched the clinkered coble, gripped blades, looked at each other, smiled at the task ahead.

They rowed a league to south, their forearms screaming, it seemed the creak of oar on wood was louder than the roar of wind and wave. But now a ghastly count, there were too many waiting. Grace steadied the coble, William passed across a mother, they filled the boat, had to leave behind two baby bodies, rowed to Longstone, and back again. Nine were saved. They had no extra beds, yet now came seven more, for Grace's brother had rowed with lifeboat into teeth of storm. So nineteen huddled in the warmth and inner calm, even as the lighthouse floor was flooded with the tide. No news could flee to anxious families, even those in Seahouses feared their lifeboat lost. Forty-three were drowned in that metal ship, and soon the story reached the national press.

The local press and London news reacted fast. Consumption would soon be cause of Grace's death, yet the architect was stress. She was claimed, a trolling public put on plays, sent letters asking for a lock of hair, requested autograph, a kiss on paper. The queen sent fifty sterling pounds. Visitors flocked to saintly coast, hired boats to gaze. Grace's fame spread across the world, some artists had her sit for days. The local Duke wrote to Wellington his own account of gallant rescue, and so she was sent a high award, a golden medal. Yet still no cease, for Grace was called to join a circus as exhibit, and Edinburgh women wrote, advised her not to go. Leading wives of fishing

Hull wrote six times, two thousand wished to meet her. Men offered marriage, they wanted her as a prize exhibit.

Grace was firm and said to William and Thomasin, 'I have not married yet, for they say the man is master, and there is much talk of bad masters.'

At the Fish Heritage Centre of Grimsby, the displays centred on those ways of sea life. The constant fear of death, yet strong community. The slaving system, the work for boys and men. The fearless rescuers. The fifty pubs on Freeman Street, the shadow of the Mission Man knocking on the door. In the pub was an old advert for cigarettes: 'Player's No. 3, for your throat's sake, smoke!'

Said one woman of her husband, 'I thought I could change him, you do, when you're daft and young.'

Said one man, 'I'd never let my son go to sea, I'd chop his legs off.'

Mostly they had no choice.

Actor Tom Courtenay grew up in Hessle Road, an ill-lit and cold house near the dock. His aunt was grandmother of skipper Charlie Waddy. A teacher gave encouragement, so he left his fishing future to live in London, exchanging letters with his lonely mother.

She began each reply, 'Dear Tom, When I get a letter from you, I don't just read it and put it away, I read it scores of times.' There were more dense fogs over the city and dock in those days, and the damp house left her permanently ill. 'I always have a feeling when you don't write it is because you are unhappy. I hope it is not so.'

After six years of war and no fishing, they called that time of plenty dip and fish, it was so easy to fill the trawler pounds with fish. They remember cods a fathom long. But the commons soon were over-fished. When the ships came home, the dock bell rang, and the white decks and polished brass were gleaming. 'They used to look fantastic, so bright,' said 80-year-old Syd.

> *A flying arrow, a falling tide,*
> *Ice a night old, a snake when coiled.*
> [Sæmundr Sigfússon, *Hávamál, Sayings of the High One, Poetic Edda*, c1290]

CHAPTER FOUR

SAGA VI

GRIMSBY EMBARK

This saga happens at the deepwater port of Grimsby, in the late 1930s. The boy was fifteen, and signed to sail as the threat of war grew. Freddie the deckie would become a timeless wanderer. The ship Epine leaves the port one autumn dawn, and steams for Iceland. Claud the cook tells Freddie all the tales, how he lost his fingers. The skipper Syd knew where to find the cod, in those days a fathom long. The trawl comes up full, throw back one cod says Syd, that one's for the sea king. A crewman's hand is poisoned, so after filling up the pounds they moor at Flatey to meet the doctor. Alf the mate takes Freddie ashore, and he gives a book to the waiting girl on a horse. They sit in the quiet church, and Alf tells his stories of rescue by Iceland farmers. 'You should not dwell long, on sorrows of the past,' says Alf, for he was one of Grimsby's slave apprentices of the 1880s.

Well a deepwater port expanded, its sailors searching far for fish,
And fear began to stalk, the hearts of every father,
For their lads had watched, young deckies walking tall,
Along the street with wallets full, their words had wings,
They freely spent at bars, have a beer on me,
Those princes called, again across the smoke,
Yet their sleeves were long, buttoned over boils on wrists,
None could hide such freedom, from the growing boys of Grimsby.

Alas as fishers better understood, by battling frozen fingers,
The life at distant waters, chilled and cold inside the ship,
They would pause, troubled at a bed that never pitched,
At armchairs laid with lace, forgot that wives and mothers,
Had been craving, for any tidings from the shadows,
So those very sailors by-passed home, took to pubs in port,
And now the country's leader, told all his citizens,
Go quietly sleep in beds, for he had guaranteed the peace.

The boy was fifteen summers old, so he signed to sail,
There was no money for his mother, his father long since flown,
'You must go to college,' said his teacher once again,
But the boy turned to younger sister Iris, 'It is now for you,
To stay at school, so go to every lesson,
Look after mother, I will fish to end our hungry days,'
So Freddie bought his bedding, boots and gutting knife,
He shrugged on sweater, and hoisted bag upon his shoulder.

Freddie the deckie would now become, a timeless wanderer,
Of all the northern seas, he will crew six years of war,
And after bells of peace are rung, two ships he sails,
Will be lost as wrecks, upon the rocky shore of Iceland,
And fellow sailors' bones, will roll and rot,
In salt sea waves, as wet-foot men and women,
From their vintage farms, will hurry over heath and lava field,
And deeply wade in water, to seize the stranded fishers.

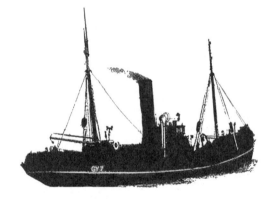

SAGA VI

Sure enough an autumn dawn, brought neither song nor ceremony,
This crew had come in ones and twos, cloth caps pulled on tight,
Their serge was sharply creased, each a choker at the neck,
The lean skipper wore a suit, tilted head toward the radio,
This ship *Epine* will wallow badly, in the Iceland waters,
They were coaled so black dust, covered deck and darkened soul,
Below were ice blocks in the pounds, outside the mist laid on the dock,
Radio ops spun his ceramic dial, there came a stream of buzz and bleep.

'Slow ahead,' Syd the skipper called, and this horse-of-sea,
Slipped from berth, glided into lock,
Alf the mate stood by, wearing hidden hammer,
An amulet about his neck, he whispered rural charm,
'Thrice I smite the Holy Crock, with this mell I thrice do knock,
One for God and one for Wod, and one of course for Lok,'
Yet the crew complained, would a coming war collide,
Would the cod be caught, as soldiers fought for land not fish?

Called the skipper, 'Full ahead, and wash away that coal,'
Since the end of sail, Cleethorpes beach was stained with dust,
Diesel soon would shift, those sands to desert yellow,
Now came a rising throb, the ship's own thumping heart,
As firemen shovelled in their lair, lonely in the vessel deeps,
Skipper eased the wheel, screws thrashed at sea,
On the bridge, the cabin door was wide,
Letting in the day, the ship was creaking as it breathed.

From above the gannets gazed, on empty sea to hooped horizon,
And saw this single questing horse, of hissing hemp and brass,
A spreading wave from bow, an arrow shaft of white stern trail,
The *Epine* toiled to Shetland, black bars out of reach,
Fair Isle fell away astern, a bright foam skirt in silver moonlight,
They passed the Faroe summits, under stars the crew,
Now wore high-necked sweaters, rubber boots cut ankle low,
Around the deck at dusk, flew fulmar soft as moths.

Below the galley glowed, the alum kettle full,
The cook was pounding dough, at his lips a nodding fag,
'Nice cup o' tea, that's what you want in this weather,
Nice cup o' tea,' he called to deckie Freddie,
Wedged at table, wooden fiddles crossing top,
To grip the sauce that spiced the fish, metal cellars for the salt and pepper,
One thing first advised his mother, make friends with cook,
So Freddie asked, 'What's it like at Iceland?'

Cookie Claud raised an arm, held out a hand,
Of one thumb and two smaller digits, so commenced a tale,
'It was a doomed ship, yet the *Dominican* was daring,
We were running fast before a gale, but struck the Blinders,
The sea poured in the fish room,' he paused,
Freddie knew of Iceland, some magnetic sites,
Where the compass simply spun, or perhaps the skipper was a drunk,
'That sea gets in the boiler, the ship will blow apart.'

'We launched the lifeboat, in the blinding blizzard,
The coast was miles beyond, so bending backs,
We rowed all day, our bloody hands were raw,
The mate a decent lad, for a Lowestoft boy,
He shouted 'do not doze,' he slapped us on the shoulders,
But the second engineer, closed his eyes to sleep,
Bleedin' terrible it was, hours of bitter cold,
His eyes we rubbed with rum, but soon his breathing ceased.'

Deckie's tea had cooled, 'The rescue party dragged us in,
Took us to a turf-roofed farm, a lovely fire was blazing,
But it was too late, that's how I lost my fingers,
Black they were by then, the doctor cut them off,'
Claud called up the well, 'Pot o' tea skipper?'
The fish pounds echoed, ice awaiting pick and axe,
They had steamed, past pulsing jellyfish,
And soon would shoot for cod, at the richest banks of Iceland.

Iceland's cliffs were grey, skipper traced the warmer current,
Steered up the eastern coast, this was the deal,
An equal share for all, so the crew dreamed up the fish,
One raced a motorbike, another bought a fitted suit,
One was on the train, with mates to London town,
'You said you'd get your teeth fixed,' Claud reminded him,
'Yet you'll spend it all on beer,' and replied that seaman,
'Yes well I've learned my lesson, this time I'll save it all.'

Alas it always seemed, the fish were all concealed,
Inside the three-mile limit, so fingers crossed and cheerful,
Ships hurried in and hoped, the one gunboat would hound another,
Yet certain skippers always lied, especially to each other,
From the speaker on the bridge, a voice now rumbled,
'Bloody poor laddie; a few baskets of sprags,
And bloody soldiers, keep smiling over,'
'We'll cast here,' smiled the skipper.

The trawl was tipped, overboard and towed astern,
The forecast warned, gale force eight was imminent,
And hours later shouted mate, 'Heave up, haul away,'
They pulled on winch, and turned with feral roar,
Foot by wet foot, the twine-net splashed on deck,
It should be cod, but could be red-fish soldiers,
Or only jellies, a rock or even whale,
This bag was heavy, the crew were pulling hard with hope.

The ocean poured on deck, they saw the mouths agape,
Eyes wide and air-surprised, yelled skipper from the bridge,
'Bloody good catch, throw back a lucky cod,
That one's for the sea king, to keep his daughters pleased,'
And now for hour on hour, by hand they gutted,
Each and every fish, swaying on the deck,
'We'll have another go,' laughed the skipper,
The net was shot again, the catch now laid below on ice.

Radio ops flung livers in a pail, poured them in the boiler,
On the worst of trips, crews made more from liver oil,
The ship often out of coal, just limping home,
Yet today a man was singing, and another shouted back,
'Bleedin' awful noise, make all the fish sit up,
I shouldn't wonder,' Freddie kept on gutting,
And asked how many, 'Ninety boxes' shouted singer,
'Good-oh,' said skipper to the mate, 'Our lips are sealed on this.'

So the men pulled and heaved, sliced and stamped,
For twenty hours straight, the wind shrieked in the rigging,
So the crew ate fast, and out they flaked,
And by late afternoon, they were crowded in the galley,
Ops had patched the radio, fish stew was steaming on the table,
First calamities on continent, on the hour the football scores,
One man could not hold his spoon, weeping blisters on his hand,
'What a world eh, what a world lad!'

Said one fireman, staring out of porthole,
'Well I suppose we'll have to go, lend a hand,'
They listened more, the Czechs had mobilised,
The Reich had sent an ultimatum, the grave voice ceased,
The men stared at space, 'Oh bloody hell!'
A new voice soon was reading, the names in pairs,
Of football clubs, Grimsby up against the Arsenal,
They thumped the table, bouncing mugs and plates.

'Must have been a fine game, wish I'd gone,
But Chamberlain's flown home, without seeing Hitler,
One–nil, bloody good eh?'
The crew swallowed tea, guessing shares of fish,
The man with black teeth grinned, 'I'll put some on the Town to win,'
Alf the mate stood on the bridge, reporting to the skipper,
'Cleethorpes Levi's hand, it's poisoned he can't use it,'
'Well the fishing's far too good, we will fill up first.'

The wind had fled, the trawler steamed up the flat-calm fjord,
Tied up at Flatey's jetty, a doctor stood at harbour-side,
Fair children watched in silence, each with blackened teeth,
Gulls screamed above, oars clacked on sixæreen,
The cod crew leant on rail, a comfort at this tiny isle,
The dark-skinned Doctor Annarr said, 'I have lanced and stitched it up,
Why will you go for war, surely you should stay,'
'Well we're going home,' said the skipper counting out the fee.

The crew stayed aboard, they could not buy a drink at Iceland,
So Freddie came ashore with Mr Mate, who'd said to bring a book,
Men were mending nets, saluting as they passed,
A girl about the age of Iris, rode up on fine white horse,
She put out her hand, an old man smiled,
And Alf said, 'Go on give the book to Unni,'
Freddie watched a beetle land, upon her sleeve and climb a finger,
Unfold its wings, and fly into the autumn sunshine.

SAGA VI

Walking past an elfin borg, they gently pushed,
At wooden doors of eggshell blue, Alf the mate now said,
'Let's wait inside, whisper word or two of thanks,'
The tiny church was place of peace, quite a shock,
For on a ship was endless hissing, of hot boiler pipe,
And wind in stays, the constant growl of wave,
Yet here was silence, it seemed this could be why they came,
Why they crossed the water, why they wandered far in search of fish.

Alf told this tale, for he had been aboard,
When *Hilaria* was defeated at Medallandsandr, off black volcanic coast,
'We were steaming fast at night, heeled hard to port,
The skipper thought, we'd simply shipped a heavy sea,
But a hole was ripped along the flank, we had no wireless,
So we tied on flares, burned them from the mast,
The rising tide washed us shorewards, farmers waded into winter sea,
Ropes around their waists, they rescued fourteen crew by breeches buoy.'

'Iceland horses soon were hitched, and for three hours,
We took the track up over bog, until we stood before a farm,
It was soft inside, they fed us soup and lamb,
The family sat on floor, so we could rest on beds,
Next came two-day trip to Vík by horse, fifteen snowy hours by bus,
From Reykjavik we flew to Renfrew, took another bus,
Three hundred miles on south to home, yet as we brought no cod,
In any of our pockets, the Grimsby owners gave us not a penny.'

'You should not dwell, too long and often,
On sorrows of the past, I was on the smacks,
From age of ten a slave,' Alf explained,
'Yet those days have gone, the Fourteen War,
Ended youthful times, engulfed those unfair ways,
I can say for certain, life for us is better now,'
No doubt this clarified, why mates like Alf,
Could command a ship, work the *Epine* crew so well.

Years later, will come another test,
For Freddie will be trawler mate, of well-known *Notts County*,
When three ships of Hull will sink, and every man but one will drown,
Their trawler will run on rocks, heavy ice on deck and every surface,
It will be the coldest ever storm, their rescue by the gunship *Oðinn*,
Now Alf the mate was finished, he stood from wooden bench,
Both his knees were cracking, and they saw a flock of birds,
Black and blurred by window glass, the whole isle swirled beyond.

'The war's off,' shouted radio op,
'Good job too, who wants a war anyway,
Coming to the match on Saturday, we're against the Leeds?'
The minds of crew had flown, free on Freeman Street,
Would they make the port, in time to see the match,
Or would the cruel sea god, rustle up a wind,
That's the next part, of any tale,
When men assume the journey's over, so a fall occurs.

The ferocious gale struck, all was gust and spindrift,
Frantic squall and water high, each wave a test of their resolve,
'We will turn and run,' shouted skipper,
They cast out anchors, each a tonne,
Run far astern, to wrestle with the storm,
A skua planed before the bridge, led the ship downwind,
Heading far from home, adding days and hungry hours,
It was Ægir's choice and now the fish, might spoil and fetch no price.

And so one still morning, the trawler grumbled up the sandy estuary,
The green light on the dock was blinking, and standing on the quay,
Leant a man with megaphone, 'Right up the end right ahead,
Close astern, whoa that'll do,'
The older crew laughed, the skipper crimped his eyes,
There was only one other trawler in, the yawning market waited,
They moored at Pontoon head, this mile-long city on the salty water,
Where a fortune could be made, by owners not the fishers.

On the whaleback the crew were dressed, brushed up bright,
The brasses shone, the ship had safely found the land,
On the dock a group of women waited, and called the skipper,
'Well here we are an' all, how are you keeping, love?'
'Can't grumble Syd, how's yourself?'
Called the mate from on the bridge, 'That gale has brought us luck,
See long merchant faces, and we'll have hit the jackpot,'
And Freddie hoisted his three cod, the allowance for his mother.

SAGA VII

HULL CRY

This saga happens at the port of Hull and nearby Hessle Road, in the famed year of 1968. The hope in every fisher's heart was always to turn for home with fish in the hold. Yet many thousand did not return. The triple trawler disaster that winter provokes Lily the fish gutter to join with friends to stand up for safety rights. Long before, Iceland made each ship carry lifeboat, lifejackets and radio. The Hull trawler owners lagged. The first to sink is St Romanus, *then* Kingston Peridot, *and finally* Ross Cleveland *in the worst storm ever known off Ísafjördur in the Westfjords of Iceland. The coastguard* Oðinn *rescues the crew of the* Notts County, *and the mate Fred forms up the Englishmen to clap the crew ashore. The mate survives the* Ross County *sinking, yet is ostracised at home. Why was it you survived? The women raise a petition, meet ministers in London, and Lily says, us women have achieved more than all the industry in sixty years. But they lose their jobs in the factories of the owners.*

Ever since those ancient days, the hope in every fisher's heart,
Had been to sail a sea of plenty, turn for home with fish in hold,
And when the others came back blank, they would laugh,
Look toward the sparkle on the brine, for it was ship on ship,
Fishers battling one another, and so it was today,
Safety trailed behind, a loss was half-expected,
Those Merchant Shipping Acts, smartly stifled labour action,
So to Hull strode desolation, the triple trawler drowning.

There was once a wife and mother, who lived on Hessle Road,
She should have worn a crown, been a queen for all she did,
Lily was a child between the wars, worked the factory lines,
So she married young, a Maltese merchant seaman,
And carried on her shoulders, fishers into common cause,
Even as the silence of the owners, dimmed each salty soul,
Soon her name was on a blacklist, unfit to work they said,
For she had stood for civil rights, at fishing street and dock.

There never was a season, when sorrow should prevail,
Hessle was a cobbled village, far from merchant quarter,
At its end was lock to rushing river, inland routes to coal and cotton mill,
To yeasty northern sea, were twenty leagues to steam,
Each terraced home was damp, a colder back-yard plot,
With outside toilet spider-spun, the newsprint hung on string,
And running from the bunker, the winter rain turned black,
Yet it was escape for countless men, their secret life in pigeon loft.

Lily's friends took in nets, fixed a hook to cupboard door,
Their fingers braiding as the babes, played in tin baths by the fire,
In afternoon they carried, hardback chairs outside on street,
Beyond front porch and facing west, warming in the sun,
Yet in a murky pub, a flushed crewman swayed in smoke,
For beer and bookies snared his pay, a pale wife held the bills,
She would keep a shilling back, a rabbit bought for Christmas lunch,
'We're having chicken,' skipped the eager children.

Yet those very children, learned a social skill,
They could tell if father, had come back home,
For the house now smelled, of creosote and salt,
So there might be sweets, they imagined bar of chocolate,
Yet inside was swelling fear, just beside each tiny heart,
Mickey's father left a hole, gone with all the other hands,
His brother stuck his gutting knife, in mast and sprung away,
His sister served, crying at the long bar fishers' pub.

Bert's brother laughed and swung, the youngsters round in circles,
Katie's uncle was a golden skipper, go with you they begged,
Choker Charlie also drowned, off Iceland's Northern Cape,
Lily's neighbour wished for silken blouse, but she cried aloud,
'What should I do, with a bloody barometer?'
Her husband paid instalments, then he too was drowned,
And all she had of him, was the wooden weather-watcher,
That sea was often cruel, it claimed the men who caught the fish.

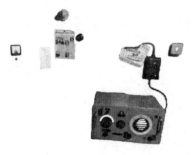

Long before in law, Iceland made each ship,
Carry modern life raft, yet the country with an empire,
Allowed their ships to sail without, so in warm dawn light,
The fishers muttered, they did not need their sons at sea,
They had seen a boy, caught by swinging otter door,
A crewman mauled by winch, another cut in two by cable,
Alas it was a harsh dilemma, women wanted men back safe,
And if those men could talk, they'd reply they needed drink.

Three ships now strode onstage, they were slow sidewinders,
Philip Gay of *Ross Cleveland*, admired and feared by all,
The young skipper of *St Romanus*, Jim Wheeldon said to owner,
'The radio's playing up,' and he in turn was told,
'You don't need a radio, to catch a fish,'
Skipper of the *Kingston Peridot*, Ray Wilson sung with mate,
The night before they sailed, save the last dance for me,
Each left a wife at home in port, all would soon be widows.

It was the second Sunday, of the shortest month,
Soon to lose three crews, was fleet of twenty British trawlers,
The skipper of the gunboat *Oðinn*, had just detained,
Six Icelandic inshore ships, for fishing in the limits,
The horror now unfolded, a tempest had been forecast,
It would be foulest ice-storm, to strike for a generation,
A memory to last a lifetime, said chairman of the local chapter,
Of lifeguards out of Ísafjördur, 'I had never seen such weather.'

Lily Bilocca slapped down, her fillet-knife on skinner's table,
Pulled on large white coat, secured her headscarf under chin,
She later looked to camera lens, 'I've always been concerned,
But I'd never done a thing about it,' for these cod-skinning women,
Who wielded blades of steel, whose pay was less than men,
Wore rubber aprons, outdoor clothing layers beneath,
They endured a daily grinding chill, snow gusting into open bays,
Just a stride from home, they stood in icy slush.

The first to sink was *St Romanus*, unstable in the calmest seas,
Known to men as yellow submarine, lying in the water low,
Its radio was limited in range, despite the rules of Board of Trade,
Half the crew were under twenty, the final trip for engineer,
Iceland trawler *Vikingur*, heard the mayday morse,
And in a silence north of Isafjördur, a Dutch ship caught an empty raft,
Yet a trawler owner said, to the young wife of the skipper,
'I do not see, why you should be worried.'

Fate took next the *Kingston Peridot*, it reported fishing slack,
The cook had slipped, his broken ribs now saved his life,
The ship put in at Reykjavik, swapped in a cook,
It was the first shore call, for their teenage deckie learners,
They steamed back to north, as Arctic storm was striking,
The bow climbed waves, three times higher than the mast,
Yet only twenty tonnes of ice, could topple such a ship,
A heavy slick was found, an owner said there still was hope.

Black were the letters, large on first sheet of *The Post*,
Two trawlers missing, that was it,
Lily saw the headline, walking home from work,
Her mind went to her husband, to deckie son and skipper brother,
The fleet was seeking shelter, ducking icy waves,
In the fjord by Hornstrandir, all their snubbing anchors down.
Ross Cleveland put ashore at Isafjord, another ailing cook,
And now was struggling, at that very moment for survival.

SAGA VII

At home again, what options does a mother have,
She was stirred to write, a letter and petition,
As distant trawlers thrashed, four friends gathered names,
In pubs and rain-swept streets, they carried scrap and sheaf,
Any piece of paper, and ten thousand women signed,
That night the women's army, in smart shoes for once,
Went forth wearing headscarves, tied beneath their chins,
To take their wooden seats, in unheated meeting hall.

On stage was Chrissie, a waif about to suffer second loss,
Her nephew crewed on *St Romanus*, a brother on *Ross Cleveland*,
But for fifty hours, it had been dodging seas,
Behind *Notts County* out of Grimsby, and soon would come a giant wave,
Skipper Philip will shout on radio, 'We are laying over,
Give my love and the crew's love, to the wives and families,'
They will be three leagues from the shore, it could have been three hundred,
Coastguard *Oðinn* bears the message, on the airwaves back to Hull.

'You will not have heard of us', the women said onstage,
'Now look again, we are here before you,
We have gathered, many thousand names,
Of voters who now believe, we can be a force for good',
Perhaps some were also children's names, for there comes a time,
When the moment appears, often midway through a life,
Though events conspire, each will face alone a test,
Yet now rose a strength in crowd, to wade this rushing river.

At dawn a trawler left the dock, the crew on bridge and foredeck,
Were watching Lily braced by railings, she was yelling questions,
'Do you have radio op?' but their eyes were blank,
For the skipper gave the work, and owners made it known,
They should fetch the fish, so fighting with her,
Were dock police in uniforms, dragging at her coat,
The police constables, being neither stock nor stone,
Sighed inside for parish deaths, yet also kept their faces passive.

She faced the pop of bulbs, and figures flashed in misery,
For more than ever, the women hoped for kindness,
Longed for someone big, just to listen with respect,
The news that many sailors, had perished in the ice,
Was about to wreathe them, in so great a weight of grief,
The mission offered solace, looked around to seek the words,
The roads that night were quiet, nothing hindered travel,
Yet songs still leaked from swinging doors, of pubs along the street.

The youngest of the gang of four, Yvonne with golden voice,
She was eating out with friends, when yes a trawlerman,
Punched her in the face, shouted fishing was the business,
Of only men, and one reporter asked on film of Lily,
'And do you regard yourself, as some kind of suffragette?'
An owner looked to camera, standing tall in suit and tie,
'The ordinary fisherman, is frankly a bit sick,
Of these women, interfering in their business.'

The Prime Minister was informed, of their petition by advisors,
So he in turn instructed, two ministers to meet these women,
And fill the room with union men, fetch the city MPs too,
Lily's letter called for every single ship, to have a radio op,
For rocket flare and beacon, one lifejacket for each man,
Surely this was not too much, in this very age,
But some wives were worried, as Lily also pressed,
For blanket ban on fishing, at Iceland now a danger symbol.

Lily spent the night planning, what to say when asked,
How to show the leaders, how the women were neglected,
Yet their expedition, gathered up in Whitehall,
And ministers and officials, sat on far side of the table,
When the women travelled north by train, they were giddy with excitement,
The hundreds in the hall, let out a cheer,
Lily called for order, and to the sparkling crowd she shouted,
'We've met with parliament, we've got what we had wanted.'

Dawn struggled up one Sunday, for that winter storm,
Had swelled in force, so four hundred men,
On trawlers and the local gunboat, were wielding axe and pick,
Yet all were working blind, and the weight of ice was building,
The sky and land were bleached, the waves were black as ink,
There was so much beauty, the crews might have thought,
Yet the vessel *Heidrunn II* had vanished, it was a dreadful loss,
Of skipper Rögnvaldur and two sons, for village of Bolungarvik.

Sigurdur the skipper of the *Oðinn*, grimly watched the wilds,
Waves were pounding steel, pouring over gun deck,
The driving snow was dense, the air seemed broken,
The sea froze solid, when it struck the metal,
Of deck and superstructure, he knew few ships were built for this,
On land all roads were shut, so Þorður phoned report,
Of flying frost at Látrabjarg, they couldn't force the farm doors open,
So they abandoned livestock, their vehicles blown across the fields.

Night came early, the *Ross Cleveland* was at half speed,
Mate Harry, was out in duck suit,
The ship took a sea and laid over, desperate calls from other ships,
Joined the fray, 'Come in *Ross Cleveland*, come in,'
There was only airwave crackle, the ship had sunk in seven seconds,
Three men scrambled into life raft, pitching on the sea,
The boy Barry was just eighteen, Walter the bosun,
Had only shirt and underwear, lucky Harry was protected.

Meanwhile *Oðinn* searched, across the fjord for *Heidrunn*,
And luck struck the *Notts County*, for now she ran aground,
There was metallic screech, jolting from the rocks,
Yet no longer might they sink, even as the engines ceased,
Inside was eerie knocking, ticking fading into silence,
There was no light, the radio op was calling,
Into darkness and repeating, 'Mayday mayday,'
And so the *Oðinn* steamed to north, striding cross the sound.

Some sailors of the *County*, fought to launch a life raft,
The wind tore and twisted, killed the foremost man aboard,
The officers of the *Oðinn*, later thought it inconceivable,
How two ships had sunk, all hands drowned,
And another grounded, and all in sight of busy Ísafjördur,
Yet they too were lucky, they were half-submerged,
They knew it best, for crew of *County*,
To stay aboard, at least the upper decks were dry.

In that *Cleveland* life raft, somewhere in the tumbler,
Harry and the two, used rubber boots to bale out water,
They tried to talk of family, shared boyhood days in Hull,
But the boy Barry must have known, he never could survive,
And after nine icy hours, he slid and curled in ball,
Walter baled for hours more, and often Harry cried,
'Hang on hang on,' but he too died and after hours passed,
The raft ground ashore, far to south in Seydisfjördur.

At Hull the day before, rugby players bowed their heads,
Mourners filled a church, the service for two trawlers,
A mother on the factory floor, was summoned by the Tannoy,
She had returned to work, another said on street to Chrissie,
We're sorry for your Philip, and word arrived at Rita's home,
Her husband had been drowned, all she had was tiny babe,
Each person seemed to knew, a fisher on the list of sunk,
And standing at front doors, mission men were fearful silhouettes.

Harry had been thinking, of trips he always took,
Ashore at Ísafjördur, each time he walked the spit,
To call on policeman friend, and each time Kristjan the detective,
Ran a hot bath for his friend, and Harry lay in silence,
Could dwell on life at home, to think of wife and baby Natalee,
And each time Harry brought, spare papers and short stories,
To help with Kristjan's crime novels, so they talked for hours,
Over coffee cups and sweet pancake, there in view of wooden hospital.

Harry saw a distant light, struggled through the snow,
He climbed a rocky slope, on cliff top was a shepherd's booth,
But he couldn't break the lock, so stood all night,
In lee of hut, he dared not close his eyes,
This was the farm of Kleifar, where lived Gudmundur,
The farmer and his wife Karitas, twelve children strong and true,
And at the dawn, two older boys Gudmann and Haraldur,
Found Harry as they searched, for sheep and cattle lost in drifts.

Harry had no gloves, he could not move,
Three days had passed, since the stranding of the *Cleveland*,
The boys wrapped him, each took an arm to guide their walk,
The two leagues home to farmhouse, they chattered constantly,
To keep this man alive, it was their brother's birthday,
They slipped his frozen clothing off, gave him cups of coffee,
And Harry fell asleep in chair, so the family waited,
The phone was down, searchers surely soon would come.

By now the crew of *County*, were maddened by the stress,
So Fred the mate calmed them, for he had stranded,
Years before in trawler *Epine*, they could see no lights,
Fred said 'Don't even jump, or think to swim to land,'
And the *Oðinn* sent a warning, 'Wait for us,
And do not get too drunk,' for stories did abound,
In Iceland's salvage circles, of fishers far too drunk,
When they were offered rescue, by farmers on the shore.

Hell is our home thought Sigurdur, if there was a time,
To take a risk, this was it,
It was what we coastguards do, so they dispatched,
Their rescue boat, twice across the bay,
And Sigurjon and Palmi, fetched the men,
Each frozen and exhausted, they had stared at death,
Now climbed aboard the *Oðinn*, the *County* after all,
Had been inside the twelve-mile limit, so they expected worse.

Oðinn skipper and the crew, now could breathe,
Yet there was no word of *Heidrunn*, so they steamed for safety,
Of the harbour, all thirty crew still shocked,
At how poorly dressed, were some men of Grimsby trawler,
They led the crew ashore, and Fred stopped the troop,
And the ragged army turned, to form two lines,
On shore they cheered, the crew of gunboat *Oðinn*,
As they staggered, sleepless down the sloping gangplank.

Now the Sudavik searchers, spied the orange raft,
And found two frozen bodies, so stiff the undertakers,
Had to massage limbs, so they could bend them into coffins,
The party followed tracks in snow, to the farmhouse of the fjord,
And when the vessel docked, word spread fast in Ísafjördur,
The *County* crew burst out from hostel, 'That's Harry Eddom,'
Shouted one fellow man from Hull, 'He looks like a ghost,'
And on a stretcher, Harry was carried to the wooden hospital.

On that actual day, Lily and the winning crowd,
Had dispersed from hall, had they ever smiled and sung this way,
'Us lasses have achieved, more in one single day,
Than all the trawler industry, did in over sixty years,'
She said to press, but all their hopes were dashed,

By news of one rescued man, how Rita had herself become,
A two-day widow, and reporters rushed for Iceland flights,
Then scrapped again for places, on the tiny plane to Ísafjördur.

Ólíni was the lead nurse on the ward, Ulfur was the doctor,
She wheeled Harry to a phone on wall, and so he called,
And spoke to smiling Rita, who now with aunt,
Would take to air, for the papers sought,
A picture of the pair together, the sailor who'd been dead,
Then come alive, another of him holding,
Their seven-month baby girl, meanwhile in beds beside,
Were men who'd seen it all, *County* skipper George and Fred the mate.

Those three men in hospital were happy, they were breathing,
Yet they dared not smile, for their luck,
Had been unfairly drawn, away from other men,
They could hear outside, scuffles as reporters shouted,
Ólíni and her nurses bolted doors, the white wooded walls,
Three storeys high the hospital, with steep pitched roof,
Had never seen the like of this, though Ulfur let inside the back door,
His brother Kristjan, who gave to Harry a copy of the Bible.

Rita sent her thanks, to the family farm at Kleifur,
Grimsby Council chose to honour, the rescuers on *Oðinn*,
So brought over, Captain Arnason and mates Sigurjon and Palmi,
For a fine reception, where they were given plaque,
Which to this day, still hangs aboard the *Oðinn*,
They met again, the mate and skipper of the *County*,
And later on the *Oðinn*, the ambassador to Iceland,
Awarded medals to the skipper, and to the first and second mates.

Lily said to the press, 'You called us silly women,
Yet we fought and have succeeded,' but were also sent to her,
Poison letters, another form of trolling,
Some scrawled by hand, one a telegram hand-delivered,
'Trawler owners hate you, trawlermen hate you too,'
It might have been better, at this very moment,
To say a prayer, may the gales be gentle,
May the weather forever, carry sailing ships to home.

The Board of Trade announced, eighty safety measures,
And Iceland fishing was suspended, Lily was sacked from factory job,
Harry signed his copy of the Bible, and gave it to the mission,
At the Court of Inquiry, convened again at City Hall,
Inspector Naisby refused, Lily's request to speak,
She was not he said, 'An interested party,'
He concluded 'the efforts of the master, and crew of *Oðinn*,
Were worthy of high praise,' yet said no word of women's safety hopes.

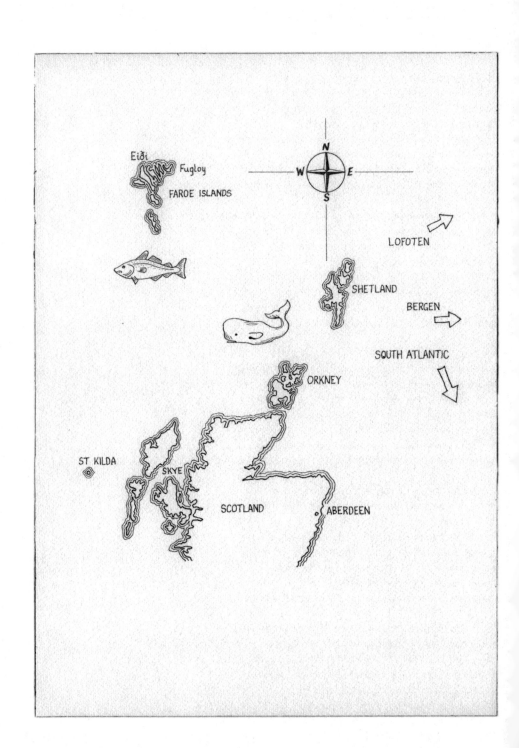

THE ATLANTIC ISLES

Fugloy island, Faroes

A day of happiness, springtime in the spirit,
Springtime in the world, at one inseparable.

[George Mackay Brown, *For the Islands I Sing*, 1997]

Eight winds always seem to blow, from the north and western compass points.

The waves and swell have travelled far, yet these Atlantic isles still stand firm. Rain falls, trees thrive in only gullies.

Birds are drawn from seas to nest, and long have been a vital source of food. There is cliff and peat, sheep that once were gold, intense events and many memories of drownings.

It all started on Sjælland, where long ago the Stoor Worm, the girder of the earth, fell back after a brave farmer's boy sailed in its mouth and fought fire with fire. He pushed burning peat into its liver, the sea rushed in and created the Øresund and Baltic Sea. The serpent's teeth dislodged so far they fell to form these two hundred isles. The teeth were large, and the ocean wide. Nowhere on these Atlantic isles of Orkney, Shetland and the Faroes is more than five leagues from an ocean shore.

And when home is far from the ermine courts of kings, it seems, people can retain an independent spirit.

No one is coming to help. The islanders travelled out to fish and crew, brought back earnings to the ports and farms, raised sheep and tilled the soil to bring forth angelica and barley. Over time, local languages diverged, but were then suppressed. The Shetland and Orkney language, Norn, became extinct, Faroese came to the brink and escaped alive, as did Gaelic in the Western Isles. The Faroes sought independence, yet were crushed by financial crisis. Shetland was under Norway rule for centuries, then bought and sold by kings. There was a time when the Earl of Orkney and Lord of the Isles were as powerful as the king of Scotland.

Highland author Jim Hunter has always supported national independence, and one day was talking to an elderly crofter. There was some speculation, would this be a time for more political devolution from London to Edinburgh. He thought the smallholder shared enthusiasm. The reply was stern: 'In London they might not give a damn about folk up here. But in Edinburgh they hate us.'

There was once a lonely white whale who wandered in the ocean waters. He was pursued for oil, as was every school and pod, each beast was snared to fuel the lights on modern city streets, to fertilise the fields. Yet for all the crews, this type of snowy whale became a test, a sign to the hunters of something greater.

'How will you now respond,' they asked the captain, 'when our feats might be followed by a fall?' Said Ahab after a silent pause, 'I think that I shall praise it.'

This perhaps is why, people in the past would say any kind of chase required a calm and empty mind. A respect for fish and whale and bird, a request that they might give up themselves, and in return the hunter would never speak unkindly, would suppress conceit. Nowadays, this is why the weeping of these beasts can still be overheard.

Small fishers and farmers of these isles counted on the commons. They climbed down cliffs for the spring harvest of egg and bird. They rowed and sailed and steamed the inshore and the distant waters, bringing back the fish. They herded whales to shallow bays, chased them cross the ocean currents. They shared the grazing lands for sheep, came together for the hay harvest when the sun was always shining. On the long winter nights they told stories, danced in chains and circles, fetched another piece of peat to burn.

Still the Faroese say, everything I need is in sight of my eyes.

Yet over time, they all have seen the fish grounds emptied of cod and herring, whales disappearing, the crofting lands cleared by laird and landlord for big sheep, the seabirds themselves starting to fall in numbers.

Kathleen Jamie wrote about 'The Gannetry', a teeming bird terminal on Shetland: 'It was exactly like a fun fair, the closer we got to the cliff edge, the more we could hear of the racket.' But then, too, close-up to the gannet nests stitched with seaweed, she saw woven into nests:

Shreds of nylon rope, orange and blue,
Scraps of net, a blue line against the white cliff.

[Kathleen Jamie, *Sightlines*, 2012]

There were two gannet birds of six-foot wingspans, fighting over a piece of coloured plastic, one had stolen it from the other's nest. All these isles are rock ships in the North Atlantic, sailing nowhere, the current and wind racing from another place. There are birds and seals, and now the modern ways have come too.

George Mackay Brown wrote of the way fishing brings people together. One fisherman of Greenvoe village lived in the row of cottages by the pier, his voice was of 'an old seaman who had been sailing all his life; it was seasoned with Geordie and Scouse and Cockney and Clydesdale; a voice that belonged to the brotherhood of the sea.' And next door, old Samuel returned with a basket of haddocks. 'Praise be,' said Rachel his wife, as she strung three to four together, and took them to the neighbours.

'We own nothing, do we,' she said. 'The Lord gives us this and that, and we must divide what is left, so there's nobody who won't have a little.'

Said Samuel, 'That isn't business.'

She replied, 'The miracle of the loaves and fishes is never done.'

Author of the east, Ronnie Blythe said to me that when he visited George Mackay Brown in Stromness, he found he was writing in the house facing away from the windows. So many people would be walking past on any day, he'd have to stop writing just to say hello to each.

So many people. And living by their own choosing. Yet other isles to the west were less fortunate.

Arran, Harris, Islay, Lewis, Mull, Rum, Skye, and later St Kilda: all depopulated. And whole Highland vales, countrysides once teeming with the cheeriest sounds of rural life were converted into social deserts. It began in the 1700s not long after the first Enclosure Acts had begun to be signed by the London parliament. New sheep had been bred, the *big sheep* Blackface and Cheviots, more productive of both wool and meat, and so the lairds and landlords saw they could obtain more income if they rented out their land to one large sheep farmer than have many hundred crofters. And so began the Clearances.

Farm families were forced from the land, the very bog and peat on which they and ancestors had continuously lived for several thousand years. Sheep numbers dramatically increased. Soon farmers were hunted down with dogs. One observer said in 1802, 'I have not a doubt that the whole race of Highlanders will, in a very few years, be extinguished.'

Orcadians and Shetlanders were forced to leave for Canada. This was not the eviction of an occasional farmer or village, it was the systematic clearance of tens of thousands. It would be hard to avoid calling this *cleansing* if it occurred today, not least because of the language deployed at the time. There was talk of the 'inevitable advance of civilisation,' and that the local people were

CHAPTER FIVE

'aborigines,' characterised by 'sloth, poverty and filth,' they were 'a parcel of beggars' with 'an obstinate adherence' to the Gaelic language.

They were called 'savages.' The echoes from the enclosures far to south were strong.

The Gaelic poet John MacLachan wrote in the early 1800s from Morvern looking over to Mull:

> As I look down over the pass,
> What a chilly view I have!
> So many cottages in disarray,
> In green ruins on each side…
> Where the fire and children once were,
> That's where the rushes have grown tallest.

[In James Hunter, *The Land of the Free*, 1999]

Fishing from Shetland and Orkney isles had been by the *haaf* beach system. This was open-ocean fishing by fourern or sixern, and men rowed thirty to fifty miles into the Atlantic to find the cod grounds. This was in the summer months, unlike the open boat fishing in Iceland during the winter, so daylight was long and storms less frequent. Yet they relied on waterproof oilskin and seaboots to survive, and at the shore were beach communities of women and children awaiting their return.

Then across all of Scotland's isles, lairds took control of the crofting system, and deliberately cut crofts too small for families to live off by farming alone. They had to fish. The lairds set the price to buy the fish, ran the shop for food and goods, added expenses to the rent.

Somehow the crofters could never get ahead.

Two and a half centuries later, Jim Hunter has had to conclude, 'Much of Scotland is a desert still.'

Out beyond the sunset isles, out from the Viking ship canal dug from shore to safe inland lake at Rubha an Dùnain, and from hillsides of Skye scattered with sheep and wet crofter ruins, out through the Sound of Harris where currents clash, out beyond the setting sun.

For one hundred leagues and more the boat slapped down on inward ocean swell, the grumbles from an air storm gone days before. The white spray thumped high, breached the cloud low and grey. A single gannet followed, a fulmar swept around the bow wave and was gone. On return there would be Risso's dolphins rising and falling from the clear waters, scarred white by deep squid battles. There would be whales, a minke with her calf, slow arch and fall again of sleek water beasts. Meanwhile, ahead lay the North Atlantic Ocean, and the isles and stacks of St Kilda. Peopled since the Neolithic, adopting Norse and Gaelic names, evacuated in August 1930, now a World Heritage Site.

Beneath the cloud appeared at first a dark blur and already the lee swell was behaving better. The boat motored for northerly Boreray and the two tallest stacks in Britain. The black granite wall rose out of ocean, far above were grassy slopes and feral Soay sheep staring down.

And on the cliffs, here was the greatest seabird station in all of north-west Europe.

There were great puffin rafts, damping down the waters, gannets darkened the sky. There was northern fulmar and guillemot. Out of no place we could see appeared skuas, suddenly mobbing a single bird, crushing it down on the rising falling clear waters. There was call and cry, squabble and quiet circling round the thousand foot cliffs. Common seals were hauled up on rock ledges inside a cave. Gannets folded wings and arrowed, one after another, into the water round the boat. The air vibrated as they sliced the sea.

A century ago, one visitor said, 'My view is that the people lived a very happy life, better housed and better fed than most others in the Highlands and Islands.' On these very cliffs and teeth of rock, the cragsmen climbed and abseiled, on thirty fathoms of horsehair rope, their ankles thick-end and toes splayed, thirty fulmar gathered could weigh ninety pounds. Some said the eggs of St Kilda were their staple potatoes.

Some years, the mainland and outer isles were cut off for eight months. One week-long storm left the islanders deaf, from pounding growl with whine and whistle. Sheep and dogs were blown off cliffs, the waves crashed over the five-hundred-foot summit of Dùn isle and directly onto houses of the single settlement.

This day, puffin beat across Village Bay and all was quiet. The main isle of Hirta comes, some say, from the Gaelic for earth itself. The way ashore was by rib, a policy to keep rats on boats and away from the million eggs and young birds. Ahead was the ruined human city, the curve of Main Street following a contour up from the shore, from the manse and church to more than a thousand stone storage cleits. These storage huts are unique to St Kilda, built of white stone and turf, huge flat slabs for lintel and ceiling on which sat turf to draw up moisture by translocation. In this wet landscape, the inside of cleits was always bone dry.

And ahead too, in the middle of such world heritage, the military base, the new buildings of wood and roofed by turf. In the 14–18 War, a U-boat drew up and the captain instructed through a megaphone, take cover, and seventy shells destroyed the wireless station, killing a single sheep. A four-inch gun rusts ashore, it was installed in response and made ready to fire on the very day of Armistice. There on the rocks, said the skipper, in the gabions, that's where I took that picture of the tiny bird.

And onshore, flitting to a nest in the stones of a cleit, the St Kilda wren, heavy with strong bill, a unique subspecies for a cut-off land. There were also burrows of the field mouse brought ashore from Viking longship, now evolved to be twice as large as those on the mainland. The Soay sheep were moulting wool, yet they have shrunk over the decades, for smaller lamb survival is more likely now that they can shelter in the dry warmth of cleits. When the last evacuees were removed from Hirta, they were given jobs in the Forestry Commission.

'What use was that?' later observed one man. 'I had never seen a tree in my life.'

Yet they needed to enter the wage economy, of course, for the island laird and civil servants had allocated the full costs of evacuation against future wages. None of them had ever spoken English.

It had been true, too, that the religious life of St Kilda was strict, brought from the mainland and isles in the early nineteenth century. The church was austere, no altar, no decoration, no fixed pews. To the right of room was the door to the schoolroom, also with high ceiling and tall windows. Diarists later wrote, the children clamoured in winter to come to the front of class to read from the Bible, for then they could stand before the fire. Like every small community, you need something to stick everyone together, to give a common sense of purpose in this microcosm of earth. They attended church daily.

Yet the missionaries of the 1800s broke violins on knees, banned song and dance, persuaded people with a sharp sword, on one side reward for adherence, on the other eternal hell. A minister wrote in 1841, he wanted 'To raise St Kildans to the scale of thinking beings.' In God's acre, above and behind the black houses on Main Street, each roof tied down by warps, were nettles and irises in the oval cemetery. Writers of the 1600s and 1700s recorded song, poetry, dance and and summer games on the beach.

Each morning, the St Kildan men met to decide on tasks and fair work allocation. All had an equal vote regardless of croft size and status, and this came to be called the St Kildan Parliament. On the other hand, one man wrote, everyone just talked as loud as they could, at the same time.

Each day they watched the children climb the hill to cut and carry peats, the job before school. Fires were in the houses burned all year, and had been for two thousand years. None would let them go out. As they drew away that August ninety years before, the women turned to one another, pointing at the cold chimneys. The men wept too, for their sheepdogs, for these were gathered and thrown off the jetty, each with a great stone tied around its neck. The next ship calling into Village Bay to escape a storm found their carcases washing at the shore.

Morag MacDonald was in her twenties when she left St Kilda, and later said, 'There was community spirit, everybody helped each other, there was no squabbling, we all got on so well together. Life used to be just lovely on this island.'

───────

At the far north-east of the isles of Faroe, Fugloy is an isle of steep cliff dropping into sea and sound, no harbour, and eighteen residents still in painted houses clinging to the slopes.

There was a waterfall pouring a hundred metres down to sea, and fulmar skating over the waves. The post boat did not moor, goods were swung ashore in alloy boxes, rubbish bins brought back, the passengers waiting then stepping off the boat as it rose to meet the narrow concrete ledge. Rain sluiced on deck and dock, puffins beat the breeze, stalling on the slopes where chicks awaited feed. The boat departed, there was the promise it would return toward the ending of the day.

The village houses were high above, and there was rusting capstan, for in earlier times the boats were winched directly up the cliff. This day was calm at times, in storm such manoeuvres would be unthinkable. The one-roomed shop was up concrete steps, goods on open shelves behind the counter. Woollen jumpers hung from the ceiling. Mist dropped, wrapped the whole isle, and we walked up and over the top path that was said to be indistinct. Sheep loomed from fog, meadows were dotted with orchid and buttercup. Wrecked cars were abandoned in an old quarry. In Hattarvik on the far side, we took refuge in the dry church, where the walls were sky blue and the altar painted red. The windows were thick glass, distorting sea and distant Sveinoy isle.

A man in the village said, they were down to eight residents, all of them over seventy. We ate our sandwiches, waited for the boat.

One minute, one hour, the sound was empty. Then one minute it was there. Still the fells above were hidden in hiddenness.

Wind had earlier dashed through windows of the old mission hotel, banged at fittings. A grey light glowed. In the morning rain, horizontal across the sound, a gale was tearing up the grassy slopes, over layers of basalt. Horses white and wild raced over the underwater tunnel that now linked these isles. We walked up steep Klakkur mountain, but could not reach the top. Far below the sea was grey, a hint of blue from deep, white fingers frothing at the skerries. All the clouds were charcoal, and the grass rippled as if a prairie. The ground was sodden, between sphagnum buttons and over slick mud flowed rivulets then river. Every hill has its bog and boulders, *huldafolk* in rocks, and silver-maned water *niig* ready to drown a careless passer-by. There was yellow bedstraw and the purple flowers of insectivorous butterwort. Redshank wheeled, gulls were stationary, it seemed we could be clean blown off the mountain. There are no swallows or swifts here, the tiny isles too hard to find or just not the insect food.

A farmer out west had recently lost a prize imported sheepdog, it was swept off the farm. One day a woman nearby was carrying a bundle of hay, and was flung over. She landed on the beach below, on the hay, and walked away.

At the bay in Klaksvik, a gull was mobbed and dropped its food onto a dark corrugated roof, the windows white and a flag snapping in the garden. The bells of Christianskirkjan rang. It has an octoreen hanging from the roof timbers. The wood was smooth and dark, and beyond the altar was the giant fresco of the Paradise of the Last Banquet, a time for sharing food. The font was four thousand years old, brought here from an ancient Sjælland site. In the crypt below were depictions of the life of Jesus carved from wood, one of fishers caught in violent storm on the Sea of Galilee.

Here you could sit in contemplation, listen to the sermons, yet also gaze up. This was the one rescued boat from northern Kunoy, relic of 1913 disaster when all the men of Skarð were in three clinkered boats, caught in a storm, all drowned save for two boys aged nine and eleven and their grandfather in his seventies. The sea god had created thirteen widows and forty children with no fathers.

For a small island, this was a savage blow. There is no forgetting of such tearing out of souls.

A man stepped out of the house of black rock. 'Come in,' he commanded, 'Look around.'

CHAPTER FIVE

Martin Holm was an artist, four generations before were fishers, all living in this house. There were paintings, landscapes and modern, his grandfather's peaked cap, a British soldier's metal helmet from the war. He liked best the English music of the sixties and seventies, watched football. And yes, just recently, a great victory. These isles of fifty thousand people beat Greece again, they who once had won the Euros. It was the greatest ever gap in rankings overturned. Well, he said, everyone was so drunk, the streets full and flowing and everyone laughing. They danced all night. He had also painted pilot whales. The *grindadráp*, so important to the Faroe Islands.

He stared, invited comment, banged his chest and said, 'This is our culture.'

Yes, those whales had been on the shore below, right across the way in Klaksvik, the sea running red. At the *grind* are always shares of whale for everyone, a great community event, passing culture to the children. And it is a bloody sight, but step inside an abattoir and you have the screaming of the pigs and cattle, the indifference of the workers. 'Here,' says Martin, 'the animals come to us. We don't hunt them, just encircle the school with boats, guide them to the shore.'

A German friend at home, Jutta Austin, showed her Faroe album of cuttings and postcards from the 1960s. She decided to learn Faroese when young, just a few years after the first bible was published in Faroese. A tourist leaflet contains colour pictures of St Olav's Day, the national festival in July, and on the same page children in patterned jumpers were standing on pilot whales at Tórshavn, ninety-seven brought ashore one Tuesday in August.

Every culture faces moral dilemmas, and it is rarely possible to draw binary conclusions on right and wrong.

In this case, good is celebration of culture, food from sea, togetherness. And less good is intelligent animals killed, and we do not yet know what they know. Something similar can be said of the raising of intelligent animals in the intensive conditions of factory farming.

Klaksvik is the most important fish port of the Faroes. The port was crammed with boats, at many a berth were sixæreen and octoreen, hulks in the dry dock, trawlers pushing up the sound. There were factory ships dripping wet, the odour of fish waste on the harbour-side. There was debris, split nets in piles, plastic fish boxes, rusting otter boards, remains of ships now cast away. The climate of the Faroes is stable, the weather just a little variable. A couple of years back, it is said, winds of 200 km/h ploughed across the isles. All movement was paralysed. Even driving was impossible. We travelled east, and took the tunnel to the pier of post boat *Ritan*. The postman had in former times hiked each fell and vale, walked the peaks and basalt cirques to pass the news to every distant isle, to homes across this alley of the storms.

Yet today the air was motionless, the fjord a mirrored lake. On the slope were scattered sheep, kittiwake calling overhead. By the shore were tarred timber houses with roofs of turf. Men in woollens murmured their routine on the rusty boat, and passengers ambled up the gangway, stowed their gear aboard. The sound was hazed with mist, the ship began to rumble, the hull now radiating ripples. A man hailed from the road, and the skipper slowly waved. There were banks of golden buttercup on one coastal meadow, another shimmered orchid pink, a single lamb was bleating

The ship cast off, and ropes were coiled on deck.

The engineer had skippered trawlers for three decades, he had steamed the northern seas, moored at many a raucous port and fish dock. Beneath the screaming gulls was always mayhem of a market, fishers standing in the wings. Yet protected from the ocean swell, this vessel was no longer fishy, there was smell of coffee from the deck below. The village of Hvannasund passed astern, the red church at the pebbled shore. The diesel engine thudded, screws churning the glassy sea.

These were isles of catchers, harvesters of seabirds and their eggs, and now came a wheeping call of the national bird, the oystercatcher made the people smile. For just as days grew longer, spring bringing fewer storms, so that bird of winter marsh appears on hay and sheepy slope. Its song is in their hearts, for it signifies the worst of winter now was over.

The post boat surged away, took a tidal race, we watched the plunge of prow, the roll through angry waves. A tube-nosed fulmar twisted over the wake, and sheers of rock and cliff brought surf and racing current.

Now beyond the fjord came rain, cheerless from the cindered cloud, the sea and ship were pattered, wind dashed across the water, low cloud ran to cover ridge. And beyond the bow wave, two dolphins rose and fell. Long ago this was where longships beached, Grímur Kamban brought Norse, years after St Brendan had come in search of Tir na Nóg, the floating isle of everlasting life.

But the isles were never free from meddlers on the mainlands. First the Norse then Dane, their queens and kings, restricted rights to trade through a royal monopoly. And the Faroes once were offered to the English King Henry VIII, who declined for lack of cash. They absorbed to Danish rule, and the language almost died.

Any time might come a squawk, from the radio in the tiny bridge. The skipper listening and flipping open window, calling to crew and Faroe passengers. Thumbs would be raised though no one here would make it to stand chest-deep as the whales were herded from the sound.

So at this northern edge of isles, the post boat powered on. And they will know, on an upper coastal road will be a group of men and women hunched in lee of hired vehicles. They will have glasses trained on the sea between the isles, radio poised to call their motored boat if they spied a dorsal fin of pilot whale. A west-coast actress joined one trip, she shivered in a sleeveless vest, then straightened her back, all the crew wore zipped-up jackets, and now the cameras rolled. Another day without a *grind* was a good one, she declared to distant audience. Yet in a bay will be bended backs and blistered palms, the boats with dragon-prows pushing at the whales, and all the roads blocked by local cars. The *grind* would soon be underway, fair-maned horses clattering over stones. On the shore, a crowd would be watching those in boats of wood and plastic, banging on the sides and slapping water, guiding pilot whales who slowly swim, ahead of chain of boats.

This sea would soon be crimson, men in only shirts in piercing wind, jeans wet through, children wearing rubber boots, climbing on a carcass. A tally-man will keep a record, and so divide the stock, and each family will carry home a share of meat and blubber.

At such a time, a distant man had stated, 'I don't give a damn about that people's culture,' and for the Faroe press, the actress wore a branded jacket, and called the people primitives, defended him as man of passion. A man called out from in the audience, 'You have no right to be here.'

The figurehead replied, 'No you do not understand, it is a bullfight of the sea, the world is telling you to cease.' In each home would be fresh meat hanging from the ceiling, the blubber soft and sliced for frying.

Yet at these northern isles, none could escape the wasteful world, for another deadly catcher had arrived. Inside the meat and blubber had been found mercury and other poisons, pollution posted on. So the islanders will say, this is all we have, this fish and sea, these sheep and rain. And now it might be killing us.

The *grind* is just a harvest, it is barbaric. You have no right to be here, we are acting for the world. The whale has had a good life, then we kill it quickly.

You wonder where could come some angle, some other type of kindness. In John Buchan's *Island of Sheep*, Anna describes the *grind* whale hunt, called the *caa* on Shetland, when boats guided the school of whales into a voe, trimming the leader forward. 'It sounds beastly,' says Peter John. 'Perhaps it is, but a lot of things are beastly, like killing pigs and using live bait. Anyhow, it puts money into the pockets of people, and gives them food and lighting for the long winter.'

In that sixties tourist guide, Willy Breinholst wrote: 'And in how many other places can you suddenly be whirled into the killing of pilot whales, one of the strangest sights in the world? Or be pulled into a chain of dancing people, who never interrupt all night long the monotonous gliding rhythm?'

Tim Ecott in *The Land of Maybe* watched a *grind* at a northern Faroe isle, described his own rising distress at the grisly effort. He also said, 'I have lost count of the number of young Faroese men who have told me they join with grind precisely because of the campaign of outsiders.' It is part of who were are, they said to him.

On Orkney close to the mainland, George Mackay Brown wrote of growing up, when 'Even the cities of Scotland were as far away as the moon.'

———————

High on a grassy Shetland slope, the sand tombolo far below, were the ruins of the ancient chapel of St Ninian, the Pictish saint, set right upon an Iron Age sacred place.

Semi-circular waves were advancing and lapping on the sand. Seals rose from the clear water, turning slowly as they looked around. There was the tirrick of tern, a swerve and plunge. A boy found treasure here, twenty-eight pieces of silver and the jawbone of a porpoise. The silver was carved in brooch and bowl, clasps in the style of gripping beasts. The originals were claimed, taken to a museum in the capital city far to south; Lerwick was granted replicas. What drew the boy to the hoard, was it voices in the solid air?

Those first barrow-keepers seemed to settle here just at the time that people of plains of Dog-gerland had fled from rising sea, some turning north toward the hills of Zetland. This day, on the western side, a freshly painted inshore boat, the blue *Hope III*, forged through swaying kelp forest, beyond the wedge-shaped stack of Hick Hole. The crew looked at an isle where ewes were grazing with their lambs, and skuas sat expressionless on nests.

One day, just two moons later, ten leagues from Sumburgh on route for Fair Isle, she stopped in a rip tide, took on water, and disappeared.

But at the ruined chapel, fingers of thistle had clawed from the ground, stones were slowly sink-ing, there were long-aged lichens of gold. Down there, deep down, there was no sound of bird or wave. The air had turned to stone, there was a thumping in my ears. It seemed a long way up to the rim, from this old well of time. Below were Neolithic bodies buried on their sides, knees pulled up to chests. It felt impossible to escape or speak, energy had leaked away from me. Inside the chapel bounds was a chamfered obelisk, etched with two circles of grey. Daisies lifted up the grass floor.

Here was the dense gravity of many thousand years of dying.

Later in the day, I had to lie on the grass at Humnavoe, the haven inside the bay across from Scalloway. The sun glittered on the blue sea, the far view to the past had become unobstructed. The Shetland poet, Jen Hadfield, wrote:

> I am afraid I shall have more questions,
> And not just because I hope to keep you talking…
> Until the sun is definitely down –
> Even if I must see you turned to stone.
>
> [Jen Hadfield, 'Drimmie', *The Stone Age*, 2021]

Jarlshof at the southern tip of Shetland mainland had also been home for four thousand years to stone wheel house, quern site, whalebones in the walls, warm hearth, and also broch tower and Viking longhouse. Here had been found, three hundred and fifty kilometres from Bergen, the same distance from Tórshavn and from Aberdeen, a stone game of nine-by-nine squares with nine white stones and four brown.

A Bronze Age smithy had worked here, by these deep waters, forging sword and strapping each axe-head to a wooden shaft. People of the village had scratched pictographs on slate, longship with oars, waves curled to crash, ley-line maps on water. The Viking longhouse was sixty ells in length, the stones borrowed from the older huts. The broch walls were inward-leaning and double-thickness, this day topped with nesting fulmars. A starling flock foraged in the algae on the shore, chattering up the sandhoppers and flying back to nests inside the ancient walls. Sum-burgh Head rose to the south, residence to a thousand guillemot and puffins, a lighthouse for the whales to spot from far, to help them steer around the head.

It was the time of the year for the summer dim, the long grey dusk and dawn that never quite is light.

There were men and women of the farm herding cattle in the hour before midnight. On the rocks of Spiggi beach were iron wheels, bent by rock and wave, rusted by a patch of pink-flowered thrift. There was an engine-block, quite cold, relic of the nearby army base. And all along the tidal line, quite unstained by sea or salt, in snared circles and twisted rope, washed ashore was shrapnel from the modern market. In the oceans half-cleared of fish, now gyres of plastic will swim for longer than the oldest whale. At the hotel, there was a wide bay window overlooking loch reserve and beach far below.

The Arctic whaling came to Shetland first. At distant Dundee, Hull and Whitby was chandlery and loft, rail and counting room, yet the whaling ships were short of men.

So on northern ocean roads, captains docked at Lerwick to take on food and water, and hurried to the hiring fair, twenty men per ship were signed. And so the whale directed wages back to Shetland, for months the men away for winter. Another established custom, perhaps in haste you might have thought, was young men signing for the merchant navy. And to each mother's doormat would come the airmail letter, the scratchy news from distant port, they could be gone for years.

Wretched whaling days they might have been, in wooden ships and risking wreck. Each day dawned with peril, sharp blade and foggy bank, ships crushed by floe, men dodging slice of flensing knife, harpoons slung from open boat, often ill of scurvy and starvation.

Yet they were iron men of rolling gait, the crew with quiet courtesy of isles. They took their fiddles, danced at dusk to stepping jig. As summer days drew on, they were home for harvest of the corn. The sea would later weary, worn out by these actions. None had seen the like of gun and whaling rocket, and now no longer could a whale pull down a ship. Sven Foyn fitted a flexor joint to harpoon head and shaft, installed fast-firing cannon, pistons in the hold to cut recoil. The scale of whaling leapt again, at Iceland fjord and Norway firth, at Faroe sound and the voes of Shetland. One of the last whale hunters met us on the dock at Lerwick, and Gibbie and Laurena Fraser took us to the silent whaling stations. At Olna Firth, sunshine glittered on the voe. When the whaling still was active, this firth was filled with smoke and blood pollution.

In Neil Gunn's *Silver Darlings*, the young men knew the inshore herring boats often came home empty, and they were off the Caithness coast just ten leagues from the Pentland Firth. The nets were hanging straight in the water, so they slept, they waited, the currents passed, they hauled strongly. Tormad appealed softly to their god, and would later shout, 'It's herring, boys! Herring! Herring!'

Near whaling stations, for the whalers brought in whales from fifty leagues away, the herring fishers lost.

At Olna there had been a factory, shanties for the workers, grand home for manager, store-houses, oil vats and meat pots, boiler house. It was the longest running whaling station. Now the site was concrete blocks at broken pier head, whale vertebrae in the grass by storage site for salvage. Every whaling station needed water, and here the stream passed through iron waterwheel. A whaling ship had been hauled ashore, more rust than iron, more blistered paint than shine. This was a ship that Gibbie had skippered, it saw service as a minesweeper. There was a yellow diving bell, twelve porthole windows, once dropped to North Sea bed by rigs in search of fossil oil. This site produced oil for soap, powdered meat and bone exported to Japan for rice-field fertiliser, whalebone baleen cleaned and cut in lengths, it was only blood that had no use. At Collafirth, there was little sign of thirty years of harvest at the start of 1900s.

There had been a dozen factory buildings, coal smoke from every chimney. Here too had been flensing on the plan and metal scent in air, the blood trail drifting slowly in the tide. At Ronas Voe were two whaling stations, further from the sea but near to streams, the voe now filled with fish farms. A great black bull stood on guard at the shore.

These four whaling stations landed four hundred whales a year, and over time local protest grew against the smell, the voe pollution, the whaling profits going to distant businesses, the disruption of the herring stock.

Perhaps it was this that did for the *caa* pilot whale hunts, the last events in Shetland recorded in the early twentieth century. After whales and free-swimming fish came the farming to the Shetland Isles, first salmon penned and then mussels on long lines of plastic rope. Seals learn to stay away, for there are guards with guns. The salmon, it is known too well, and like many an intensive livestock unit, require imported feed and are themselves food for lice. The mussel farms are cleaner on the water, long lines strung out, no feed and no waste, though guards still prowl at night to keep away the eider duck, for they will strip a farm at a single sitting.

Not far north of Lunna, the wartime depot for the Shetland Bus, was Sullom Voe, where first came ashore the fossil oil and gas in the early 1970s. The Zetland County Council had been well prepared. Yet post-war, things looked bad. Prosperity of any sort was a distant hope. First came the Shetland Folk Society, then the *New Shetlander* periodical. Both built identity and pride in the 'Auld Rock.'

Then the 1962 Yell Conference sent a delegation to the Faroes. It was, reported Thomas Henderson, 'A revelation.'

The Zetland visitors found 'energy and keenness evident in Faroe,' with the 'young folk staying on.'

They came home with confidence, and immediately asked the London government for Faroe-style autonomy.

None were really surprised. It was denied.

But they reorganised fishing and processing, placed knitwear on a commercial footing. They looked inward, and sought to make the most of island assets. Then the critical law, the 1974 Zetland Act allowed the local authority control over negotiations with multinational companies. They imposed a local tax on fossil oil. Today the oil tanks seemed small in that landscape of sky and water and green hills, by the zebra-striped accommodation ship, under flaming gas flare on the skyline. Yet Shetland invested, as did Norway, they created a fund for the island culture. Now grew a sense of shared identity, the folk music revival, the flaming barrels run through streets for Up-Helly-Aa, a Viking longship burned each year. The investment was used for social welfare, art and sport, environmental programmes and financial development.

CHAPTER FIVE

Gibbie with the scar across his face, who returned from southern whaling with enough to buy a motorbike, still sped around the island roads, for those ways had also brought to them a sense of freedom.

Jim Hunter says, 'The last thirty years have brought a striking revival of fortune.'

We met the last whalers at the old Lerwick ice-house. Not much whaling history has been written by the crews, yet these were the men who left the peat and sheep in the 1950s, and sailed across the equator to the South Atlantic.

Over hill came this whisper, go south and cross the roaring forties, three thousand leagues, past rocky Capes of Horn and Hope, where Captain Cook of Whitby whalers had searched for a new continent on *The Discovery*. It was not long after when Edgar Allan Poe's *Arthur Pym of Nantucket* came to sail those vast waters, encountering whales and white birds, but also bears and native people rowing canoes. Go south was now the offer, to South Georgia's eastern coast, to harbours named after Leith and Stromness, after Husavik and Grytviken.

They lived in constant light. It was a gift.

They worked the boxy chasers and factory ships from South Georgia, and returned north to harvest hay in Shetland summer. For years, they never saw the dark. There was Gibbie Fraser, crewman John Winchester, David Polson a captain and then a harbour-master, Tony Jarmson and Alistair Thomason smiling with Norn accents, Davy Cooper of the Shetland Amenity Trust. They left these isles and followed Arctic terns, as far south as was possible to imagine. It was harsh, they said, all those bloody broken whales. Norman Leaske spoke of the hell of the bullfight in Spain, what was the point of that blood sport. They have written two books, collected five thousand photographs. They take their tales to youngsters in the schools, for this was just their way of life. There were at the height twelve thousand whalers in the Southern Ocean in the 1950s, on the largest factory ships seven hundred men alone, the youngest mess boys of just sixteen.

The whaling ended for South Georgia in 1963, for the clearance of the oceans was complete, and Norman was now fashioning ships in bottles. We could build anything down there in South Georgia, he said, we built an iron lung for a Norwegian lad, repaired ship and engine, each machine in factory and cookhouse. They all were experts of the still, you could make an alcoholic drink from almost anything, from rice and raisin, oatmeal, compass fluid and hair-cream.

Yet accidents were few. Once a fin whale, long white stripe upon its jaw, dived under a chaser, towed the ship till lines were cut. Once a harpoon bounced off a sperm whale head, its mouth scarred by kraken hooks, signs of combat in the deep. The bomb exploded in the air, shrapnel pinging off the deck, perhaps it was a son or daughter of the white whale who swam in waters west of Chile. One swam around a catcher, pulled the rope so tight it took a man's leg right off.

Gibbie said, 'The sperm whale was the cleverest, they seemed to know how to beat us. We knew they felt pain and fear, we prayed for a quick kill.'

He also said, 'We loved our job, and the isolation and hardship forged a great camaraderie. However, there is no place for our type of whaling in the modern world. We were glad we stopped when we did.'

We stood outside the ice-house green doors, gulls crying above, and lined up for photographs. On return, fog poured over the hills, filled the vales and smothered the land. We crossed the 60-degree north latitude line again. There had been talk of the aurora coming south, the islands' merry dancers, but the fog stayed dense. Coming to Shetland in the *Orkneyinga Saga*, Earl Rognvald, the great grandson of Thorfinn and nephew of St Magnus, wrote:

> The breaker battered our boats,
> Cracked in sleet-storm our two sisters,
> Our ships curling, the killer wave crushed lives,
> The crew endured, the undaunted Earl's story won't die.

> [*Orkneyinga Saga*, c1197–1206]

As we have heard, the people of these Atlantic isles had long lived by fish and sheep and bird.

The birds were more reliable. When Joseph Russell-Jeaffreason of the London Geographic Society travelled to the Faroes in the 1890s, he said people were 'pessimists of the most pronounced type, they invariably look on the dark side.' Yet he also said their principal amusement was dancing. The men worked in fowling pairs to gather birds and eggs from the cliffs, six-hundred-foot ropes letting one over the edge to swing a twelve-foot fowling net to snag the petrel and the puffin. Each swung with deadly deliberation. It was said a crew could catch a thousand puffin in a day, though the beating of their wings could knock a man clear off a cliff. Birds were eaten fresh, salted or dried, nailed by beaks to the wooden sides of houses.

An old proverb says, *a Faroese without a boat is a Faroese in chains*. And this brings people together.

In one western harbour, there were six men in a sixæreen, gliding gently across the harbour in the rain, each white oar sliding smoothly into sea. Now the small boat travelled around the Vestmanna cliffs of Streymoy. A great swell pitched the boat, there was only ocean between here and Labrador. Gannets arrowed into the sea and the nesting cliffs were streaked with guano. On a slope, near-vertical it seemed, two roped men dropped toward a single sheep stranded above the black cliff. They waved, we wondered, does a sheep feel fear? On the route back, there was a steady stream of cars heading south. There were pilot whales, said the hotel owner, we keep it secret from the visitors now.

At Saksun in the west was a great amphitheatre of layered rock and tumbling waterfall above an inland beach of yellow sand, and here was Dúvagarður farmhouse of lime-washed stone and pitched roof of turf.

At the centre of the longhouse was the *roykstova* living area, the beds in alcove cabins set along the wall. It is said some people slept sitting upright, for you only lie down when you die. At one

CHAPTER FIVE

end was the kitchen, at the other the barn for six warm cattle. The family and visitors sat at the benches to eat from wooden bowls, and there were long views from the small windows. In the yard there was meat shed and fish shed, hung to dry or salted in kegs, hay barn, angelica vegetable garden, channel for drinking water, and hollow in a rock for crushing tormentil used for tanning leather for shoes. There was a shed with fire for drying green barley.

In Iceland they used to say, you will only have dry feet when you die.

The mid-1960s brochure for the Faroes proclaimed in English, Danish and German, 'In how many other places can you find a country where it rains for two hundred and eighty days of the year? But it must be added, it doesn't rain the whole day.'

And so it was the time of haymaking, and the sweet sward makes community. The grass was propped on net-racks, covered with green netting to dry in the wind. There were many oyster-catchers and orchids in each meadow, spotted orchids on the grass roofs of ancient houses. Higher in the hills were men and boys trotting across the bog and watery meadows, waving arms and fluorescent jackets. They ran as a broad line, then broke into smaller groups to chase the scattered sheep. At the top of the pass were the concrete shearing pens, the holding bays and neck braces in a line. The mist was thick. All ages were here, all the men and women and the children. This is the *skinn*, the culture of sharing. The sheep bleated, lambs separated from mothers. They were hand-sheared with clippers, the back wool cut first, then around the sides. Mist dripped moisture from the shearers' faces. On the road the national cycle race dashed past, individual riders then a group, chasing cars rattling over the cattle grid, then silence fell. They clipped the wool, and doused each sheep with medicine.

The sheep bounced into the meadow, nimbler and cooler. Sheep were once Faroese gold, but now the wool was tossed in a pile, later set alight. It burned to ash in the cold mist. George Mackay Brown remembered in his autobiography, *For the Islands I Sing*, the time when 'The hammers in the boatyard were finally silent.'

Distant forces are always at play. Now they were at the sheep.

The sheep shearing station looked down on Eiði. Many a village churchyard has statues staring out to sea. At Gjógv, there was a woman and two daughters moulded out of bronze, the metal streaming tears, dripping from their chins, for they still could see the drowned fishers in the waves.

On the shore, near the old concrete fish factory with blackened windows, by the church with glossy gravestones, was a grave with name, occupation as skipari, and schooner etched for ever in the marble. A man of the sea, lost at sea, an empty grave by this Atlantic shore. It was a restless sea. A half of the population of this village of Gjógv were drowned when two octoreens were swamped in sight of shore. Today eider ducks burbled at the shore, gathered ducklings into nursery groups. Eiði church itself was full of inner colour, cream with three votive ships hanging from the sky-blue ceiling, one day in the 1880s a beam of sunlight came through those large windows to shine on the secret sermon spoken for the first time in Faroese.

This is the thing. Great tales of these Atlantic Isles were told in the *Orkneyinga Saga*, stories of the earls of Orkney when they were as powerful as any kingdom looking inward to the North Sea and North Atlantic.

In the centuries that followed, all was decline as the isles faded from the memories of distant kings.

The sagas were written at the Icelandic literary centre of Oddi, begun by Sæmundr Sigfússon and given greatness by Snorri Sturluson at Reykholt. The earls may have centred on small isles surrounded by ocean, but they were known across Europe and all the way to Jerusalem. One earl said to Svein Asleifarson of Gairsay, 'It is hard to tell what comes first, old fellow, death or glory.' Svein was a leader who fished and farmed, stayed on his land from sowing to the harvest, entertained all winter in his hall that held eighty men, and took two trips a year for raiding, his spring and autumn trips to the Hebrides and Ireland.

Earl Thorfinn was the mighty, raiding further into Scotland and England, and across to Kattegut and Sjælland. His sons Paul and Erlend were 'tall handsome men, shrewd and gentle,' said the saga, and were the only leaders on Norse King Harald Hardrada's side to survive the Battle of Stamford Bridge. The English King Harold allowed them to leave the bloody site and sail back to Orkney, where they ruled together. But Paul's son Hakon and Erlend's son Magnus soon had gold in their eyes. Each wanted to rule alone.

Magnus was betrayed at the chosen site for debate on an Easter Monday, killed by the cook Lifolf with an axe. Hakon went on to bring peace to the land, making 'new laws for Orkney which the farmers found they liked much better.' Magnus, though, became the saint, there were miracles and his bones were buried in the cathedral walls at Kirkwall. The nephew of Magnus was Earl Rognvald Kalson, and he was famed for being a leader with grace, good at politics and poetry, he was a fisher, a skier on the slopes of Norway, and spent three years on pilgrimage to Jerusalem and back.

The saga said, 'He breathed sweetness and fragrance,' in all his doings.

Yet this kind of leadership and benevolence was little in evidence during the dark eras of crofting clearances. The *Orkneyinga Saga* had said:

> The bright sun will turn black,
> The earth sink into the dark sea.

As at Iceland, the Faroe Isles were prevented from trading by the Danish king's monopoly.

Escape came close in the second war, for Britain's soldiers instructed the Faroese to fly your flag, not the Danish under Nazi rule. The Løgting parliament immediately voted for independence, but was turned down after the war by Denmark. The Faroe language now was slowly written up, but the island state had to take the grants, and was forced to kneel once more. From high on slopes of layer cake, the sea below always looks benign. Just water, not much tide out here in the middle of the ocean. The new undersea tunnels have transformed the Faroes, linking isles and making travel largely independent of the weather.

CHAPTER FIVE

Yet on distant Fugloy, a sheep farmer had said, these might help people move from the edge to capital. It might mean the outer isles are abandoned faster.

Yet smallness helps at times.

The leader of the Shetland Bus, junior naval officer, David Howarth, declared, 'Every person in Norway knows about us, and we had succeeded in inflicting enough flea-bites for the invaders to know very well what kind of insect we were.'

Norway had been invaded, and the Milorg resistance movement needed arms, radios and intelligence. Norwegian inshore fishers sailed for Shetland, and now emerged the secret sea road between Lunna Voe and every cove and isle from Bergen to Lofoten. Agents were delivered on darkest nights, refugees plucked from under hunt of Gestapo. The radios helped coordinate attacks on Narvik, on Lofoten isles to destroy glycerine factories, on the heavy water facility at Vemork. The inshore fishers faced the worst of the North Sea, violent storms and winds that persisted for many days, yet were shot and bombed when the weather calmed. The worst of events: the *Blia* sank with forty-five crew agents and refugees on board. The best were numerous: repeated travel under darkest cover, the tying up of a Nazi army of three hundred thousand troops, drawn away from the battlefronts elsewhere in Europe.

Back at Lunna, at the farmhouse where the secret service operated, there remained:

> *The surge of surf at foot of cliffs,*
> *The course winter grass bending,*
> *To the blast of wind from sea, and in the air,*
> *The undefinable smell of the first snow.*

And now across these Atlantic isles, new stories are being created.

Now has come land reform and new community ownership. The distant courts of kings changed the land rules, and island communities in the west began to buy the empty acres. The land is being re-peopled. The first was at Assynt in 1992, since then the isles of Eigg and Gigha, and estates of Knoydart, Melness, Valtos and Borve. When Ulva church was built on Mull in 1828, it could call on six hundred islanders. Now it has come into community ownership, it is hoped the population will grow back to thirty, perhaps fifty, before long. The West Harris Trust purchased three estates, and the population has already increased to one hundred and fifty.

There are now six hundred thousand acres under community ownership, offering ways of life close to fish and farm and birds, once again.

For Jim Hunter, spending public money to let people live in ways many urban dwellers would envy is a matter of maintaining diversity. It has also brought self-belief and confidence, now people can tell a story about themselves and believe it. 'Time was, after all, when it seemed not so much improbable as impossible that emptied places would ever be resettled. But they were.'

These isles, after all, were under Norse control for longer than the time since they became part of the United Kingdom in 1707.

In a Faroe hall, after food was served and eaten, men in black tunics with golden buttons, their white beards trimmed, stood in a circle and joined hands with women in long dresses and pina-fores. There were folk songs, and then the chain dance began, two steps left then one right. The wooden black shoes of dancers clumped and creaked on the polished floor. It was the rhythm of the oar, creak of oarlock, the splashing of the old Atlantic. A chain dance can have two hundred and fifty verses, and on nights of summer celebration the dancers might find they sing without repeat.

It is more than just a national day said that sixties guide: 'It is a day for the joy of living.'

On St Olav's Day, in the streets of Tórshavn, all the people will still be dancing, flowing back and forth, the singers forming circles and chanting sagas. There will be swell, the rise and fall, the chain dance shifting, wooden heels cracking on the cobbles.

There never will be darkness, just a dimming as the sun briefly sets and rises, as singing fills the streets and alleys.

> In the morning, as soon as it was light,
> They set out, and scoured the world.

[*Orkneyinga Saga*, c1197–1206]

CHAPTER FIVE

SAGA VIII

GIFT OF LIGHT

This saga happened at the isles of Shetland, then in the South Atlantic, in the 1950s and 1960s. No doubt you will have heard of a lonely white whale, wandering the ocean waters. Now whaling rose and fell on Shetland, and the young men are hired for whaling out of South Georgia. They travel over the equator for the southern summer, returning home in time for the hay harvest of the northern summer. Those boys, they live their lives in constant light. Gibbie works the catchers, it is a brutal time, the task of cutting whales to pieces. The whales themselves, at times, exact revenge on catchers. Years later, the last whalers meet at the old ice-house on Lerwick dock to tell their stories. Gibbie raises sheep, and races the island roads on his vintage motorbike.

No doubt you will have heard, of a lonely whale,
Wandering long the ocean waters, an albino white,
Pursued he was for oil, as was every school,
Each beast was snared to fuel the lights, on modern city streets,
Yet for all the crews, this snowy whale became a test,
A signal to the hunters, whose searching was a gift,
How will you now respond, when feats are followed by a fall,
Said Ahab after silent pause, 'I shall praise it.'

This perhaps is why, people in the past would say,
Any kind of hunt, required a calm and empty mind,
A respect for animals, a request that they might,
Give up themselves, and in return the hunter,
Would never speak unkindly, would suppress conceit,
So it was a shock when whales, saw the chase,
Was led by harsh harpooner, by fleets of sailing ships,
This is why their weeping, nowadays can still be overheard.

Unlike the cod and herring, whales saw in the worlds of air,
Above the water-tops, a bright domain of colour,
More than filtered blue, that fades to dark at crushing depths,
These ocean giants, rolled gently with their infants,
Yet on all the distant isles, a stranded whale was treasure,
A shawl of food and fat, abundant uses for their keratin,
So onshore men and women, of the meagre crofts,
While cutting wet-foot peat, watched for shoal and water sign.

At Shetland's isles, lands of chambered tomb and cursus,
Once hills at edge of Doggerland, where Norway was a shorter sail,
Than south to cities of the mainland, so for half a thousand years,
The Viking kings were rulers, yet a pauper court pledged away the isles,
People might have mourned, but nothing much had changed,
All this time, gust and storm were unimpeded,
The brunt was borne by cliff and skerry, by people of a barren land,
So they took to oceans, hired as hunters of the whale.

At Collafirth and Ronas Voe, were built the bloody stations,
Units billowed steam, by shore and sheepy slope,
For set by flow of steady watercourse, whales were flensed,
In sea were carcase queues, blood pouring into clear marine,
The inlets brimmed with metal scent, the stench of death,
And sure enough the herring fishers, protested at pollution of their sea,
So by the second war, as whale numbers fell away,
The quays were quick deserted, concrete soon absorbed by grass.

Those on isles had come to feel, they could never leave,
The long dark days of winter, when soil had turned to iron,
There was work in spring, on herring boats,
There was digging on the croft, putting in potatoes,
They could shear a sheep, learn to drive the tractor,
Yet men and women, wondered how they could survive,
What futures held for children, on their windy shores,
Alas many soon were migrants, fleeing Shetland's isles.

Over hill came this word, go south and cross the roaring forties,
Three thousand leagues, past rocky Capes of Horn and Hope,
Where Cook of Whitby whalers, had searched for continent,
Where in richer waters, he wrote of albatross and the petrel,
And schools of giant whales, in seas around the southern Arctic,
This is why were built, on South Georgia's eastern coast,
Harbours named after Leith and Stromness, for Husvik and Grytviken,
Echoes from the northern ports, these edged by ice and snow.

An older brother waved two years of wage, so Norman signed,
Jimmy stood in a three-foot ditch, wet to knees,
His brother strolling up in suit and tie, passing drinks around,
Tom hired to dodge the navy, Joe became the only British gunner,
Other Shelties signed as mess boys, phoned agents down at Leith,
They would crew as seamen, sit as watcher in the barrel,
As flenser on the dock, as steam-saw man and carpenter,
So Gibbie signed at sixteen, there was no work at home.

In years beyond the war, it seemed the world knew more,
Of satellites in orbit, of plans to race for moon,
Than lives of thousand men, in distant southern ocean,
The Shetland boys joined the Norse, learned somehow to speak,
To men from nearer Argentine, to crews from Tyne and Wear,
Now all their lives, would soon be lit,
By years of sun, now they could forget,
The hard embrace of winter, the endless dark of daily night.

So the men who beat the plough to net, tarried now with penguin,
The fishers who had hailed, 'It's herring boys, herring,'
Now would chase the blowers, under swelling cresting wave,
Beside the blue-black bergs of ice, yet alas for anxious whales,

Who never upset people, they could not survive,
This onslaught from the ships, could not copy terns,
Birds of snowy feather, flying north to south and south to north,
Birds of bloody bill and snug black cap, now imitated by the whaler men.

The catcher cast off, easing into sludgy sea,
Gibbie stood at stern, watching coal smoke lying low,
From the harbour wall came cries, *Fuld fangst* good hunting,
They left the belching works, the sickly sloping plan,
By giant boiler building, a whale was being hauled,
By hawser on a winch, flensers stood aside,
A flipper still could kill a man, a carcase might explode,
The graveyard at the timber church, extended every year.

He observed its skin so smooth, polished black and blue,
Knives sliced the flesh, a towline pulled away,
A strip with rending crash, the blubber cutters,
Now carved square blocks, fed them into hopper,
There was din and rattle, crack and hissing steam,
Life ebbed to crimson sea, one hundred men upon the plan,
He could not rid the taste, of blood between his teeth,
There was laughter in the bitter air, below the snowy mounts of Georgia.

Now at sea the catcher, surged from mother ship,
Crewmen watched with awe, the surface-skim of albatross,
Locked wings and seaman's eyes, motionless yet on the move,
Shouted Gibbie 'Hvalblast,' from the pitching barrel on the mast,
A whale spout spurred adrenalin, four ship rings for the chase,
Tension grew in crew, at masthead he was air sick,
A dark curve slow appeared, he smelled the oily breath,
Called the Norse gunner, 'Slow ahead.'

SAGA VIII

These boxy chasers, tailed the whales,
That rose and sank, the harpoon-man standing,
At platform-prow, he was still and patient longest,
He commanded highest wage, the other crew were paid,
By success of hunt, they had to hope,
He would send, from plunging deck,
The half-tonne arrow flange, with explosive charge,
That he would strike the whale, so they could haul the carcase in.

Now the catcher wallowed, spray furling over gunner,
Foam at nearby iceberg swirled, and harpoon streaked,
With crack and whistling rush, there came explosive thump,
Rainbows formed above the waves, the flat head pivoted,
And the whale dived, leaving slick of oily water,
Down a mile and in the dreadful dark, Gibbie now imagined thrashing,
Minutes before that whale, knew not of human world,
Yet seventy kilogrammes were lodged, the harpoon weight in body.

Crewmen sighed on foredeck, they could not help,
But wince and shudder, it was a brutal way of earning,
The winch rattled, the line pulled tight the whale,
The skin was stabbed with lance, the carcase filled with air,
Jabbed with flag and left to wallow, the ship rushed off for more,
Catchers often clashed, always piercing competition,
Yet certain times a whale was passive, it just stopped and died,
From deck they watched commotion, as killer whales sped in for tongue.

The Shetland men on factory ship, all they ever saw,
Were dead whales, they never felt their freedom,
At the shore station, the meat was dressed as steak,
And deaf to their distress, alcohol was quite forbidden,
So each man built a secret still, became an expert brewer,
Fermented drink from rice and raisin, from oatmeal and potato,
They longed to hear, the voice of wives and lively children,
Longed to sit with pipe, watch the sun set on the northern waters.

Yet some would say, they lived in grace,
For twilight joined to dawn, there was salt-dried cod,
Eggs powdered from a tin, eggs from penguin colony,
At sea they watched for slushy film, that split to pancake,
For quickly plates of pack ice, could jostle up and clasp,
The ship soon motionless, each listening to the scrape and rasp,
So the men climbed out, on ice pack under blazing summer sun,
And kicked a football as they waited, icebergs slowly skirting by.

Some men chose to winter out, months of darkness on repairs,
Most steamed away, to meet the northern summer,
These men of everlasting light, they set on deck,
A canvas pool, to celebrate the crossing of equator line,
And for a while, they could forget,
The task of cutting whales to pieces, those walls of cold,
And corrugated iron, that one day soon would be abandoned,
To the Arctic terns, migrators too of polar flights.

Gibbie did hear tell, of a long white whale,
That swam Antarctic waters, up to west Australia,
But no one wished pursuit, of such a beast,
They could see it was a gift, it helped the whalers,
Make it to the end, and when all was said and done,
The Norse company penned letters, offered to each man,
Low interest loans in Shetland Trust, to help them buy,
Trawlers and a fish boat, machinery and a net.

Long years later, the last whalers met at Lerwick dock,
In ice-house block, to tell their stories,
Their part of island history, they wrote a book of fables,
And at the rural village hall, a whaler's daughter-grand,
Played the fiddle, on accordion was paired a grandson,
The day was mild, not a hint of autumn gale,
Soon would come, the days for winter celebration,
So Gibbie raised his sheep, and sped the roads on vintage motorbike.

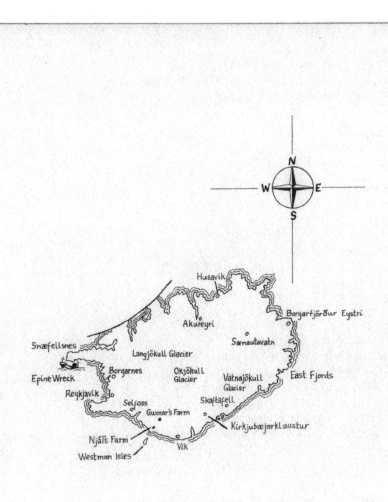

Husavik

Borgarfjörður Eystri

Akureyri

Snæfellsnes

Sænautavatn

Langjökull Glacier

Epine Wreck

Borgarnes

Okjökull Glacier

Vatnajökull Glacier

East Fjords

Reykjavik

Selfoss

Gunnar's Farm

Skaftafell

Kirkjubæjarklaustur

Njál's Farm

Vík

Westman Isles

CHAPTER SIX

ICELAND ICE AND FIRE

Dyrfjäll mountains, Iceland

How do you say goodbye,
To a glacier?

Asked Andri Snær Magnason, in *On Time and Water.*

And how, too, to say farewell to the reindeer calving grounds drowned by a reservoir, to all the herring and each blue whale?

To cold winters and low-lying shores, to an ocean free of plastic?

This is a sea that formerly was dry, yet is rising once again. Far to north a new isle has also risen, boiling from the ocean rock and sediment.

How should we say goodbye to all the insects, how to the deserted and cleared villages, how to the old fish dock? How do we say goodbye when the coffin is given heft by stones, and still the bearers stumble? The famed seafarer was buried sitting upright in a mound, with a ship, with a story. But what about the others who were lost, who were taken by the waves, whose life-tales we have now forgotten?

There will be chaos in the smoke, you suspect, when the wyrms find out what happened to the treasure. Was it used to help the people, what might they see, how would they frame advice? This might be all we can do, slide the oar into water, steer this ship, find the one route, hold on tight until the sun has fully risen on the rime-cold dawn. What should we carry on our crossings, over life and land?

At a certain place, the ground is hot and steam rises round the lava. At another, snow that fell a thousand years ago has not yet reached the glacial face.

Alienation from nature may have contributed to some of our problems today. Until recently, our daily lives were intertwined with living things. Have we suffered from an extinction of experience? Thomas Berry wrote, 'We are in between stories. The old story, the account of how we fit, seems no longer effective.'

Attentiveness and immersion can bring respect, and if we are lucky, we will find that animals, plants and places intercept us in our wanderings, helping to bring forth distinctive stories of the land. This creation of story and knowledge arising from local circumstances could be called ecological literacy. We might add the terms land and sea literacy.

These are best thought of as not a particular body of knowledge, but the process of coming to knowing. Land and sea literacy is not just what we know, but how we respond, how we let the natural and social worlds shape us and our cultures. An acquisition process such as this inevitably leads to diversity of culture, language and story about land and nature because close observation of one set of local circumstances leads to divergence from those responding to another set of conditions. We become tied to our pieces of land, and to one another. So when landscape is lost, it is not just a habitat or individual species. It is the meaning in our lives. Writing of American geographies, author Barry Lopez said, 'To come to a specific understanding… requires not only time but a kind of local expertise, an intimacy with a place. There is no way round the former requirement: if you want to know you must take the time.'

We might conclude that this land and sea literacy is not just knowing the names of things and their functional uses, but putting ourselves in an animate, observant and talkative world. The world was never inanimate, with natural resources only to be exploited, gathered, shot and eaten. If these things are done, then it should be only in certain ways, so respecting nature. Indigenous people believe that if they cause harm to nature, then they will themselves come to harm, whether it is speaking without respect of certain animals, or whether it is over-fishing a lake or hunting out an animal.

Yet in the shadows of affluence, it seems, we have come to believe that harm to the Earth is inconsequential, or at the very least trust that if something is lost then it can be replaced.

We chose to think the consequences will never haunt us.

For the Western Apache, wrote Keith Basso in *Wisdom Sits in Places*, landscapes are never culturally vacant. Animals, places and whole landscapes have meanings, sometimes sobering, sometimes uplifting, but always with a moral dimension. Living is not just about knowing, it is about knowing what to do, and when to do the right thing. Places and things 'acquire the stamp of human events' and memorable times, and people wrap these into stories that can be myths, historical tales, sagas or just gossip.

For the Apache every story begins and ends with the phrase, 'It happened at…' And so this anchoring of narrative to places means mention of a place evokes a particular story, which in turn carries a moral standard, and implication for certain types of social relations. Some Apache dialogues come to comprise only of a sequence of place names.

After one such interaction, Lola Machuse explained, 'We gave that woman pictures to work on in her mind. We didn't speak too much to her. We didn't hold her down.'

Keith Basso observed that there is an assumed courtesy in not speaking too much, and in not demanding that the listener sees the world as the narrator wishes. Too many words also smother the audience: an effective story-teller seeks to open up thinking, letting people travel in their minds. These stories are never definitive, they shape-shift over time and are regularly changed in detail. He also wrote of the class of arrow stories, a particular kind of story designed to have strong consequences. They are fired like arrows, and are intended to provide moral guidance to listeners, and thus influence their behaviours.

Annie Peaches said, 'The land is always stalking people.'

And Benson Lewis added, 'Stories make us live right.'

Above all, said Charles Henry, 'Each place still looks after us.'

For the Apache rightly say, if places care for us, then each must be treated kindly. The names of places do not lie, but if younger generations do not know the places or the stories, then the names will no longer evoke respect and understanding. Keith Basso concluded, 'Knowledge of places is thus closely linked to knowledge of the self, so to grasping our position in the larger scheme of things.'

In the hottest place in the world, and one of the lowest, my friend Pauline Esteves, tribal elder of the Timbisha Shoshone people, said Coyote the trickster was always seen before a story.

Coyote readies us for the story, in the sagebrush, on the playa, in the cool pinyon forest high above the place that was called by incomers Death Valley. There had always been water in the desert, said Pauline, until it was stolen. Every place has a story, and the most powerful in the desert are at water sources. Oases have spirits, water babies, little people, and before we consume, we ask for acknowledgement, sprinkle a little on the land, give thanks for the water. Wherever we go, she said, we are reminded to be respectful, as water is not just for cleaning or drinking, it is medicine.

Yet people from other places just walked in and used the water, they dammed it, channelled it: 'That is a bad thing to do, they will experience something bad in there.'

CHAPTER SIX

She added, 'You know the playa over by Windrose Canyon, that dry lake; when I was a child we used to play in the water there.'

The whole valley is a spiritual place to the Timbisha, it has power, it is protective. 'Maybe that's the reason we're still here,' she said.

Stories that inhere in places are both currency and commons. Something happened here, and over there. Thus we should listen in a certain way. This is right and that is wrong.

About a thousand years ago, there were 4,560 farms in Iceland. There are 4,500 today. Farms named in the Book of Settlements, the Landnámabók, are present in today's landscapes. There are sagas written a thousand years ago. Their locations are entirely recognisable. This cannot be said for many other affluent countries, where farm numbers have fallen sharply, landscape features removed, the commons enclosed and field sizes increased. Economic growth brought many things, but it took away the old stories. And if we have no story, we might find we no longer care enough.

Here are the boulders Gisli and his wife Audr scrambled up, where he fought to his last.

This is the great rock that Grettir lifted, this is meadow where Unn the Deep-Minded lost her comb, called Kambsnes ever since.

This the farmhouse where Njál and his wife were burned to death, this the nearby farm from which Gunnar the archer could not stay away, the place he loved so much, and where he too was killed.

These are the stones outlining the basement where Snorri Sturluson was struck down. This, too, is the borg where was an elven church, a further reminder for protection. Here a Hebridean woman called Thórgunn was showered by a skyfall of blood during haymaking; here a Scottish thrall called Nail fought off horse thieves, but was captured and jumped off a cliff; here a russet river flowed over eddying amber pools among beds of white pebbles, across which Björn jumped to woo Thuríd.

In 1897, W G Collingwood and Jón Stefánsson undertook a *Pilgrimage of the Saga-Steads*, and drew and painted 150 detailed scenes, most of them the very places where events in sagas occurred. Recently Richard Fidler and Kári Gíslason undertook a similar trip in *Saga Land*, to locations of the sagas of Gisli and Njál, also to places of their childhoods and early working lives. They reported a local idiom: 'Every Icelander walks around with a book in their stomach.'

Two things are clear: the encountered scenes were recognisable from the written records from nine or ten centuries before; they remain close to identical today. Iceland landscapes and land use have remained largely stable for a millennium.

But then came the flooding of the treasure of Kringilsárrani, an arrow to the heart of Iceland. It was a commons, a place of goose-nests and lava-red bedrock, crowberry meadow and roaring rapids, the calving grounds for the reindeer of Iceland. When Sabine Baring-Gould travelled in search of sagas in 1862, he reported, 'Reindeer were tolerably numerous.' Yet like many other affluent countries,

Iceland had been attracted to the selfishness of the late twentieth century neoliberal project. Just four years before the economic crash of 2008, it had built the 190 metre high Kárahnjúkar Dam to channel subsidised electricity to a multinational company smelting aluminium. Soon a fifty square kilometre lake had drowned Kringilsárrani. A world treasure was lost.

Politicians had talked down the region, saying it was nothing special. They accused photographers of exaggerating the natural beauty by using photoshop methods: either way, it was farewell. These assets of the Earth, this capital, were lost forever. Andri Snær Magnason observed of this destructive episode, 'Now that the Earth is in trouble, should we call an economist or an ecologist?'

And for the world economy: it gets a light metal for making soft-drink cans that would contain a drink harmful to the consumer, and then be mostly thrown away. Each year, the water levels vary so much that kilometres of grey silt are left on the landscape.

One evening on the south coast, at Kirkjubæjarklaustur, we climbed the hill to the marsh above the fire church, up the edge of rushing waterfall, through a forest of humid birch and spruce.

The forest had been planted by local residents after 1945, and now has the tallest tree in Iceland, a Sitka spruce of twenty-five metres. On the slope was the singing cave of Sönghellir, where nuns from the convent at Klaustur would chant to monks who had travelled from afar. At the summit were banks of thrift and lady's bedstraw, cotton-grass and waves lapping on the glassy lake of Systravatn. It is said *nykur* dwell here, the water horse and kelpie. Here the nuns often bathed, and one day two saw a hand rise from the water wearing a fine golden ring. One tried to grab the ring, but was dragged down by this show of mortal avarice. Inland was still the white daze of Vatnajökull. The light held below the cloud, slowing time itself.

To the south spread the wide lava plain of Landbrot pseudocraters, mossy hummocks and enclosed troll-caves where farmers kept their hardy sheep and cattle. In the sea was rock bank and lava that could gash the side from any trawler searching for the cod, and fifty leagues beyond was the newest land of Iceland.

This isle appeared at the time of cod wars and a decade before the eruption of Eldfell on the Westmann Isles, when six times the amount of tephra fell on Heimæy harbour as did land on Pompeii. One day, there was clear water, the next a bubbling burning sea. Out of depths came Sutr's fire, hot lava, and the rising isle of Surtsey. Since the early sixties, it has grown to more than a league on each side, risen one hundred and fifty metres from the sea. Moss and lichen appeared after four to seven years, willow after twenty-five, and there are now seventy species of plants. Fulmar and guillemot nested first, then in flew ravens.

Everyone knows ravens understand human language. They can call to bring on rain or snow, especially at their nesting time.

Down below the lake and waterfall was the wooden church where a fire priest once stopped the fiery lava with a mass. Here had been an ancient monastery, yet there had also been five hundred years of woe, Iceland bonded to the Norse and Danish thrones. And so it was in 1783 that Mount Laki erupted, tore off its top, threw cinder in the sky. For those centuries, Iceland could only sell to royal merchants, and now the eight months of eruptions of Lakígigar broke this stranglehold. First a warning, a blazing fireball flew across the Arctic stars. The people were astounded, silenced by the sight.

Now burned the Skaflá fires, and all of Europe's air was dimmed. Smog bound the Faroe Isles in ash and acid rain, darkened streets of London, then was tasted in Moscow and Aleppo.

It killed one in five of Iceland people, half of all the livestock. Falling strands of molten glass stuck in people's hair, scorched their skin. The harvest burned in fields, ash charred each bilberry on the heath. Fish lay lifeless in the rivers. Their island air was filled with fluorine haze, so the skin of horses flayed, the teeth of sheep were shattered. At Klaustur on the shore, Jón Steingrímson chanted verse and called on God. He stopped the magma at the door. The sun was blood-red for two whole years, the moon stained too. And from every North Sea port, ships sailed with aid, and so was ended crown control of Iceland farms and fishing fleet.

One day a trader opened hands, his dark skin cupping beans and he instructed, these were for the roasting not the eating, and so coffee took on a taste of freedom.

And this, the true nature of things. Reynisdranger black-sand beach was known as the most beautiful to gods. At the green headland were the giant trolls, four basalt stacks in mist, turned to stone at dawn as they raced for home in Utgard. This was Vík, the southmost village of the mainland, and we walked through stands of purple lupin to the shore. Here was the largest colony of Arctic terns in Europe, and they chattered over silver sea, beat hard the air and peeled off to dive, cutting water as a knife. On the beach was a silvered statue of a leaning fisherman on plinth, its twin installed in Hull to gaze this way. The froth of waves was molten on the charcoal beach. There was oystercatcher and piping redshank, and puffins dashing for their burrows chased by skuas. You could see how the birds got here, how the lupins too, imported from Alaska to stop erosion. But all the other plants, the insects, what help had they?

Look back a little further, past the hundred metre coastal arch of Dyrhólæy, past the shoulder of Ejyafjallajökull that closed the skies of Europe, and there flows the Markafljót, the Mart-fleet of *Njál's Saga*, the great river that takes to marshlands and skirts the farms of Njál of Bergthórshvoll and Gunnar of Hliderendi. It is the only saga set in the south of Iceland along two hundred leagues of coastline with only Vík beach and the harbour of Hæmey for fishers' safety.

The saga calls the coast, 'Nothing but sands and vast deserts and a harbourless coast, and outside the skerries a heavy surf.'

This was the landscape near the literary centre of Oddi, where Sæmundr came back to Iceland aged twenty after study in Europe, and where his great grandson Jón Loptsson fostered Snorri Sturluson. Sæmundr wrote the *Elder Edda*, Snorri the *Prose Edda*, two of the greatest works of literature of the time. Njál's farm is on a low hill two leagues from the sea. He was a man of peace, even as endless conflict seemed to drive the times of the 990s and early 1000s. He was burned to death in his farm, climbing into bed with his wife with stoic resignation, and submitting to fate. His friend Gunnar was also killed by treachery, having been outlawed by opponents who won an argument at the Althing.

Gunnar should have stayed away, but had to see his home at beloved Hliderendi:

> How lovely the slopes are,
> More lovely than they ever seemed to me before,
> Golden cornfields and new mown hay,
> I am going back home, and
> I will not go away.
>
> [*Njál's Saga*, c1200s]

Forty men came down the *Iá* hollow road to the farmhouse from the fell pastures, enticed his dog Sám away to kill him, and Gunnar said, 'you've been cruelly used, my foster-child Sám, and it is expected our deaths are meant to be close together.' They attacked, he repelled with his bow, he injured fourteen and killed two, but his bow was cut by Thorbrand.

'Twist me a bowstring out of your hair,' said Gunnar to his wife Hallgerd, 'My life lies on it.'

'Now I remember that slap on the face,' said she to this her third husband, and watched on as they killed Gunnar. He was buried by Njál sitting upright in a cairn on the hill above. Gunnar loved that place too much, they said.

One day at Hliderendi, it happened that a shepherd and a servant woman were driving cattle past Gunnar's Mound. Gunnar seemed in high spirits and was reciting verses. They told Gunnar's mother, who told Njál, and his two sons went to the mound on a clear night with the moon shining brightly. The mound was open and Gunnar was looking at the moon, four lights burning in the mound. They saw that Gunnar was happy and had a cheerful look.

But trouble today is brewing. Inland and east from Njál's burned farm and Klaustur lies an icy realm, great Vatnajökull, Europe's largest glacier. It used to cover a tenth of Iceland, but in the past twenty years has shrunk in volume by a tenth.

The world's heat has come to Iceland.

We approached by southern ring road, over black sand wash and past the torn wreckage of Skeidarí Bridge, washed away by boiling flood, not so long ago. The volcano under Vatnajökull had roared, icebergs broke the bridge, and pushed back the sea before a plain of gravel. The Skeidarí had once been so effective a barrier that mice had never reached the land to the east. At Skaftafell, we walked the trail around a hill, east toward the glacial front. Winter advanced, and there across a playa of old growth birch, no taller than a horse, was the melting face of ice, thirty metres high, a league wide. It was scarred black, lattice lines of scoured sand, and a polar wind was blowing off the ice. Icebergs had calved into the milk-grey lake, as large as office blocks, the ice itself was vivid white.

CHAPTER SIX

The glacier had travelled through a different time. It was slow moving, and yet far too fast. The chief of Hel waits, for frayed bones had been broken on the stone and rock.

This fractured ice before us once was falling snow one thousand years ago, just as Iceland had been settled and new farms laid out. Above a falcon keened. It should have been a wild place far from human will.

Once all was well for these many species of glacier, ice-cap and outlet, mountain cirque and stream. Long ago, the gods could recall when great trees fell layer on layer, and were crushed to ancient carbon, yet they never expected reckless burning. Now the world has warmed by one degree since the start of industry. Not much, if you measure by the daily weather. Author of *On Time and Water*, Andri Snær Magnason, says, try this. Go inside. Our warm-blooded kind of life relies on homeostasis, it tries to bring back every change. Yet if your body temperature rises by one degree, you are ill; it is fever at two degrees; at three to four, and it could be fatal.

There are two hundred and seventy glaciers in Iceland, and now one has died.

Okjökull, the Ok-glacier, lies north-west of Vatnajökull toward Reykholt and the Hvíta River. Now there is only rock and ash. W G Collingwood and Jón Stefánsson described in 1899 the snowy domes of Ok: 'It stands, as it stood in ancient days, on the confines of the world. The wild land is not without wandering sheep, and flocks of ptarmigans and swans, the water teems with trout.'

Twenty-seven years earlier, Sabine Baring-Gould had travelled by horse train over the mountain pass by Ok, 'We toiled for some hours up the flank of the jökull, over soil spangled with golden marsh saxifrage, and with beautiful tufted saxifrage. On the far side of Ok we rested at a little patch of turf and low willow, where grows an abundance of water avens.' They sat and watch red bursts of sand blown around Skaptafell.

There is now a memorial plaque, one Andri Snær was asked to write as a letter to the future. Was this farewell or a funeral for such eternal symbol, this white giant of frost?

He wrote, 'This monument is to acknowledge that we know what is happening and what needs to be done. Only you know if we did it.'

There is a hole in Langjökull, Europe's second largest glacier.

On the eve at base camp, we lay in hot pools that fed the Hvítá River, steam smoking over the green hillside of meadow and rustling poplar, and at dawn had parked on dirt sand and crushed stone. We climbed aboard the fat-wheeled missile launcher, converted for this glacial work. The cloud was thick, rain lashed against the windows, and water lay on the top of ice. At a certain high place, fifteen hundred metres up above the Arctic sea, a single metal tunnel was gaping in the blizzard. Inside the glacier, dripping rivulets ran down the walls and carved hollows. A crevasse split to one side, the floor was slick and slippery. There were neon lights to mark the route, and even these had sunk into the ice.

The tunnels were arched, and off to one side had been carved a chapel, a blue room with wooden benches.

A lad stood at the altar and sang a folk song, and said 'I've got to tell you something serious, very serious. In seventy-five years, there will be no glacier here.' And then, perhaps, he might have said, 'I know some of you might not believe this will happen, if you work for corporates and kings, but I am Icelandic and this is my glacier.'

Later he whispered, they mostly do not like to hear that bit. We, you and me and all the gods, will have to limit warming of the world. In the Himalaya and the Hindu Kush, there are forty-six thousand glaciers, considered sacred for the fresh water they provide for free to one and a half billion people. Yet seventy to ninety per cent of these glaciers will have disappeared by the end of the century.

Outside again, all was intense and white, and cold wind tore at our faces. Halldór Laxness, Iceland's first Nobel Prize winner, wrote that glaciers in his day were 'illuminated at certain times by special radiance, and stand in golden glow.'

At one edge of this glacier, the water on the surface was pooled into an aquamarine lake. It poured off the ice in torrents. As it hit the sludgy rock and dust, it turned brown, and churned downhill.

———

At the East Fjords, there were streaked skies and screaming birds.

Bales of white silage were spaced across the meadows, and two girls were playing football on the rough grass by the shore. The sun was hot, but the air cold.

Out on the Norwegian Sea was a stable wall of fog, the southerly wind held it back. This time of haymaking used to bring people together, now a single tractor ferried through the tall grass.

Hey, they said, don't walk on that farmer's land, around the bay beyond the fish factory, he will run out with a gun.

Seyðisfjördur were playing away, and the team had driven in and out of fjords, across volcanic plain, and back out again across the northern coast to Borgafjördur Eystri. By the time of their top-of-the-table clash, summer had departed. The west wind tore down the pitch. Seyðisfjördur wore green and white stripes, Borgafjördur were all in red. A quarter century ago, Robert Putnam observed that people of Boston were bowling just as much as they did in the past, but now played alone. The league structure had once aided cross-community understanding and trust, and social capital had been higher because playing away meant going to another place with differing identity and story.

Cars were parked facing the pitch on a slope, spectators huddled inside to watch. There were children running around in T-shirts, but the substitutes for the away team also sat in vehicles with engines running. On the wings were speedy lads, in the midfield solid enforcers long past forty. The cook was the referee, a waiter ran the line. The home team were leading, enough to win the league. But penalty, and dismay. The keeper dived and saved, and all the home cars bounced, piping horns in celebration.

At the other end, the ball was often taken by the wind and flew into the grassy bog by the Álfaborg, the hill-home of the elves. No one seemed to be able to find the ball fast, wandering through the grass to waste a little time. Then the home team was celebrating, and the away had a hundred leagues still to drive.

By then the rain was driving hard across the hills and village. The girls had given up with their ball, but now were laughing and turning somersaults.

You could conclude, there was nothing special here at Bakkergerði, a fishing village at the north-east edge of Iceland. No saga had been written here.

Yet there was modern fish factory, a ring of rhyolite mountains, puffins beating at the wind, a polar light so brilliant when cloud and fog had cleared, oxbow streams glittering in the vale. When we came, the village had been filled by three thousand visitors for a music festival in the old herring factory. There had been slow movement in the fields, deliberate packing of tents, caravans hitched to cars, and then silence for another year. This was village home of painter Jóhannes Kjarval, he was raised at Geitavík down the fjord. The café in the village had striking portraits, the local people captured in ink and charcoal wash in the 1940s, their faces torn by wind and weather. In the grey church with white eaves and windows was a Kjarval painting, it was Christ giving the Sermon on the Mount, standing right here on the Álfaborg, and saying something about the importance of sharing.

In the fish factory, the floor swilled with seawater, young women and men dressed in blue uniforms and white aprons stood and gutted cod and catfish.

Their knives flashed over the white surface, lit from below and translucent, and a glove tree stood to one side, each metal branch ended by a drying red rubber hand. Blood covered aprons and arms. Here was half the football team and their support. The single computer had yellow sticky notes around the screen, and plastic crates were full of fillets. And hanging from a spike was the traditional food of *hákarl*. The Greenland shark is toxic to eat, at first, as its flesh contains antifreeze. The shark is buried in the ground for sixty days so urea can break down the flesh, then hung to cure for another four months. It was safe yet pungent.

The factory foreman sliced the red shark, and handed over strips of rubber flesh. From the window was a rainbow rising over the Álfaborg.

We walked over the mountains, coming down sharp and steep, and rising once again. There were meadows of flowers on the slopes, pinking stone curlew and whimbrel calling.

In the remote bays of Brúnarvik and Husavik were abandoned farms. That was where my grandmother lived, said Magnus. There were remains of beach fishing village, and windrows of driftwood on the grey sand. The layer of polar fog rose high, but stayed offshore. We lay in the lush grass and among blue harebells, in the sun, listening to the water rush from the hills. The blue sea was stretched with clashing currents, travelling north around this eastern side of isle. We walked until the sun was below us, shining shadows upwards, up to the cathedrals of rock and snow, passing over alpine pastures yellow with sulphurous bedstraw. The snow glittered mica-bright, and iron in the soil had leached one snow-edge red, the bloody rill running down the slope. One day we ate lunch in the moraine field of Stórurð, the troll-flung boulders from the Dyrfjäll Mountains. The glacial pool was emerald green, harsh enough to strip the skin off any swimmer.

The valley of Eiriksdalur was full of willow and birch, none higher than an ankle, and all the meadows were a surface lake of pouring hidden water.

The mountains fell dark, and the clouds were patterned with white and orange light. Ingunn Snædal of Egilsstaðir wrote in her poem 'Icelandic Landscape':

> Icelandic landscape
> Half sky
> The other half
> A memory.

One day it rained, on the weathered shale and layer cake, on thousands of feet of scree, on the green bog and white waterfalls.

The sea seemed still far below.

There had been a sect from Canada, preparing for a crystal ceremony in the valley. We walked out on the Ósar River toward the black sand beach at Stapavik, ripped and smoothed by wind and rain. A cairn marked the site of *hvalreki*, where a whale had washed ashore. Two men from Germany came and paid the farmer to remove the teeth and bone. Now a cone of pine trunks marked the grave. At the point, the wind rose and thrashed at coast.

There was no escape, for here too were bright plastic colours, smaller pieces broken into ever-smaller shards. All the saturated colours, in this land of green and brown, charcoal cloud and grey river. Around the shoulder, where deepwater ships could moor, sacks of coffee, flour and barley were winched up to the cliff top, carried inland on horses clattering over slate. It was their window on the world of trade and goods from far. At the café in the village huddled by the fire, drinking coffee and hot chocolate, we looked closely at Kjarval's heads, the women and men of these remote farms and fish.

Across the bay that filled with ash when Laki erupted was the wooden turf-roofed farm of Sænautasel. It was by the cold lake of Sænautavatn, the infield surrounded by stone walls. We dipped to enter, the floor was beaten earth, some inner walls wooden slats, some stone and turf. There was the earthy smell of being underground. It is said this was the inspiration and model for famed *Independent People* by Halldór Laxness. At the far end was the byre for sheep and cattle, in the

CHAPTER SIX

centre the *badstufa* and kitchen, steep stairs to the single bedroom. There were churns for mik and skyr, a piece of lamb nailed to the wall. The cots in the loft were packed together, and there were lace curtains at the window of glass.

This farm was in the Landnámabók, part of the *hreppur* commune system unchanged since those days. The highlands and outfields remain common grazing today, and the *hreppur* organises round-ups when the sheep are brought down in autumn, an occasion for socialising, for jollity and celebration. People dress up for the sheep, and for each other. It was a farm like this where An the servant grew up, the place he left to study as a doctor in Copenhagen, later which he inherited and then went on to live on Flatey, treating injured British trawlermen. This day, the family brought coffee and pancakes served with rhubarb jam in the old sheepcote.

It was not far south that the *Saga of Hrafnkel Frey Goði* played out at Adalbol, where today there are twenty farm and temple buildings in the grass of a glacial vale warmed by geothermal heating.

Icelandic horses have been bred for strength and endurance, unique for their five gaits and smooth movement, and Hrafnkel was a worshipper of the god Freyr, so called his own horse Freyfaxi, it had a dark mane and dark stripe down his back. Hrafnkel forbade his shepherd Einar from riding the horse, yet Einar took it to search for thirty missing sheep. He rode for two days, up the glacier, down to the Jokulsa River, and found the sheep in a steep ravine. He thought Hrafnkel would be pleased, but he was killed with an axe. Samr the shepherd kinsman had Hrafnkel punished at the Althing, took his land and property.

But we have heard of such a person, who had a great temple built and acted as superior to all the people of the vale. By treachery, he acquired back his land and farm, but in life never seemed to be content.

On an isle upon the place where tectonic plates grind and pull apart, you are never far from fire.

To the east of Akureyri, the northern capital deep inland on Eyjafjördur, are the smoking lands of Krafla. The ground beneath our feet was hot, steam hissed from vents, risen from the magma chamber, a fissure to the core of earth.

From a distance, little seemed alive, save the boiling ground itself. The cooled lava was charcoal black and fractal, not a single surface smooth. Mud pools bubbled, there were opalescent ponds, yet up close you could see fine biofilms. The ground had once caught fire, and stone swallowed up by smoke, yet there by red rock was a meadow bright of moss. And there too, on lava by a hissing fumarole, was a single tuft of fescue, a viviparous grass of green. Thirty eruptions have occurred at Krafla, right above the mid-Atlantic ridge where is fought the fiery clash of plate tectonics. The lava fields stretch ninety leagues, and nearby was a geothermal plant, all silver pipes and steam.

At blue bathing pools, we took to the hot water, and a cold breeze blew down from Arctic. In many a place you can watch the water boil and churn, suck back and then advance, bubble more. The ground growls, and water blasts high, the steam sheared away by wind. It often leaves behind the smell of sulphur in the geysired air.

It is said the weather is better at northern Akureyri than at western Reykjavik, and so the sun shone.

It was bright on the green hills and fjord, dappled in the forest behind the town, glittering in the harbour where Níels Einarsson and friends were preparing the yacht *Gógó* to sail for Greenland. There were friends on the pontoon, boxes being secreted away, rigging and sail checked, motor run again. Níels is director of the Stefansson Arctic Institute, and has written how Iceland found a new species of fish. It won the cod wars, up against the naval might of Britain, it had cut the trawling gear, the British ships having painted out their names. Young deckies threw potatoes and coal at the coastguard ships that darted inside the trawling fleet as fast as sharks.

But as in life, when you win you often lose. Now there were no foreign fishermen to blame for falling stocks, and so Iceland came up with the clever plan for transferable quotas. These would limit fishing effort, reward those who worked the market best.

There were loud local advocates of ITQs still writing favourably in 2008 that quotas created living capital, that they were working to generate financial capital in other sectors. There was the belief that indebtedness in the fishing sector was a good thing, and even better that it doubled over ten years, as this borrowing meant others benefitted too.

History is often so unkind.

Andri Snær Magnason begins *On Time and Water* with some words of an Iceland bank chief executive from October 2008: 'We are doing very well indeed,' he declared. Days later, the three big banks collapsed. In January 1989, the East German leader, Erick Honecker had also said, 'The wall will stand for fifty years, and a hundred too.' It had gone by that November.

The quota advocates had forgotten one simple thing.

The paper fish can only thrive if there are abundant fish in seas. Yet the paper fish soon outnumbered real cod, and so helped bring down the world economy. At the time of the crash, Iceland quota was worth fifty times the annual profit of all its fish industry. There should be, on the harbour-side at Patreksfjördur, a statue to those two small fishers, Erlingur and Örn, who had sailed on behalf of the earth commons.

The poet Jón úr Vör grew up with fifteen siblings over at Patreksfjördur, and wrote:

> I search for a break from work, and the bustle of the day,
> In a flower garden by the road, and I lie face-down in the grass.
> But an old man with a stick, walks up to me says in a broken voice,
> It is forbidden to lie here.
>
> [Jón úr Vör, *Patriotic Poem*, 1942]

We sat with Astrid Ogilvie in the Hof Centre by the harbour, let the sailors continue preparations. There were sunbeams lancing, smiling faces.

She studied at Reykholt, later joined Níels' institute here in Akureyri. The overland route north will swing past Reykholt, home of the most famed scald of all, Snorri Sturluson, on the plain below the glacial falls. Eight hundred years ago, he was elected twice as law-speaker at the Althing, an author of the *Prose Edda*, the *Heimskringla*, the circle of the world, yet was killed by rivals. Mostly stories keep the tribes together. Here Astrid walked in Snorri's footsteps. She was once of Norfolk in England's east, then Oslo and Denver, now in Akureyri. Both Norse and Anglo-Saxon sagas have a thread of wisdom sayings, moral tales on how to live.

'Health to the givers! A guest has come in,' says the second verse of the *Hávamál*, the Sayings of the High One.

What of the good life, I asked Astrid, what are the things that matter most in life? Well, it was connection and belonging, togetherness, natural surroundings, healthy food. Like others, she found the things that make us happy, seem essential for life, these are mostly low in carbon too.

One day, Cousin Jon and three fly-fisher friends sent news, they would arrive in two days. Friends in the village found spare beds and bedding, installed them in her apartment. The men stayed, woke her early to ask how to make breakfast, and then the Pastor Geir Waage knocked. Come, he said, I'll show you round this place of words, where sagas were composed and flew outwards to the world. Bjarne the actor from Oslo sang *'O sole mio'* in the church, and beyond the church-yard was the site of the fortress farm where Snorri lived. His life had ended on the night after St Maurice's Day, when Gizur came with seventy men. Pastor Geir called out the names of the well-armed mercenaries who found Snorri in the cellar, and they walked in footsteps over stone and grass hummock.

'Do not strike,' had said Snorri. The one called Árni struck, and then Þorsteinn and the others flashed swords and axe. Justice may occur in other realms of life, but did not happen in a tale like this.

In the *Hávamál* was spoken this verse:

> *Livestock die, kinsmen die,*
> *One day you die yourself,*
> *One thing I know that never dies,*
> *A dead man's reputation.*

Ahead lay the great dome of Snæfellsjökull.

And this tale is almost done.

You could not, though, imagine a better natural place to bring the people together than at the Assembly Fields of Thingvellir, where the Öxará river, the axe-river, flows between league-long cloisters of basalt pillars, past Flosí's *gjá*, the crevasse across which he leapt in full armour, to the Logberg Rock. Below lay the broad plain where the water oxbows past the church to the wide blue lake of Thingvellavatn. There were turf mounds over rock walls, the *búd*-booths where *goðar* gathered their clans for the three weeks of summer Althing. For eleven hundred years, now, the island has come to this open-air cathedral. Hokusai designed and published his *Hundred Views of Fuji* in 1834, some with cone volcano small in distance, some filling scenes with fiery sunrise slopes. You can pick as many views for Snæfellsjökull.

On a clear day, it is on the horizon from the streets in Reykjavik, it is a powerful presence from a plunging whaling ship south of cliff-wall of Látrabjarg. It is surrounded on three sides by polar water, it has watched many a trawler limp across Faxaflói bay to safety of the harbour walls of Reykjavik. From Thingvellir, the road skirts the southern peninsula, past isolated red-roofed farms to the village harbour of Arnastapi.

The cone slopes rise high and bright, the lower meadows covered in yellow hawkweed. Here lived Bárdár, half-troll half-man, who left the world to live inside the glacier. Oðinn's son was called Baldr, and there was much good to say about him. He was beautiful and bright, wise and merciful, but none of his decisions were effective. He was buried with his horse, and waits to ride from Hel after Ragnarök. Bárdár will also be released, if his glacier comes to melt. Here was set by Jules Verne his journey to the centre of the earth, the fissure going down and deep.

Far away, though, in the seaman's mission at Grimsby is a stained-glass window of the steam trawler *Epine*. It was a rusting sidewinder, a ship that long has lain upon the sacred beach of black basalt pearls.

Ten years had passed since a deckie learner had taken a first trip on the *Epine*, and now began a descent to hell. The *Epine* was six times sold, served in the war, and now under the white cone mount by the ragged shore that could tear the skin from any swimmer, the guts of ship were spilled for ever. The *Epine* had been a toiler, no mystic clipper of the sea. It was a less than average ship. Leading craftsmen had never laboured long to hone and varnish wood, to polish brass. No smithies had poured their skills or raised with pride a mallet over molten iron. The ship was named after a spine deployed to catch a fish.

But the *Epine* became a thorn that stuck in the skin of sailors.

At this beach of Djúpalónssandur, on those pearls of black basalt, were three pools of sky that rose and fell with tide. And at the cliff were four lifting stones, *Amlóði* was the weakling just of twenty kilogrammes, *Fullsterkur* was a colossal one hundred and fifty.

Grettir lifted a stone in his saga, and here with bursts of breath, their shoulders popping, with crack of hip and knee, the beach fishers plucked them from the pebbles. There are, it is said, hidden powers at Snæfellsjökull. These were the very men who waded in to rescue sailors from the wreck. On the bluff was a lava labyrinth, a *völundarhús* built by elves. It was a crossing point, an entrance to another world. At this lovely beach of Dritvík, the three hundred men for three centuries of the fishing village would lay their clothes on stone to dry before the sky.

Yet to this very day, rusting shards of ship lie cast upon the pebbles. It has become a hallowed site, where those seamen lost their lives in sight of safety of the land.

CHAPTER SIX

In Hull, the lean inspector's suit hung loose, a cut too large. He had walked the streets to the Guildhall, wreathed in a smog of green. Ghosts loomed and vanished, there was cough and silence. A policeman peered from porch, counting names from list. The chill committee room was lit by single bulb, he switched on the electric fire, lit a cigarette, and cracked his gavel down. J V Naisby set out his instructions, let the court begin. He called for statements, each witness would be heard in full. It had been a Saturday in March, a south-west gale and rough stuff sea. The trawl nets had been shot, hauled and still were empty.

The *Epine* skipper snarled, so steamed north on ship Hargood's recommendation, for they reported better fishing up at Adalvik on Hornstrandir. He set the shortest route, close to shore and disappeared below.

On that winter night, the conditions worsened. Wind was roaring in the rigging, surf poured across the deck, so far, just a normal night at Iceland.

The youngest deckie called the mate, worried at the readings. At the end of first watch, progress still was bad. The mate Freddie called the skipper, he staggered up. Yet in only minutes more, the weak screw thrashing, the ship was on the rocks of Snæfellsnes. Sea filled the engine room, and the lights shorted out. In hellish cold and dark, the firemen both were drowned. On the deck the crew fired six distress rockets, lit a fire on the whaleback. The lifeboat had been smashed, and they could make out a cliff, could not know the beach was close, just forty steps, they could have waded through at the lowest tide.

The crew and mate fought to save the ship. But the storm redoubled fury.

Freddie the mate staggered on the falling deck, he had not slept for days. Some men bound themselves to rigging, but their hands froze and were washed away. Freddie saw lights appear ashore, and by the afternoon, the rescue party had attached a line. There was one giant man who walked into the waves, and hauled four sailors in by breeches buoy. One seaman leapt and swum. But by then fourteen crew had drowned. The survivors rested at a farm, and were ferried back to Reykjavik. Those men had beaten the war, yet did the captain lead them to a grave?

The judge wrapped up, 'The area is well-known for abnormal magnetic disturbance, but we are reluctantly driven to conclude the cause of stranding was an error. The dead-drunk skipper was responsible. All other conduct, all members of the crew was in accord with high traditions of their calling.'

As we have heard, some inspectors sent silver plate or case for cigarettes. But this inspector, hasty to conclude, appended a simple clause, 'This was a stranding of a British vessel where yeoman service was rendered by the Iceland rescue service.'

And the Grimsby sailors' mission installed a stained-glass window, for six of the drowned were married, and two were boys of seventeen. Would the widows tear their clothes, pull out hair in clumps, sense they should be shouting at the sky and gods? The mourners knew the silence in return was endless. Yet the skipper's fault was not so clear. Freddie knew he'd been down below and sober, lying in his box bed. He had simply seen too much at war and in these dreaded fishing grounds.

And sure enough, a monster of the deep now prowled the cobbled streets. One berth at the dock was blank, yet the church pews all were full. Each coffin was empty, so the groups of bearers carried one whole life, and they stumbled often in the space for anguish.

They all felt it had been a wicked ship.

> Summer is dying, is dying, and cold is the breath of fall,
> I am the bird that passes, the ships that the tempests blow,
> My song is a song of parting,
> I came, and I go.
>
> [Davið Stefànsson, *Eg sigli i haust/I Sail in the Fall*, 1895–1964]

Bergthora was well liked, Njál her husband too.

He never lifted his hands with a weapon, he was respected for his wisdom in the law, for his good will. Gunnar was the famed fighter of the friends, winning battles in southern Norway and Denmark.

Njál lived contentedly at the farm of Bergthorshvol in sight of the southern sea. But he had the power of prophecy, and could see he would one day burn in fire. Time passed as do events, and the fire came closer. Sæunn was also wise, and could foretell the future, and though she talked too much, most was true. The old woman was worried about a large pile of chickweed outside the farm: 'This chickweed will be taken and set afire when Njál is burned in his house,' she spoke. She nagged all summer, but the weeds were never taken inside.

Flosí was the man who jumped the ravine over the Öxará River, and he was offered money at the Althing, then much more, and Snorri Sturluson urged him to accept. But Flosí did not know the meaning of enough, when to stop, and so led a force south of one hundred of men. They arrived at Kirkjubær, and all the men went into the church to pray. Then they rode past the upland lakes, around Eyjafjallajökull to their left, and then came down the Markafljot River.

The whole world of these people was about to end, in fire for some, in dishonour for others.

Inside at Bergthorshvol, Bergthora spoke to the large household, and said, 'Each of you is to have what you like best, for this evening is the last time I will serve food for my household.' This cannot be, they cried.

In the night, Flosí's force surrounded the well-built farmhouse. 'We could fight,' he said, 'but we might lose. The other way is to burn them inside.' They took the chickweed and set it alight in the loft.

When the whole house began to burn. Njál went to the door and said to Flosí, 'Are you willing to make a settlement with my sons?'

CHAPTER SIX

And Flosí said, 'I will not. But I am willing to let the women and children and servants come out.' 'I want to offer you free exit,' said Flosí to Njál.

But Njál said, 'I will not leave, for I am an old man.' Bergthora spoke, 'And I promised him that one fate should await us both.'

The two of them went back in. 'We will go to our bed and lie down,' said Njál, and their grandson said, 'You promised me grandmother we would never be parted,' and so young Thord joined them.

They lay down in the bed, and placed the boy between them. They crossed themselves and put their souls in God's hands.

The house in which they lived burned down.

Thord's father Kari escaped, but Njál's other two sons were also burned to death. One attacker, Gunnar Lambsson, taunted Skarphedin from the roof timbers, and Skarphedin took from his purse a human tooth and threw it so hard it knocked Gunnar's eye onto his cheek, and he fell from the roof.

Flosí spoke of his use of fire, 'Men will call this both a mighty and an evil deed.'

And this is why they also called this the *Saga of Burnt Njál*. For the people had unleashed the fire of the world.

> *All things on earth are transient,*
> *The days of your greatness and glory,*
> *Flickers like flames in the night,*
> *Far in the depths of the past.*

[Jónas Hallgrímsson, *Iceland*, 1807–45]

DROWNING OF DOGGERLAND

This saga was the first, and it happens on the steppes of Doggerland, long ago, the dryland that would flood and form an inland sea. The Sky People had been numerous, but now are migrants escaping the rising waters. They arrive at the cliffs, and the forest people strain their bows. But Erce the Queen says, wait, there are infants in the boats. Herne the King invites Sky-Rider, the shaman leader of the people, to tell her story. They are dark-skinned stalkers, chasers of the horse and broad-browed auroch, they roamed the plains. But they had to dig up ancestral bones, move in and up. One day, the sun rises from the water, sets too in western seas. Gulls seethe, cold calls the cormorant. Silence follows her tale, and Herne says we will take you to the hills of chalk. Sky gives him in return a tight-sewn leather bag containing seeds of corn, given to her by traders from the hot lands far to south. Herring now would follow, in that novel northern sea.

It is said the Sky People, once were numerous,
But they had drowned, and every dark hide,
Of land and fire pit, each vale and fell had been seized,
By the rising flood, the swell of sea had beaten down defence,
So they launched their boats, lashed and loaded auroch-skin,
And flexed the oars, among the furs and flutes,
Were sobbing infants, fastened tight to strakes of birch,
At last ahead appeared a strip of land, they saw a hall upon the cliff.

It seemed no spell they cast, no cry to gods,
By these blue-eyed people, who could beat the wind,
And slip with bow inside the range, of creatures on the hunt,
It seemed they could not counter, how a poison had been cast,
That sunk their world, their land that fell,
Before the ceaseless tide, as does the oak before the axe,
The brine now bore them on, toward a beach where figures stood,
In shadows under sighing pines, the squadron now drew near.

The forest people watched, this ragged fleet approach,
They drew ash bows, for this had been a year,
Of shore attacks and sorrow, so took the strain,
Herne the King called to arms, 'aweigh the anchors,
Sail around the flanks,' yet Queen Erce was renowned,
Her long sight best in tribe, and she now observed,
'There are babies in those boats, I see no shields arrayed,
We should pause and help, these people come ashore.'

After countless battles, Herne the fabled hunter,
Now could see these folk, were people fleeing demons,
And to elite platoon he ordered, 'Stow your bows and lance,
But be on guard, send reserves to ride and help,'
A tall woman stepped ashore, from the leading vessel,
Others staggered at the land, hands pulled the boats through breakers,
An infant fell and Erce shouted, to the rescue party,
'Watch those children,' one was face down in the wash.

The boat people scattered, over sand and dunes,
Gazed up at mottled sky, muttered thanks to gods of solid land,
And drank from skins of water, that the forest people proffered,
Who now could see, this was the hour,
For a rescue, not an echo of the days,
When flames were lit, on seaward ridge and summit,

To wreck on rocks, such passing ships,
Nor would they need to darken skies, firing arrows at marauders.

'Sit with us,' hailed the green king of wood and swidden,
From his splendorous hall, 'here is roasted meat and honey,
Our trees are dense with fruit, here is draught for all to drink,'
And the dark-skinned woman, her one eye crimped,
Stood tall before her people, bowed to king and queen,
Thanked them for their kindness, said quietly 'we have come far,
Our homes have drowned,' and the king motioned,
'Lay your goods on polished floor, you are safe to rest with us.'

The king paused by his sergeant, 'send a party to the pines,
And dig the pits, for those bodies lying on the shore,'
And said to leader, her name was Sky-Ryder of the shore,
'Our people live in marvelled woods, we will tell,
How our children run with deer and elk, how this to us is paradise,'
And Erce smiled 'when you've fully rested, you must voice the story,
Of your people and this soak, but first we all will walk,
And give our prayers together, for those babies laid in tiny graves.'

A dream near dawn, appeared before the migrant leader,
Sky-Ryder heard a whispered warning, 'you have endured so much,
Yet must fly upslope, scramble up the cliff,
At far Valhalla, sheer has slid Storegga,
Three mountainsides of rock, have toppled into Arctic water,'
At the hour of the hare, the clouds a rosy hue,
She dabbed on drops, of sea-lavender oil,
And sought the antler-king, 'we all must climb again.'

Herne was a wise king, and turned to Erce for her counsel,
'We should trust this leader, she seems to know,
Most about the water, why the waves have risen,
How this curling current, has forced them from their camps,'
So Herne walked before his woodland people, 'pick up your sandals,
Tie them to your feet, set off uphill,'
He told Sky-Ryder and her people, 'outside our upper hall,
Let us gather, where fragrant blossoms lie upon the roof.'

The assembled crowd on cliff top, saw the tide retreat,
It did not stop, the sea disclosed,
An old land and rotted homes, a dry steppe east to rising sun,
Sky-Ryder unwrapped a beaver skin, revealed ancestral bones,

And ribs of people, let them breathe again,
There came cries from children, some were far below on beach,
A distant surf appeared, a grumble from horizon,
And now the tidal bore advanced, pouring over sandy flats.

This was the sea, yet not the normal sea,
Before the wave, was billowed cloud of dust,
Matter floated in the air, the crowd stood and pointed,
They could hear a roar, as ocean ran at land,
Young men rushed down paths, grabbed up the children,
And all were scrambling, up the sandstone cliff,
None had heard such sound, never seen such wall of angry water,
The breaker raced ahead, soon would drown the infants in their mounds.

The water tore at amber trees, ripped roots from ground,
At the base of cliff, the lower hall was struck yet stood,
They could smell the brine, the churning mud,
Then all fell silent, now the middle land was shallow sea,
Doggerland was bank and swale, where once the horse had run,
Sighed the oaken-king, 'light the fire pits,
Bring food and vintage mead,' he called on Sky,
'We hope plain words, will help us apprehend this mess.'

Sky-Ryder stood with staff, that fit so well her grip,
A shield of four-fold hide, slung upon her back,
The birds of shore had flown, yet above them larks were singing,
Herne cried to servants, 'fetch more logs,
Stoke the blaze, come forward out of shadows,'
Sky saw the hunting dogs, were wagging tails,
Running through the crowd, she saw the sea had calmed,
It seemed they now were safe, even as the waters lapped at cliff.

Her tale commenced, 'you will recall,
It had been fearsome cold, tundra-chilled this far south,
We the People padded north, mammoth numbers poorer,
On hunting hill and grassy plain, on Doggerland we camped,
At salty-marsh and wide lagoon, by a million whistling waders,
At the still point, lovely ash Yggdrasil propped up the sky,
And serpent circled brine, the guard of all our ground,
In those distant days, Dogger was a wide dry plain.'

'You can see, we are dark-skinned stalkers,
And were chasers of the horse, the hackneys and their mares,
The broad-browed auroch, great bison herds,
And harried by our dogs, were giant elk and reindeer,
Yet we later learned of creeping shift, icebergs severed free,
Though eagles planed serene, above the stormy shore,
The waves we begged to wait, would bring a great betrayal,
The seas were rising up, we sensed a warp of salt and sand.'

'Let me tell of my grandmother, flyer of our tribes,
Sky-Runner of the steppe was wiry, her skin was scorched,
And wearing amber brooch, loose-limbed she led the clan,
Across the rippled grass, around the lakes,
They sang by fire pit, flickering by the canvas camps,
At the end of ropes, the children spun their flutes of bone,
It was the sound of prairie wind, it called our roaming herds,
We tossed our laughing infants in the air, never wearied of those ways.'

'Every place to us, was protected by a spirit guard,
Each spring and cave a link, between the inner–outer worlds,
We always paused to pay, respects and place an offering,
Where lancing from a cloud, light rays shone on grass so lush,
It might rain for days, the dry gulch flooded,
In a drought, we called on clouds,
And stamped to rain dance song, till the rose of dawn,
Our tents were warm, though in winter grey hair comes to all.'

'The air was life, the wealth of sun and rain,
Yet also fetched our greatest fear, green funnel-clouds,
Yet as the gannets screamed, a storm was beating at our home,
My mother was a shaman too, and travelled far in dreams,
She checked the tides, watched them sink a saltmarsh,
And heard the tales, strange from southern marches,
Where had hunters settled, and carried soil in baskets,
And by some magic, trained their cattle into passive herds.'

'Still we Dogger People cheered, and honed the sharper blade,
Battled bear and browser, it had always been that way,
Yet flighting in, came a flock of snowy herons,
Each with crest of feathers, standing tall upon the mirrored marsh,
Now waves were rising, the height of me,
In half a hundred years, so in and up we carried camps,
Where elders warbled, their lovely lullabies,
So washed the rising waves, the currents lapping at our gate.'

'We were not alarmed, just now shifted often,
We Skys had always trekked, but routes grew shorter,
Our world was shrinking, so we stirred some ochre,
With water drawn, from sacred spring,
And by a holy cave on scarp, we all were taught to hold a palm,
Upon the sacred rock, and blow a fine red dust,
So by an auroch hands were painted, arrows in a roaming horse,
We wanted each to have the spirit, of a summer evening cloud.'

'I was a little taller than my mother, and I sang before our yurts,
We had to hurry, dig up a hundred holy graves,
Bury bones once more, lay the bow of ash,
Beside the red-deer skull, set antler harpoon by the axe,
Yet one day braiding baskets, a willow withy speared me in this eye,
Its liquid life drained out, my sight now halved,
I called on Oðinn, desist and stop the sea,
Still the surge poured in, league on league not letting up.'

'Gulls seethed about the shore, sooty petrel plunged,
Cold-cried the cormorant, I knew it was another sign,
We could not tame this tempest, all our shamans tried,
Had we eaten fish forbidden, had a snake,
Whispered in the grass, no one could recall,
It seemed we had been fastened, inside a frightful spell,
And one sharp dawn, came a shocking sight,
The sun-star rose from water, later slipped into the western waves.'

'I dreamed our world would drown, yet one tribal clan,
Refused to see, they stood and shouted,
Why us whyever us, we'll not dig another bone,
They said it had been shamans, who brought disaster on them all,'
She gazed around, at the audience with her eye,
And the king and queen nodded, for they too had seen,
How people at their camp, started with complaints,
When their stable worlds, seemed to snap apart.

So Sky-Ryder recommended, 'when the night-lion roars,
Your senses sharpen, for this was growler grabbing land,
Our ground had shrunk, a lean breach at first,
And in came spacious yeasty sea, grave and yard were lost,

We searched above for signs, in hoops of moon and sun,
Sat trembling in the sweat lodge, red and raw each glowing stone,
Watched cloud and soul-bird, counted days both long,
And short, saw fire streak across the starlit sky.'

'I called my four scout-boys, fetch the rangy dogs,
Those lads were knappers, experts of the flint,
They could split a stone, find the blade inside,
So their feet would hardly touch, the rippling grass below,
They mapped the land, measured shore beneath the rain,
And at the camp they sang, our whistling beating music of the steppe,
But that clan of hostile vipers, crept and pounced one night,
And three were slain, their bodies thrown in mere.'

'Lame Deer was the youngest boy, he folded into shadows,
Fast across the steppe, he raced to bring the news,
We were surrounded, it was a wet world now,
I called on tribal carvers, gather teeth and tusk,
Groove the faces of the boys, each beside a stag,
Now we had to fish for wrasse, saithe and long ling too,
We returned to salt, whelk and oyster shell,
Our people had been crushed, and Dogger Isle was disappearing.

Silence followed story, Sky's tale was near complete,
Gripped by spell of words, the forest people then applauded,
Tapping hilts of knife, on hollow blocks of wood,
She had filled their sinews, with every kind of sorrow,

SAGA IX

So the people on the cliff top, passed from hand to hand,
More horns of mead, and turned the spits of meat,
That soon would fully roast, and reclined in humming meadow,
Building back the tales, about the flooded people of the plain.

At last Herne stretched his tendons, 'true wealth is not the gold abandoned,
In your graves and ground, it is our sons and daughters,
It is the land secure, and safe beneath our feet,'
But then he stepped up and said, 'so why did the sea rise,
And will it ever stop,' and now Sky-Ryder opened hands,
And shrugged in silence, so he called on heralds,
'Blow on trumpet shells, for now you Skys are safe,
We all can see, you have suffered more than most.'

Now Sky-Ryder gave to Herne the hunter, a tight-sewn leather bag,
'Here are seeds of grass, good sized and golden,
Clear the clods, sow them after winter,
And these bright ewes, they each will birth in spring,
Two leaping lambs apiece,' and the oaken people were impressed,
Yet she warned, one pale-faced trader,
Sneezed a killing kind of ache, she had mixed more herbs,
Yet many of their band of wind, rattled lungs and died.

Herne cupped the seeds, rose to his feet,
'How awful when the wealth, of worlds is laid to waste,
When hall and tent are rime-encrusted, when waves will wrap our bones,
This is reminder to us all, our own chill winters fast approach,
I see the fire splutters, the children deep in dream,
We will heed and set a sentry, hope we have the ear of forest gods,'
From their camp was silence, not a fly was buzzing,
A cuckoo called three times, and settled on a nearby branch.

Well Herne declared his plan, 'We will take you,
To the land of cloud, to meadows blooming to horizon,
The time for grief is gone, you can mark each place,
Mend the moon and heal the land,' and perhaps one day,
They would sleep, without a troubling dream,
For that sea did stop, even as it had been deaf to cries,
Can you imagine, herring now have followed,
And they will swim, far across that novel northern sea.

BEFORE RAGNARÖK

Vík beach, Iceland

A fire he needs, who has come in,
And is chilled to the knees.

[Sæmundr Sigfússon, *Hávamál, Sayings of the High One, Poetic Edda*, c1290]

No, surely not.

Those prophecies of the boy with green eyes, Merlin, that recovery work of Hildr, what the gods of Asgard said would happen to the world, surely the end will look different. How did they know, back then, that our house would also come to burn?

The Wanderer, the Strider, the Weary Walker called Gangleri asked, 'What will be, after heaven and earth and the whole world are burned? All the gods will be dead, together with the warriors of Valhalla, and the whole of mankind.'

And Thriði the Third, a minor god of the Æsir, replied, 'There will be, at that time, many good places to live.'

There is glory in the earth, said the scald in the Old English poem, *The Wanderer*, yet also:

The man without friends awaits once more,
Sees fallow waves in front of him.

And in the vellum codex called the Exeter Book, the story-teller in *The Seafarer* had spoken, 'I can sing a life story about myself.' He had spent winters on the ice-chilled sea, on the exile's roads. He was crushed with cold, bound up with frost, with cold chains, hunger tore within. It felt like winter, precisely because, 'Friends and kinsmen [had] fallen from me.'

The wanderers and seafarers of those days knew something else. So did those who stayed behind. Happiness would not be found in treasure. Fill your bowl to the brim, and it will spill. *The Seafarer* said, 'I will never believe that earthly wealth, stands eternal for a person.' He also spoke:

The heart's desire, each season urges,
The mind to sail, that far from here,
I may seek the homeland, of foreign people.

Long long ago, a thousand years and more before these tales were told, Lao Tzu in the *Tao Te Ching* said, 'If you aren't afraid of dying, there's nothing you can't achieve.' A verse goes on to say:

People enjoy their food, take pleasure being with their families,
Spend weekends working in their gardens,
Delight in the doings of the neighbourhood,
And even though the next country is so close,
That people can hear the roosters crowing and their dogs barking,
They are content to die of old age,
Without ever having gone to it.

On the Gosforth cross in Cumberland, on the Easby pillar in the lower Yorkshire Dales, there are beasts bound in the final struggles of Ragnarök. Are they holding back the end of the world, or have they turned to be destroyers? Can we find a way to live with the wild, in short, rather than be the end of it?

Gangleri the Weary Walker asked High, what is to be made of Ragnarök?

The end of the world begins with *fimbulvetr*, the great winter to remind all the people how the earth had suffered at their hands.

There are to be mighty earthquakes, darkening of the sun, the serpent will leave the sea and then allow the waters to rise. One wolf will swallow the sun, and the people will feel they have suffered a terrible disaster; the other wolf will catch the moon, causing ruin. The giants will arrive aboard the ship *Naglfar*, made from the uncut nails of the dead. A great conflict follows. There is Oðinn wearing a gold helm and chain mail, there is Skaði and Ran, there is Thor and Freyr and Loki, and all the other male and female gods, all the frost giants and Midgard Serpent, the troops of Hel, the elves and dwarfs, the giants led by Surt. The battlefield of Vigrid extends one hundred leagues in each direction.

So. There comes calm and a lovely picture of renewal.

The earth rises green and fertile from the sea, and the surviving children of the gods all sit together and talk among themselves, sharing stories and speaking of what had been, as Snorri Sturluson said in *The Prose Edda*. And yet there are hints of another way, the building of a bright hall beside the wild country, the synchrony of oars pulled and the ship moving smoothly onward. The gods and people still can have their starry heaven, and the mighty tree its blossom, the horse can still gallop through the air, and all the given gifts be shared.

The greatest terror to be faced will not be disintegration in the dark, the emptied seas of fish, the scramble to find the treasure hoard.

It is the fact and fate of death for each of us. On the way, stories will be told, becoming gifts of currency themselves. On a famed ship, a good wind blows whenever the sail is raised, no matter where it is headed.

And so Gangleri smiled and said, 'The people passed these stories down, from one to the other.'

And the Wanderer spoke these final words:

> *Often a lone survivor experiences grace,*
> *Across the paths of ocean.*

CODA SEVEN

END NOTES ON THE CHAPTERS AND SAGAS

The Subtitle

1. The subtitle of the book contains the preposition 'at' rather than perhaps the more expected 'in' or 'on'. This is deliberate, as fishermen always talked of going to the fishing at Iceland, or at the Faroes or Greenland. I wanted the 'Travels and Tales' to be in reference to specific places where there are 'Warming Waters'. The 'at' also implies you might be on the land or on the water, or indeed at the edge of both.

Preface

1. The Gary Snyder quote is from his *He who Hunted Birds* (1979), about Haida myth, and the Yellowman quote is from William Hynes and William Doty: *Mythical Trickster Figures* (1993).

2. The oldest recorded written saga is the *Epic of Gilgamesh* of Mesopotamia, its Akkadian manuscripts depicted life some five thousand years ago on smooth tablets of clay. Greek and Roman epic poems were composed by Homer, Virgil and Apollonius of Rhodes (*The Iliad, The Odyssey, The Aeneid, Jason and the Argonauts*), the conclusions already known to audiences as they settled down to each performance. From China came the two and a half thousand year old Tao stories of life in early eras, as spoken or written by Lao Tzu (*Tao Te Ching*), Chuang Tzu (*The Book of Chuang Tzu*), the folk manual *Seven Taoist Masters*, and Luo Guanzhong's epic tale of civil war, collapse of government and the voices of the ordinary people (*Romance of the Three Kingdoms*). The Japanese saga also date back two thousand years with the first *Manyóshú* songs, journey tales (*Journey along the Sea Road, The Tale of Saigyō*), and the later epics, *Tale of the Heike, Tales of Ise* and *Tale of Genji*.

3. From India came the Sanskrit epics of gods and people, The *Mahābhārata*, also written more than two thousand years ago and containing one hundred thousand couplet lines, and The *Rāmāyaṇa* of twenty-four thousand lines. In Ibn Fadlān's *Land of Darkness*, Arab travellers journey to the far north, and were early columnists of the Viking world. In the timbral and polyphonic throat-singing of the Tuvan people of southern Siberia, epics have been sung for more than a thousand years. Throat singers receive their texts in dreams: the longest transcription of the *Manas* epic of the clans of steppe contains half a million lines of verse. The Faroe chain dancers are accompanied by Kvædi ballads, led by skipari scalds who know all the versions and sing all night. The *Kalevala* epic poem is derived from oral poetry of Karelia in eastern Finland, often attributed to Lönnrot, who sat down under a tall pine in the 1830s to write the archaic songs of the hunters and fishers Juhana Kainulainen and Arhippa Pertunen. At the time, singing matches were held in villages, the Ingria-based Larin Paraske was nationally known for her repertoire of more than eleven thousand lines.

4. The idea of the monomyth originates with Joseph Campbell in his 1949 classic, *The Hero with a Thousand Faces*; see also *Myths of Light and Pathways to Bliss*. The folk tales of Alice in Wonderland (via Lewis Carroll), Cinderella and Goldilocks are well known and widely told. Janet Yolen (in *Folktales*) has counted more than five hundred variants on Cinderella told in folk tales across Europe. The hero's journey into nature is discussed and practised by Bill Plotkin in *Soulcraft*, and across our lifecourse by Stephen Gilligan and Robert Dilts in *The Hero's Journey*. Hero can be a troubling term, seeming to imply male and not female (hero, heroine); yet most uses today imply hero works at a meta-level to cover all people. Trickster tales can be found in *Trickster Makes This World* by Lewis Hyde, and in many accounts of specific tribes, indigenous groups and cultures of the land and sea: see especially *Make Prayers to the Raven*

(Richard Nelson), *Wisdom Sits in Places* (Keith Basso), *Medicine Man* (John Fire Lame Deer and Richard Erdoes), and *A Story as Sharp as a Knife* (Robert Bringhurst). See Italo Calvino, Lewis Hyde, Janet Yolen, and Richard Erdoes and Alfonso Ortiz for further tales of tricksters worldwide. See also Ruth Sawyer's *The Way of the Storyteller* (1942), and *Mythical Trickster Figure* by William Hynes and William Doty and the Trickster Myth Group (1993).

CHAPTER 1: The Westfjords of Iceland

1. Iceland was a rare piece of earth territory uninhabited by ancient humans. The first to set foot were monks sailing hide boats, but they did not establish a growing human colony. Naddoð is reported to be the first Viking to arrive, followed by Flóki the Raven in the later 800s. There are many accounts of Iceland's early history: see *The Viking World* (James Graham-Campbell), *Viking Age Iceland* (Jesse Byock), *Wasteland with Words* (Siguður Gylfi Magnússon).

2. The population for the whole of the Westfjords of Iceland in 2020 was about 7,000. Avalanches remain an existential threat to many homes and villages in the region.

3. A chapter on the Innu country life and their enforced settlement can be found in my *The Edge of Extinction* (2014).

4. *Gisli Sursson's Saga* is one of some 150 Icelandic sagas, and one of the most famed. A caring farmer in Haukadalur, forced into family conflict by circumstances, declared an outlaw, living fourteen years on remote fells and fjords, and eventually found by mercenaries. His wife Audr spoke famed words when Gisli was killed.

5. The triptych of novels by Jón Kalman Stefánsson, beginning with *Heaven and Hell*, contains dramatic accounts of fishing from the beach camps of Iceland. Halldór Laxness was the first Icelandic author to receive the Nobel Prize.

6. There is some controversy about the landscape of Iceland and if, when and how trees disappeared. At land settlement, woodland was cleared for housing, heating and charcoal making. Imported grazing animals would then have suppressed tree regeneration. The landscape today looks largely devoid of trees: there are patches of woodland in steep vales; there are low willow and birch species that grow to only ankle height (the joke runs: what do you do if you are lost in an Icelandic forest? Answer: stand up). But the truth is more complex. Woodland cover was never static before settlement, ebbing and flowing with climate. From the period 1250-1900, the Little Ice Age brought periods of severe cold, with drift ice at the coasts, hampering regrowth and shortening growing seasons. Some valleys have maintained large-scale native woodland over a thousand years, comprising mainly birch, willow and rowan. Archaeological and written records also show that there were many deliberate local efforts at sustained conservation of woodlands. There was irrigation of woodlands, restrictions on grazing, and use of manuring. Some woods, such as at Hofstaðir farm near Mývatn have been in constant and sustainable use from 940 CE to the present day. Nonetheless, birch woodland covered 28% of land area in the 800s (2.8 million hectares), and today covers 1.5% (150,000 hectares). See Emily Tisdall et al. (2018); Arnór Snorrason et al. (2019); Rupert Bates et al. (2021).

7. The two trawler rescues occurred on the peninsula of Látrabjarg in the southern Westfjords of Iceland. Four hundred metre cliffs along a fourteen kilometre stretch of coast contain some of the largest colonies of seabirds in the world. Farmers of this coast long had learned to abseil down the cliffs to gather birds and eggs in spring. The trawler *Dhoon* from Fleetwood was wrecked at the base of south-facing cliffs in late 1947; the *Sargon* was stranded in Patreksfjord facing north a year later. The *Sargon* wreck is

visible still at low tide. The film of the dramatic rescue of the *Dhoon* led by Þórður Jonsson and local fyrd of more than thirty farming men and women was produced and directed by Óskar Gíslason. It can be viewed at the Hnjótur museum, two kilometres from the *Sargon* wreck. The Icelandic writer and journalist Óttar Sveinsson has written an account of the dramatic rescues in his book, *Við Látrabjarg*. Accounts of the rescues are in the *Lowestoft Journal*, *Weekly News* of Fleetwood, *Fishing News* of Grimsby and *Evening Telegraph* of Grimsby. When the *Sargon* was lost and found in the Arctic Sea in the late 1920s, skipper John Caton was carried shoulder high in Grimsby's Riby Square. The Court's formal investigation of the *Sargon* was chaired by Judge Kenneth Carpmael, and occurred in May 1949 (no S.411). The Látrabjarg rescues became a foundational myth for Iceland, just after Independence. Outside of Fleetwood and Grimsby in England, they seemed hardly to be noticed, and within a decade the first cod war had begun.

8. Kristín Svava Tómasdóttir's poem 'Austurvöllur on the Day of the Wake' is in her book *Stormwarning*.

9. Hornstrandir is now a national park, and the lack of modern development and livestock grazing is notable in the fabulous biodiversity and grand silences.

10. Many former whaling ports of the north have transitioned to whale watching, a huge financial success. Whale watching trips can be taken from Ólafsvik and Húsavik in Iceland, and from Andenes in the northern Lofoten Islands of Norway.

SAGA I: Crossings

1. Skaði continues the tradition of female shamans begun by the Sky tribe in Doggerland. Iceland's Thingvellir was established in about the year 930. Viking governance centred on open-air assembly places called *Things*, specified places where collective decisions were made and agreed. There were a number of regional Things in Iceland. It was at Thingvellir that Iceland declared and celebrated independence in June 1944.

2. Comprehensive summaries of Norse mythology are in *Gods and Myths of Northern Europe* (Hilda Ellis Davidson), in *Tree of Life* (Roger Cook) and the recent *Norse Mythology* (Neil Gaiman). A clear account of the life of *Women in the Viking Age* is by Judith Jesch. The story of Ingimund and Hrolleif is contained in *The Saga of the People of Vatnsdal* (see *The Sagas of the Icelanders*: Jane Smiley).

3. Flatey isle is where the Flateyjarbók was written, the longest medieval Icelandic manuscript (225 vellum pages), and is where the first public library was established in Iceland. It is where the Grimsby trawler *Epine* docks in Saga VI 'Grimsby Embark'. An, now Anarr, treats the injured sailor.

SAGA II: Settlement

1. This saga 'Settlement' centres on the farms of northern Iceland and its regional capital of Akureyri. Iceland goðar farmers had long relied on inland bonded or slaved labour, with children sold to farmers as permanent live-in labour. In the middle ages, Iceland suffered four centuries of restrictive trade by the Norway and Danish courts and kings. A monopoly on trade was granted, yet Iceland people were not permitted to import goods. The catastrophic volcanic eruption of Lakígigar (known as Laki) of 1783 darkened the skies across all of Europe, and also released Iceland from this system, but only after severe loss and deprivation. Farmers could sell sheep, and use money to buy goods. Coffee took on the taste of freedom, and soon the country had the highest rates of literacy in Europe.

2. The English author Sabine Baring-Gould visited Iceland and stayed on farms and visited Akureyri, going on to write *Mehalah* set on the Essex marshes. Other accounts of Iceland life can be found in *Iceland Im-*

agined (Karen Oslund), *Control of Nature* (John McPhee), *Viking Age Iceland* (Jesse Byock), and *Wasteland with Words* (Siguður Gylfi Magnússon).

CHAPTER 2: The Sjælland Gate and Lofoten Isles

1. The fabulous Skuldelev longships can be seen in the Roskilde Ship Museum at the shore of the fjord. The museum also houses a working shipyard, and trips can be taken from here by longship.

2. For one thousand years, the primary location of the *Beowulf* tale remained unknown. The poem was written in Old English, so many thought it could have been set in England. Archaeologists are now clear that Heorot was at Gammel Lejre, a few kilometres from Roskilde fjord. Sjælland was then an isle of many meres and marshes, and one nearby was the lair of Grendel and his mother. There have been many fine translations of *Beowulf*. Many believe Seamus Heaney's has been the best. He said it took him twenty years of work to complete.

3. For an early history of Denmark, see Saxo Grammaticus. See also Knud Jespersen's *A History of Denmark* for the rise of fall of empire, and the emergence of the modern state.

4. Meik Wiking is the Director of Copenhagen's Happiness Research Institute, and has researched and written widely on happiness in affluence economies. I write about the good life in my book, *Green Mind and the Good Life*. Meik Wiking's account of the greening of the capital city indicates how quickly a city can be transformed to promote health and well-being, and save money.

5. An account of the ice-fishers of Karelia can be found in a chapter of my *The Edge of Extinction* (2014). The ice-fisher leader, Esa Rahunen died in 2016. Tero Mustonen leads the pan-Arctic organisation Snowchange Cooperative (www.snowchange.org/).

6. Harald Hardrada had as strong a claim on England's crown as William of Normandy (whose ancestors were also Viking). Had England's Harold fought William first, history would have pivoted quite differently in 1066. Instead his loss of key troops at the Stamford Bridge victory meant he had a weakened force after they again were force-marched south to Hastings.

7. The Lofoten Isles are north of the Arctic Circle, yet are warmed by the Gulf Stream. There were many possible locations for the sources of the Viking raid on Lindisfarne in 793. The saga 'Viking Quest' simply imagines they launched from Lofoten. The Moskenstraumen maelstrom is the whirlpool and trap of Edgar Allan Poe's famed 1830s short story about the cataracts of the dreary district of Lofoten, in which the fisherman's boat was caught hanging halfway down the smooth tunnel, smooth as ebony, and fisher escaped by clinging on to a barrel.

8. The Texans came to Great Yarmouth and Lowestoft in the 1970s, and set up a football (American football) team called the Roughnecks. We were locals recruited for the team, and the league was won. The air force colonel had been generous at first, but was less content at losing. The team, though, folded when the oil men and families returned to Texas; some of the US air bases are still open. Coach Lawrence Elkins lives in Texas today after a career in the oil industry: his athletic life is celebrated in Ron Davis's 2019 book *Lawrence Elkins*. Lawrence was named eight times for sports halls of fame, from Baylor (in 1976) to the Texan Bowl (2017). He played professionally for the Huston Oilers (now the Texans), Pittsburgh Steelers and Chicago Bears, before injury enforced his retirement.

9. Norway invested oil returns, setting up the Government Pension Fund Global in 1990, also known as the Oil Fund. The aim was to keep economic benefits from oil within the country, and thus to help all citizens.

The fund gains revenue partly from taxes on the oil industry, rather than these being available for the Treasury to use for current expenditure. The Fund has now grown to one of the largest in the world, worth more than US$1.3 trillion of assets, worth US$250,000 to each person in Norway.

SAGA III: Viking Quest

1. The Norse Vikings first arrived in the British Isles in June 793, raiding the rich monastery at Lindisfarne. In the saga 'Quest', they originate in the Lofoten Islands of Norway. The clinker-built design of ships was invented by the Vikings of Norway–Sweden–Denmark. In the saga, Grim and Bolvik deployed a new long-ship template. A fine museum of Viking history and life is at Borg in the west Lofotens, the chain of Arctic isles that project into the North Atlantic/North Sea. In the saga, the *Wyrm* longship carries the first Vikings to Lindisfarne.

2. There are no written records of the first quests by the Norse to Britain. There are, however, many famed tales of Norse sagas of Iceland and Scandinavia, and Anglo-Saxon poems and tales of the British Isles. Many writers are no longer known, including the authors of *Beowulf, The Seafarer, The Wanderer, The Battle of Maldon* (Mældune), *The Lay of Wayland, The Lay of Skirmir,* and *The Lay of Eirikr Bloodaxe.* Heroic poems include *Deor, The Dream of the Rood,* and the famed short old English poem, *Cædmon's Hymn.* A modern echo of the first quests from Scandinavia can be found in *The Call of the Sagas,* the journey in an open boat from Helsinki to Iceland in 1994 by Pekka Piri and Matti Pulli.

CHAPTER 3: The Eastern Shore

1. The chapter opens with the event of the First Light Festival at Lowestoft in 2019. The metal giant was a depiction of Pakefield Man. The festival was organised and directed by Genevieve Christie. The pandemic prevented the return of the festival for two years. It returned in 2022, and there is hope that these success-es will lead to an annual event at the summer solstice at England's most easterly point.

2. 'On this eve, back on every Denmark beach, a sail's stretch and a wind's whip away': this is a deliberate rhythmic reference to the famed short poem, 'Sea Fever', by John Masefield (where the 'wind's like a whet-ted knife').

3. Across medieval Europe, St John's Day on June 24th was devoted to marking the summer solstice, and there were traditions of communities sitting by overnight fires, telling stories and leaping over the flames (see Carl Lindahl et al., *Medieval Folklore,* 2002).

4. It is not advisable to walk the Broomway on Maplin Sands without local guides. Brian and Teri Dawson of Nature Breaks helped here. Accounts of walking 400 miles of this coast in 2007–08 can be found my *This Luminous Coast* (2011).

5. The Battle of Mældune/Maldon took place in August 991, centred on Northey Island at the head of the Blackwater estuary (called the Pant upstream). The epic poem is one of the finest pieces of Old English literature, together with *Beowulf, The Seafarer* and *The Wanderer.* The original authors are unknown, and the final pages of the 325-line Maldon poem were burned in the Cotton Library fire of 1731. *The Longman Anthology of of Old English, Old Icelandic and Anglo-Norman Literature* (by Richard North, Joe Allard and Patricia Gillies) provides superb translations and commentary. The prevailing view for about a thousand years was that Byrhtnoð let the Vikings of Olaf win by his pride, and so was beaten. But the politics of the day were critical, especially the factions at the court of Æthelred. The king was content for many years to pay raiding Vikings to go away, which just brought more back. It worked for Æthelred, as he was on the throne for thirty-seven years in all. It ruined the economy, though made Olaf rich enough to acquire the

throne of Norway, and later insist Christianity be taken up in Iceland and Norway. The battle on the Essex marsh had wide consequences. The later genocide of St Brice's Day in November was led by Æthelred in 1002, as he sought to deflect attention from his failing leadership. Danes were killed across the country.

6. Canute (also Cnut or Knut) later unified Denmark and England from 1016 to 1035, and as we have seen had Harald Hardrada not lost at Stamford Bridge, he would have united Norway and England in 1066. For an account of the life of Cnut, see Tore Skeie (*The Wolf Age*, 2018), who calls him, 'The mightiest Nordic king ever to have lived.'

7. Many kennings are used in heroic and epic poems by Anglo-Saxon writers: war-god wine (poem), bee-ship's town (flowers on a grave mound), sea-stead (ship), wolf-slopes (wilds), wound-sea (blood), destroyer of timber (wave), wound-icicle (sword). Here also see gannet's bath (sea), fish-flayer (eagle), cloud cudgel (peregrine), air-scythe (swift). Key words are also used to demonstrate times of year or seasons, as are *kigo* words or phrases in Japanese haiku and epic poems.

8. The raven has returned to Essex and Suffolk, bringing back story and culture. The nightingale is the famed infiltrator in the East, being restricted now to the counties of Suffolk, Essex, Kent and Sussex. They are transgressors, says Sam Lee (in *The Nightingale*, 2021), inviting change with silence and suspense, as the spring sap rises in the woodland trees.

9. The beavers have been introduced to Spains Hall Estate in Finchingfield by Archie Ruggles-Brice. They have already had a dramatic effect on the upper watershed of the Pant.

10. There are several dragon myths in the Stour Valley, the border river of Suffolk and Essex. There are very fine medieval wall paintings of the wyrm and St Francis preaching to the birds in Wiston church near Nayland. Wormingford church on this hill contains stained glass of the green crocodile. The dragon returned to the mere at Wormingford. Two dragons fought on the water meadows at Cornard. St Edmund was crowned in 855 CE at the tiny stone chapel above Bures (though a number of other locations across East Anglia make similar claims: See Hugh Lupton on *Norfolk Folk Tales*).

11. Accounts of the draining of the Fens can be found in Lord Ernle's (Rowland Prothero) *English Farming* (1912). E P Thompson wrote about the Waltham Black Act and its role in the enclosures of England in *Of Whigs and Hunters*.

12. On pilgrimage, see Philip Cousineau's *The Art of Pilgrimage* (1998), where he says we should seek 'attentive travel.' He wrote, 'I hope it does not go as planned. Cross the threshold, and listen intently to everything around you.'

13. The many St Edmund's Ways in south Suffolk eventually join up with the Peddars Way in Norfolk. There is a St Edmund's Point at the end of the Peddars Way on the cliffs of Hunstanton.

SAGA IV: Herring for the Grit City

1. This saga is set at the former beach village of Lowestoft called The Grit. It was located on the dunes (denes) below the northern town cliffs, to the south of the lighthouse. A lattice of a dozen paths called scores (from the Old Norse *skora*) still run up the cliff today. David Butcher led an excellent oral history project of Lowestoft men and women of the fishing, producing a selection of books (*The Driftermen, The Trawlermen, Living from the Sea*, and *Following the Fishing*). In the same series is Jack Rose's autobiography. The Grit was organised into two Beach Companies. These were in fierce competition with each other, yet provided social support and pensions for all their member families. The Grit was abandoned after the Second World

War, when it had been used for army practice for street-fighting. Lowestoft Maritime Museum is on Whapload Road by the site of the Grit. My grandfather was born in a flint and brick cottage two hundred metres to the south, facing the food factory on the dunes.

2.   The saga links up the joskins men of farm and fish (often also called half-and-halfers). They walked to coast after harvest to crew the herring smacks. Many rural pubs in the region are called the Plough and Sail (at Saxmundham, Snape, Paglesham, Lowestoft, Tollesbury), showing strong links between farm and fish. There are many fine accounts of farm and rural life in the early to mid-twentieth century, including by Hugh Barratt, Adrian Bell, Ronald Blythe, George Ewart Evans, Lilias Rider Haggard and A G Street. The folk-singing pubs of Suffolk, Essex and Norfolk were well known, and some men and women toured the pubs as paid singers and dancers (see especially the Ship at Blaxhall, the Eel's Foot at Eastbridge, the Boxford White Hart, the Green Man at Tunstall).

SAGA V: Barge Requiem

1.   Barges once were the workhorses of the coast, carrying many types of farm produce and industrial goods from ports and farm quays. Most were abandoned from the 1940s onwards, as transport took to road and rail. In recent years, a number of organisations and shipyards have raised wrecks and refurbished barges for leisure trips. A number, such as the *Cambria*, still are sailing the East Coast rivers, estuaries and inshore ways. Organisations in the east offering barge trips include the Pioneer Sailing Trust of Brightlingsea and Topsail Charters of Maldon.

2.   Fine accounts of barging were written by A S Bennett (*Tide Time*) and Bob Roberts (*Coasting Bargemaster* and *Last of the Sailormen*). Both Maurice Griffiths (*Magic of the Swatchways*) and Hervey Benham (*Once upon a Tide, Sailing Craft of East Anglia*) contain particularly acute observations about sailing many types of craft in the Essex and Suffolk inshore waters. In the saga, Thora chooses a cottage on the Nore in Whitstable, facing north to Herne Bay at the mouth of the Thames estuary. In those times, the tidal part of the Thames River through the capital was called the London River.

CHAPTER 4: The North Lands

1.   The departure of the UK from the European Union was supposed to reinvigorate the fishing industry. But by mid-2021, the freezer-trawler *Kirkella* was moored and idle in a distant port, unable to work the grounds off Norway, the Faroes and Greenland. The skipper Charlie Waddy sat at home and waited, the first time in 47 years he could not be at sea.

2.   The story of the boy Merlin's prophecies appears in Geoffrey of Monmouth's *History of the Kings of Britain*. Merlin's prophecies centre on the coming of flood, especially around London, the wilds coming into the cities, and the burning up of land and forest. When Merlin becomes an adult, he leaves civilisation to live in the wilds, perhaps searching for Britain's lost miracles. Vortigern is a king in England sometime after the Romans departed. Perhaps Merlin is also the model for the Green Men of pagan symbolism [see *Pagan Britain* (Hutton)] and the Green Knight epic (*Sir Gawain and the Green Knight*).

3.   Geoffrey (Galfridis) of Monmouth's *The History of the Kings of Britain*, completed in the early 1100s, contains an account of the prophecies of Merlin, and tales of Vortigern the King. The author of *Sir Gawain and the Green Knight* is also not known. The cunning men and women were healers and shamans of England, and used herbal remedies as well as high and low magic. An account of Cunning Murrell is in *Morrison* (1990) and *Popular Magic* by Owen Davies (2003). For details of early British life, see *Pagan Britain* (Hutton), *Anglo-Saxon World* (Crossley-Holland), and *Britain Begins* (Cunliffe).

4. The Abbess Hilda of Whitby is famed for holding the Synod of Whitby in the year 664. An account of St Hildr (also Hild and Hildur) can be found in Janina Ramirez (*The Private Lives of Saints*, 2015). After Christianity had been introduced to Britain, both from the north via monks sailing to Ireland and Iona and from Rome to Canterbury, different traditions emerged. Hilda was able to obtain agreement by her political skills. She had grown up at Bamburgh castle on the Northumberland coast. The isle of Lindisfarne became a monastic centre and site for pilgrims. Many saints originated at Lindisfarne, including Cuthbert who went to live on the Farne Islands, and Cedd who sailed south to establish St Peter's Chapel on the Dengie promontory of Essex (at the mouth of the river where Viking invaders travelled to the Battle of Mældune/Maldon). The importance of medieval saints across Europe is explored and explained in Robert Bartlett's *Why Can the Dead Do Such Great Things?* At their height, there were at least 84 saints' days in the medieval calendar, on none of which should work be undertaken. It took to the twentieth century before the six-day week and then the five-day became common, before these non-work holidays were unravelled by new ways of working.

5. The museum at Lindisfarne contains comprehensive displays and objects to explain the rise, and later fall and rise again, of the monastery, priory and pilgrim isle. It is estimated that there were 650,000 visitors annually to the Holy Isle (before the pandemic of 2020–22).

6. There is a fragment of the Easby Cross in St Agatha's church by the riverside ruins of Easby Abbey near Richmond. There are also distinctive and beautiful wall paintings.

7. Grace Darling and her father rowed to the rescue of crew and passengers of the new steamship *Forfarshire* in 1838. She was 23 years of age, and four years later died of tuberculosis brought on by the stress of public and media attention after the daring rescue. Grace's grandfather was gardener at Bamburgh castle; she is buried nearby. The *Forfarshire* was an early iron ship, but used steam to drive paddles outside the hull. The design was ill-suited to the weather and waves of the North Sea. For accounts of life in lighthouses, see Nicholson's *Rock Lighthouses*. There have been many accounts of Grace Darling's life, including online; there is also a dedicated museum at Bamburgh. For more on the *Holy Island of Lindisfarne*, see Cartwright and Cartwright.

8. On Grimsby: it is said a longship captain called Grim established the town and later port of Grimsby his village, a *by*, on the marsh). Hugh Lupton (2013) says Oðinn was also known as Grimr, the marked one, the one-eyed god. Grim is the skipper of the *Wyrm* in the saga called 'Viking Quest'. In Norfolk, the famed 400 Neolithic round barrows and flint mines called Grime's Graves were probably given their current name by Anglo-Saxons. But, of course, maybe Oðinn and Grimr are much much older.

9. The apprentice system was used by Grimsby smack and ship owners from the 1870s to about 1914. It was a despicable piece of British history. It was modern slavery wrapped up as career opportunity. It is a bleak part of Grimsby's past. It helped the port to grow, and industrialists (who owned ship, shop, market, port, train and trainline) to become wealthy. A number of fishing ports in England's east had been developed with new harbours, docks, infrastructure and rail connections to provide links to the industrial heartlands. Yet many ship owners were short of labour. Through amendments to the Merchant Shipping Act of 1872, a slavery system was made legal, just decades after Wilberforce of Hull had led reform of international slavery. In the decade 1884–94, 2,000 men and boys were killed on smacks, and hundreds of boys were sent to Lincoln jail for trying to escape the life of fishing. The fleeting system had been developed by Samuel Hewett of Barking, later moving to Gorleston-Yarmouth. In this chapter, Alf goes on to help during the fishers' strike of 1901 in Grimsby, and then becomes a mate on trawlers of the 1920s and 1930s. He becomes the mate on the *Epine*. It was the First World War, called the Fourteen War by many rural people through the twentieth century, that broke the apprentice system.

10. The Grimsby Fishing Heritage Centre contains important displays on the deepwater fishing from Grimsby, and its apprentice system See also the oral histories by Nick Triplow and co-authors (*Distant Water* and *The Women They Left Behind*). Original stories in newspapers are archived at the Grimsby Public Library. For accounts of the lives and cultures of cod and herring, see *Cod* (Mark Kurlansky) and *Herring* (Mike Smylie). The actor Sir Tom Courtenay wrote an autobiography *Dear Tom* about growing up on Hessle Road in Hull. Also from the community, Jim Williams wrote about his life on ships (*Swinging the Lamp*), and provided personal notes before his death aged 90. *The Fishermen* (by Jeremy Tunstall) is a unique social account of deepwater fishing communities of the 1950s–1960s; *Rough Seas* by James Greene is a more recent account of the life of English fishermen at and off Iceland. Brian Lavery's *The Headscarf Revolutionaries* focuses on the stories of the four women who led the Hull women of Hessle Road in 1968.

11. At Grimsby, the *Ross Tiger* trawler is moored at the Fishing Heritage Centre. The *Arctic Corsair* is moored on the River Beverley in Hull: the ghost clumps and clomps aboard.

12. I am grateful to MPs Austin Mitchell and the Rt. Hon. Alan Johnson for meeting at their offices in the House of Commons in London, and to the mayor of Hull, Mary Glew, for hosting a visit to her quarters in the Town Hall.

13. When Edward the Confessor died in early 1066, Harold Godwineson seized the crown of England. But William (Guillaume) of Normandie was promised this very crown by Harold, his former friend. William was a direct descendant of Hrolf/Rollo the Walker, the Viking invaders of northern France. Rollo was given all of Normandie by the king, Charles the Simple, to prevent further sieges of Paris. William spoke French, but was a fourth generation Viking. To the north of Britain came Harald the Hard-Bargainer, the king of Norway, who also had a claim on England's crown. He was joined by Tostig, Harold's brother, who had been ejected as Earl of Northumberland for poor governance by Edward Confessor. *King Harald's Saga* was later written by Snorri Sturluson in Iceland, and contains an account of all his life leading to the defeat by Harold at Stamford Bridge. The details of court scalds appear in *Sagas of the Warrior Poets*. See also *Saga of the Volsungs* for the tale of Sigurd the dragon-slayer. It is said the Norman jester, the court storyteller called Taillefer, sang the famed Chanson de Roland to inspire William's army before the battle with Harold at Hastings (see Skeire, 2021).

SAGA VI: Grimsby Embark

1. This saga follows the first post on ship of a deckie learner, a teenage boy on deepwater trawler. Even in the 1950s and 1960s, boys as young as thirteen were employed as deckies in Iceland's waters. The *Epine* was a 350 ton slow sidewinder trawler, wrecked in 1948 on the black pebbled beach at Djúpalónssandur on the Snaefellness peninsula. The full report of the stranding is contained in the Report of Court (S409), led by Judge J V Naisby in September 1948. Accounts of the wreck are also contained in new reports of the *Grimsby Times* and *Evening Telegraph* in March and September 1948.

2. The mate on the *Epine* has an amulet hammer of Thor around his neck. Grimsby itself was named after Grimr, another name for Oðinn. Thor's hammer has long been a powerful symbol, and is inscribed on Bronze Age petroglyphs in Scandinavia.

3. The doctor of Flatey in this saga was trained in Copenhagen, and was the boy An the Black. The account of Freddie the deckie's first trip is drawn from F D Ommanney's sensitive account of a 1930s trawler trip in *North Cape*. Ommanney had earlier published an account of whaling in the South Atlantic. Triplow and colleagues also provide oral history on the fishing life based at Grimsby.

SAGA VII: Hull Cry

1. The saga 'Hull Cry' contains the story of the mothers, wives and daughters of Hull, led into civil protest in 1968 by Lillian Bilocca. It occurs at the time of the Triple Trawler Disaster off northern Iceland, and the rescue of the crew of Grimsby trawler *Notts County* by the gunboat *Oðinn*. One man is rescued from the *Ross Cleveland*, Harry Eddom the mate, the only crewman to survive from the three trawler losses. Two BBC documentaries centre on the women's movement, *Hull's Headscarf Heroes* (by Steve Humphries) and *The Last Testament of Lillian Bilocca* (by Maxine Peake). Óttar Sveinsson's book *Doom of the Deep* contains many accounts relating to the disaster and the *Notts County* rescue, particularly from the Icelandic rescuers' side.

CHAPTER 5: The Atlantic Isles

1. The Atlantic isles of Orkney and Shetland are nearer to Norway than to the Scottish capital, and were under Norse rule for longer than Scotland has been part of the UK. The Faroes never escaped Danish rule, and have today a form of home rule (as has Greenland). On all these isles, eight winds blow, and small boats are part of collective and family history. Fishing remains of vital significance.

2. Jim Hunter has been one of the foremost commentators, writers and leaders on re-peopling the Isles and Highlands of Scotland, following their clearances in the 1700s and 1800s. Landscapes that were commons became enclosed, and are now becoming commons once again. See Jim Hunter's *Land of the Free* for accounts of life on the isles of Scotland, the novel *Island of Sheep* (1936) by John Buchan, and island and coastal tales by poets George Mackay Brown (*Greenvoe*) and Alasdair Maclean (*Night Falls on Ardnamurchan*).

3. The Faroe Islands are twenty-two layer-cake mountain isles between Shetland and Iceland that long have relied on the sea and sheep for people's livelihoods. They are sometimes called the lands of maybe, as everything is driven by the weather and often harsh winds of the North Atlantic. The national bird of the Faroes is the oystercatcher, arriving from marshes to the south to signify the arrival of spring.

4. The *grindadráp* (or *grind* for short) is the name for the tradition of pilot whale corralling and harvest. It was called the *caa* in Shetland. It is a core part of Faroe pride and identity. It is also at the sharp end of international campaigning to end all forms of whaling, particularly by the Sea Shepherd organisation. Conservation organisations have played a key role in persuading national governments worldwide to cease commercial whaling. Some efforts to limit or prevent pilot whale hunts have met with dismay on the Faroes. Regardless of position, it is now the case that mercury pollutants have been concentrated in the flesh and blubber of whales, making them increasingly toxic to humans.

5. The last whalers of Shetland have published excellent books on their life in the South Atlantic in the 1950s and 1960s. The meet regularly in Lerwick. At the time, there was no other paid work for men, save for the merchant navy. A mini-series called *Britain's Whale Hunters* was made by the BBC (2014).

6. The Zetland County Council was enlightened in the 1960s to focus on building domestic pride and culture, and this allowed then to obtain tax returns from oil companies from 1974. Like Norway, they have invested these in common benefits. The Shetland Charitable Trust has assets of over £250 million, and distributes these to local groups. The most famed collective fund created with oil income is the Norwegain government's Pension Fund Global, established in 1976, and now used to fund public assets and commons in Norway. The UK government in the 1980s decided to spend its North Sea oil income on reducing taxes and cutting current account deficits. Guy Standing in *Plunder of the Commons* (2019) was blunt, and called this 'the worst economic mistake ever made by a British government.' Similar funds to Norway and Shetland have been established by the states of Wyoming (to eliminate income tax in the state) and Texas

(which distributes US$800 million each year to public schools). The Alaskan oil fund, the Alaska Permanent Fund, was set up by Republican governor, Jay Hammond, in 1976, and is used to provide a universal and unconditional annual payment of about US$3,000 to every Alaskan. This has become similar to the discussions in many countries about how a Universal Basic Income (UBI) could be deployed to reduce inequality and increase social justice. See also Rutger Bregman's *Human Kind* (2020), and Paul Mason's *Post-Capitalism* (2015). Paul Mason observes: 'It's tough being rich.' If the richest 1% gave up some income, they would become slightly poorer yet happier: 'The 99% are coming to the rescue.'

7. The Faroe chain dancers are accompanied by Kvæði ballads, led by skipari scalds who know all the versions and can sing all night. There are many forms of circle dance across Europe: chain, step, processional and promenade. The term (Christmas) carol was both song and circle dance. These were banned by the Church between 600 and 1500 CE: inside churches, in their grounds and in church neighbourhoods (see Lindahl et al, *Medieval Folklore*, 2002). In this way, dance always had a political and social content and edge.

SAGA VIII: Gift of Light

1. This saga is set in the South Atlantic, where whaling stations were established on South Georgia. Many of the crew came from the Shetland Isles, where there long was a tradition of working whaling ships and merchant naval vessels. The Last Whalers have written their accounts of the life in permanent sunlight, spending the northern latitude winter in the Antarctic, and the northern summer back home. Their accounts and photographs are in *Shetland's Whalers Remembered* (Gibbie Fraser) and *Shetland's Whaling Tradition: From Willafjord to Enderby Land* (Laureen Johnson). Fine accounts of whaling in the South Atlantic were written by F D Ommanney (*South Latitude*) and by R B Robertson (*Of Whales and Men*). Ahab, of course, was the obsessive captain of the fictional *Pequod* in Herman Melville's *Moby Dick*.

2. A gift increases in value as it moves from person to person. It has mysterious social power: see Lewis Hyde's *The Gift* (1979). It can also, occasionally, deceive: think of the Trojan Horse and the poisoned apple given to Snow White.

CHAPTER 6: Iceland Ice and Fire

1. Stories are the currency of stable economies and societies. When told, they expand. You do not use up a story when you read or hear it. The Iceland sagas emerged from a period of stability after settlement, and have become world-renowned literature. This chapter begins with accounts of the importance of stories to indigenous peoples. They make people wise, they help them care for the land, they help them look after the land. The locations for the sagas of Iceland can be found and recognised today. Three important accounts help: Sabine Baring-Gould of 1862; W G Collingwood and Jón Stafánsson in 1897 (*Pilgrimage of the Saga-Steads*), and Richard Fidler and Kári Gíslason in 2017 (*Saga Land*). See also Jon Krakauer and David Roberts' *Iceland: Land of the Sagas* (1990). 'We might develop a new intimacy with the land,' wrote Thomas Berry in *The Great Work* (1999). This is our sacred story, and only intimacy can save us.

2. Andri Snær Magnason has written beautifully of glaciers and stories in *On Time and Water*. He wrote the elegy to the first lost glacier, the Okjökul, the Ok glacier (which cannot, as he says, any longer be described as OK). The loss of a wide variety of commons during recent centuries of modern and industrial development is discussed in detail by Guy Standing in his clear and comprehensive *Plunder of the Commons* (2019), which covers the enclosures of land, sea, knowledge, urban, health system and water commons. See also Paul Mason's *Post-Capitalism* (2015). For more on collective models of social and economic engagement, see Henry Timms and Jeremy Heiman's book *#newpower* (2018), and Rutger Bregman's *Human Kind* (2020).

3. On how prosocial we humans really are, see Rutger Bregman's superb *Human Kind* (2021). The assumption that civilisation is about to crack and collapse (the veneer theory) is persistent and wrong. Everywhere we look, we find most people are not selfish. We help one another, even in the most disastrous of circumstances. What we often see is what Rebecca Solnit called 'elite panic': they see humanity in their own image, and can't believe other people will not also act selfishly. Rutger Bregman says, 'For most of our lives, we humans didn't collect things but relationships.'

4. Níels Einarsson is Director of the Stefansson Arctic Institute in Akureyri, and has written about the phenomenon of *paper fish*: how Iceland turned inwards once the cod wars were won. The privatisation of the commons into tradeable quotas allowed a few businesses to expand rapidly, and caused most small fishers to cease. Paper fish quotas contributed to the financial crash of 2007–08. Robert Wade's essay *Iceland as Icarus* is critical of the enclosing of the commons.

5. *Njál's Saga* is one of the most famed family sagas of Iceland, containing the stories of Gunnar and Njál, their families and communities. It is also called the *Saga of Burnt Njál*, as he and wife and grandson were burned to death at the farm of Bergthórshvoll. Richard Fidler and Kári Gíslason visited Hlíðarendi, Gunnar's farm, and noted the white church had been badly scorched by ash from the eruption of Eyjafjallajökull in 2010. Fire came to Njál's house, just as heat is coming to the world today.

6. Many of the major characters of Icelandic sagas were poets themselves. Famed authors include Snorri Sturluson, Egil Skallagrimson, Bragi Boðdasson, Þódólfor, Eilífr Godrúnarson, Ulfr Uggason. The skaldic poetry of Snorri Sturluson includes *Heimskringla* (*The Orb of the World*), *The Prose Edda*, and *King Harald's Saga*. He in turn drew upon the written work by Ari Thorgilson the Learned and Eirik Oddson. The scalds Kormak, Hallfred and Gunnlaug, authors of the *The Sagas of the Warrior Poets*, were known as great creators as well as difficult and awkward characters. Some tales are known for their appearance in unique and illustrated manuscripts: the fourteenth century manuscript of the Flateyjarbók found on the isle of Flatey in western Iceland, and the Gospels of Lindisfarne.

7. The beach where the *Epine* wreck lies is now a formal sacred site, with rusting parts of the ship left where the waves take them. The three testing stones are at the head of beach, and on the promontory is the labyrinth (*völundarhús*) laid out in lava rock. Local legend has it that the elves created the labyrinth. Just beyond are the meadows rising to the cone of volcano of Snaefell, the location for Jules Verne's fictional tale, *Journey to the Centre of the Earth*. As we see with the wreck of the *Epine*, the links between Iceland and Britain had always been strong. It was the crossing that brought cultures together, as the quote from fisherman Keith Mayall told in Chapter 3. It was the political interests that pulled people apart across the North Sea and North Atlantic.

8. There are many accounts of the three cod wars between Britain and Iceland, beginning in the late 1950s, and ending in 1975. An excellent display is at the Westfjords History Museum in Ísafjördur. When oil was discovered in the North Sea, Britain's position on the 200-mile limits for fish rapidly changed, as these limits included mineral rights. As oil burned up the world, so eventually wind power came to the North Sea. Now many wind turbines are tethered to the shallowest sandbanks of Doggerland, and there are plans for floating islands over deeper water.

SAGA IX: Drowning of Doggerland

1. Prior to Bryony Coles coining the term *Doggerland* in 1998, few people appreciated that large parts of the current North Sea (formerly also the German Ocean) once were dry. The melting ice sheet following the last Ice Age raised sea levels, and slowly drowned the steppe and prairie home to Neolithic people and huge numbers of animals and birds. A large archaeological survey is currently underway in the

North Sea, led by Vince Gaffney and colleagues at the University of Bradford. Julia Blackburn has written about searching for Doggerland on both sides of the modern North Sea (*Time Song*).

2. It is likely that the hunter-gatherers of Doggerland showed many cultural similarities to contemporary hunter-gatherer and nomadic cultures, such as in North America [see *Braiding Sweetgrass* (Robin Wall Kimmerer), *Black Elk* (Joe Jackson), *Wisdom Sits in Places* (Keith Basso), *I Dreamed the Animals* (Georg Henriksen)]; in Africa [*The !Kung San* (Robert Lee)]; and in central Asia [see *Where Rivers and Mountains Sing* (Sevyan Levin), *Nomads of South Siberia (Sevyan* Vainshtein), *The Shaman's Coat* (Anna Reid), the chapters on Tyva, Innu and Shoshone in *The Edge of Extinction* (Jules Pretty)]. See Vicki Cummings and colleagues (2014) for a comprehensive archaeological and anthropological summary of worldwide hunter-gatherer communities and cultures.

3. Not long after Doggerland was drowned saw the emergence of the first cities in Mesopotamia, and the first written saga about Gilgamesh. Enlil the god was irritated by the noise and dust of civilisation, and brought a flood. This and later flood narratives, including in the Bible, assume the flood is caused by persistent rainfall. Yet it is conceivable that traders took back to lands between the great rivers stories about the flooding of Doggerland, and its painful loss. Sky-Ryder was one-eyed, as was Oðinn the god. The people of Doggerland lost dry land to sea; it was not long after they came to the uplands of chalk that stone circles, barrows, cursus monuments and other celebrations of solid soil emerged.

4. The oldest recorded written saga is the *Epic of Gilgamesh* of Mesopotamia, its Akkadian manuscripts depicted life some 5000 years ago on smooth tablets of clay. The Greek and Roman epic poems were composed by Homer, Virgil and Apollonius of Rhodes (*The Iliad, The Odyssey, The Aeneid, Jason and the Argonauts*), the conclusions already known to audiences as they settled down to each performance. Modern authors and songwriters have continued these traditions: Julia Blackburn's *Time Song* and Robin Robertson's *The Long Take*; others being fine reworkings of original tales: Madeline Miller's *Circe* and hip-hop artist Akala's song 'Odyssey'. Some have corrected biases in the majority of original material, where the heroes were mostly men, the women mainly bystanders.

CODA 7: Before Ragnarök

1. The Coda to *Sea Sagas* returns to Merlin's prophecies. The account of Ragnarök, the Viking/ Norse end of the world, is contained in the *Poetic Edda* and Kevin Crossley-Holland's *The Penguin Book of Norse Myths*. As we have seen with the drowning of Doggerland, it is intriguing to reflect on the regular appearance of flood and heat/fire narratives in past cultures. Only in contemporary times have these changes been human-induced. Said the poet, Gary Snyder (in *He who Hunted Birds*, 1979): 'a curse on this monocultural industrial civilisation.'

2. Well, maybe there's another way to a good life that protects and improves social togetherness, nature and the planet. A way that emphasises happiness over consumption and the pursuit of things, a way that emphasises contact with nature, healthy food, activity, togetherness, creative pursuits and a spiritual and/ or ethical framework of coherence. See my 2023 book, *The Low-Carbon Good Life*.

THE ILLUSTRATIONS

The chapter illustrations are all photographs. The saga images are monochrome photographs with backgrounds digitally removed. These images are intended to echo the simple designs of ink calligraphy on white paper. Locations are listed below. A total of 58 of the 64 original photographs were taken by the author, with exceptions noted below.

Front Cover
This is one of the Skuldelev longships at Roskilde ship museum, Sjælland, Denmark.

Dedication Page
Lindisfarne castle and harbour, UK.

Preface
Barge in Stour estuary, Suffolk and Essex border, UK.
Dragon wall painting, Wiston church, Nayland, Suffolk, UK.

Chapter 1: The Westfjords of Iceland
Krafla lava landscape, Iceland.

Saga I: Crossings
Skuldelev ship, Roskilde ship museum, Sjaelland, Denmark.
Sixæreen, Bolungarvik, Iceland.
Sea eagle ceiling painting, Flatey church, Iceland (painted by Baltasar Samper).
Laufskálavarða cairns, Iceland.
Pink-footed geese, Essex marshes.

Saga II: Settlement
Turf-roofed fishing settlement, Bolungavik, Iceland.
Clogs, Castelnaud-la-Chapelle, France.
Herring ship, Patreksfjord (original photo at Fosshotel).
Whimbrel, Hallgrímskirkja Saurbæ, Hvalfjördur, Iceland.

Chapter 2: The Sjælland Gate and Lofoten Isles
Roskilde ship museum, Sjælland, Denmark.

Saga III: Viking Quest
Roskilde ship museum, Sjælland, Denmark.
Lofoten islands, Norway.
Mallet, Nottage museum, Wivenhoe UK.
Sea Stallion longship (replica of *Skuldelev 2* (original photo Werner Karrasch).
Tafl board, Lofotr Viking museum at Borg, Lofoten Islands, Norway.
Roskilde ship museum, Sjælland, Denmark.

Chapter 3: The Eastern Shore
Pakefield Man, First Light Festival 2019, Lowestoft, Suffolk

Saga IV: Herring for the Grit City
Faithful Friend (LT33), Lowestoft, Suffolk (permission for publication granted by Stanley Earl, Chairman of the Port of Lowestoft Research Society).
Barge, Suffolk.
Hesteyri village, Hornstrandir, Iceland.
Horse, Essex.
Barge, Orwell River, Suffolk.

Saga V: Barge Requiem
Barge, Suffolk.
Barge wreck, Colne estuary, Essex.
Wooden flour container, Suffolk.
Barge, Suffolk.

Chapter 4: The North Lands
Lindisfarne harbour and castle, UK.

Saga VI: Grimsby Embark
Home photo display, Grimsby Fishing Heritage Centre, Grimsby, UK.
Steam trawler *Epine* (from display at Djúpalónssandur, Iceland).
Ross Tiger trawler, Grimsby Fishing Heritage Centre, UK.
House, Flatey island, Iceland.
Remains of *Epine* wreck on Djúpalónssandurr beach, Iceland.

Saga VII: Hull Cry
Arctic Corsair, St Andrews Dock Heritage museum, Hull, UK.
Radio operator's desk on board *Ross Tiger*, Grimsby Fishing Heritage Centre, Grimsby.
Salary teller, Grimsby Fishing Heritage Centre, Grimsby.
Porthole, *Arctic Corsair* trawler, Hull.
Dart board, Grimsby Fishing Heritage Centre, Grimsby.
Rauðisandur church, Westfjords.

Chapter 5: The Atlantic Isles
Kirkja village, Fugloy, Faroe Islands.

Saga VIII: Gift of Light

Fin whale, Husavik, Iceland.
Barge, Suffolk, UK.
Ship, Isafjord, Iceland.
Arctic terns, Iceland.

Chapter 6: Iceland Ice and Fire

Dyrfjäll Mountains, north-east Iceland.

Saga IX: Drowning of Doggerland

Maplin Sands off Foulness Island (North Sea), Essex, UK.
Head of goddess on silver bowl from Gundestrup, Denmark (Nationalmuseet, Copenhagen; original photo from H R Ellis Davidson, *Scandinavian Mythology*, 1969). Used here to represent Queen Erce.
Rocks offshore at Vík, Iceland.
Shaman dancing woman petroglyph, Pilbara/Dampier peninsula, Western Australia.
Fulmar, Iceland.
Dancers and reindeer, Bronze Age stone carvings at Bohulsän, Sweden (original photo from H R Ellis David-son, *Scandinavian Mythology*, 1969).
Reindeer cave painting, Pla de Petracos, Valenciana, Spain.
Deer and eagle (original photo from HR Ellis-Davison, *Scandinavian Mythology*, 1969).

Coda 7: Before Ragnarök

Vík beach, South Iceland.

The Illustrations

Hesteyri village, Hornstrandir, Iceland.

Acknowledgements

Southend Beach, Essex, UK.

Walk with the Author

Image from embroidered tapestry, Lofotr Viking museum at Borg, Lofoten Islands, Norway.

ACKNOWLEDGEMENTS

In the course of writing these *Sea Sagas of the North*, I visited some 150 ports, coastal settlements and islands facing and edging the North Sea and North Atlantic: in Denmark, England, the Faroe Isles, Iceland, Norway and Scotland. I travelled on Viking longship, oyster smack and spritsail barge, lifeboat and post boat, iron ferry and wooden ferry, trawler and whaler, rowed and motored painter; and visited trawler and ship museum, whaling station, shipyard and dock. I am very grateful to record office librarians of Lowestoft, Fleetwood, Grimsby and Hull.

Many people also offered advice, stories, and their oral histories of life at the edge of land and on the sea:

Jutta Austin, Helen Band, Richard Barnard, Debbie Beckett, Joyce Benton, Julia Blackburn, Catherine Bramwell, Fabian Bush, David Butcher, Emily Crawford, Barrie Deas, Jerry DeHay, Colin Dixon, Níels Einarsson, Lawrence Elkins, Gibbie Fraser and Laurena Fraser, Vince Gaffney, Mary Glew, Jenny Harpur, Mary Hepburn, Tommy Hepburn, Mike Holroyd, Jim Hunter, Andrew Impey, Rt. Hon. Alan Johnson MP, Elizabeth Kitching, John Lane, Sheree Mack, Andri Snær Magnason, Keith Mayall, Derek McDonald, Austin Mitchell MP, Mike Mitchell, Tero and Kaisu Mustonen, Janey Mykura, Astrid Ogilvie, Karen Park, Steve Peak, Charles Pinder, Chris Pretty, Óttar Sveinsson, Emma Toulson, James Towe, Anita Waddy and Charlie Waddy, Syd Wakwerit, Frank Walker, Meik Wiking, Jim Williams, and Deborah Winter.

For wise and helpful comments on the chapters and sagas themselves, I am grateful to Glenn Albrecht, Peggy Barlett, Richard Bawden, Julia Blackburn, Fabian Bush, David Butcher, Liz Calder, Douglas Christie, Genevieve Christie, John Christie, Bryony Coles, Ruth Creasy, Uwe Derksen, Tom Dobbs, Paul Ellis, Gibbie and Laurena Fraser, Patricia Gillies, Liz Gladin Robert Golden, Ros Green, Jenny Harpur, Tommy Hepburn, Liz Kuti, Jonathan Lichtenstein, Rachel Lichtenstein, Simon Lyster, Richard Mabey, Bill McKibben, Leo Mellor, Mike Mitchell, Tero Mustonen, David Orr, Tanya Steele, Roma Tearne, Geoff Wells, Vic Wheeldon, Meik Wiking, Ken Worpole and Ron Wilkinson. The wisest advice came from Martin Large of Hawthorn Press, who knows what makes a good story.

I'd like to thank Ingunn Snædal and Kristín Svava Tómasdóttir for permission to include excerpts from their poems, 'Icelandic Landscape' and 'Austurvöllur on the Day of the Wake', and Jen Hadfield of Shetland for permission to quote a part of her poem, 'Drimmie'.

Thank you, too, to Chris Pretty for drawing the maps.

Many other astute observations on related or earlier work have been made on social media platforms and at readings or talks: to you all, again, much thanks.

I would like to thank Li Hongwen, Bin Wu and Yuelai Lu for their detective work in helping to translate the calligraphy seal used on the cover of this book.

WALK WITH THE AUTHOR

There are many tales of travel and crossings in the chapters and sagas of *Sea Sagas of the North*. If you would like to walk with the author, then suggested routes and locations are set out here.

Iceland: Chapter 1 and Sagas I and II

The content of Chapter 1 takes place mainly in the Westfjords of north-west Iceland, with the launch and return point the peninsula of Snæfellsnaes. The isle of Flatey lies on the ferry route north of Stykkishólmur. You can leave a car on the ferry and hop off at Flatey, and spend the day walking around the flat isle, visiting Iceland's first public library (tiny and wooden) and the church with beautiful ceiling painted by Baltasar Samper. It is a textured scene of sea eagle and sheep, raven, fish and seal, and Christ preaching in a knitted sweater.

The chapter follows a route through the Westfjords from south to north, via Patreksfjörður and diverts to the great bird cliffs of Látrabjarg. You can walk along the cliff tops, amongst puffins in summer, and look down a half kilometre to the wreck site of the *Dhoon*. In the vale of Hnjótur is one of Iceland's many fine and local museums, with relics from the *Sargon* rescue. From the beach and mountain road, the wreck of the *Sargon* is visible.

Gisli's Saga is set in the Westfjords, and you can walk around the vale where he lived west of Thingeyri, and visit the rocks where he died near the Dynjandi waterfalls. Each fjord has distinctive history, and has faced disasters of ship losses and avalanches. The town of Ísafjördur is a centre for fishing, and features in many historic events, including the 1968 triple trawler disaster (of Hull). You can take a boat from Ísafjördur and spend a day walking over the hills and vales of north-west Hornstrandir, a rich and wild landscape with neither settled people nor livestock. You are very close to the Arctic Circle on Hornstrandir.

The whale-watching trips can be taken from Olafsvik on Snæfellsnaes, also from Húsavik east of Akureyri. There are locations of sagas what can be visited on the peninsula. The site of the Grimsby trawler wreck is at Djúpalónssandur beach of black basalt pearls, looking west toward Greenland.

The saga *Crossing* plays out on the mainland and then on Flatey, and concludes at the Althing at Thingvellir. The saga *Settlement* takes place in the north of Iceland on a farm in riding distance of Akureyri, and then at the fishing port itself. You can walk around the many trails in the forest of Akureyri.

Denmark and Norway: Chapter 2 and Saga III

The content of Chapter 2 takes place on the Danish Isle of Sjælland (Zealand) and on the Norwegian isles of Lofoten north of the Arctic Circle. On Sjælland, you can take a regional train from Copenhagen north to Helsingør (Elsinore in the play Hamlet), and begin a journey along the north coast of the isle from Hamlet's castle of Kronberg. This is popularly called the Danish Riviera, and there are walks and cycle routes the sixty kilometres via Hornbaek, Gilleleje and Tisvilde to Hundestad. There are castles and monasteries inland, and the great forest of Gribskov contains many trails. A different train line will take you to Roskilde and its ship museum at the southern tip of the fjord. The cover photograph for *Sea Sagas of the North* is of one of the Skuldelev ships in the museum. The site of the main events in the epic poem *Beowulf* occur at Lejre 5 km from Roskilde. The beaching of Beowulf's longship could have occurred on the north coast of Sjælland or in Roskilde fjord.

The saga *Viking Quest* is set on the Lofoten isles, with the heroes travelling across the North Sea to Lindisfarne (see Chapter 4). Grim and Bolvik are imagined travelling from Lofoten to Roskilde to learn about the new technology of clinker-built longships that will allow them to travel, safely they hope, across the North Sea to the awaiting riches of England, Ireland and Scotland.

On Lofoten, you can drive from Narvik airport and visit Andenes for whale-watching, travel on various ferries, stay in the Rorbuer painted fisher-huts at Svolvær, where you can also visit the dramatic exhibition of Gunnar Berg's paintings of sea life, and then travel to the far west of the isles to Á. The magnificent longhouse museum is at Borg. The Norwegian isles and coast feature strongly in the history of Shetland, including the Shetland Bus of secret trawler travel during the Second World War, bring supplies to Norway and taking refugees out.

Eastern Shore of England: Chapter 3, Sagas IV and V, Saga IX

The content of Chapter 3 takes place in north Kent, and then the counties of Essex, Suffolk and Norfolk. Saga IV is set at the site of the Grit village (beach fish village) at Lowestoft, and begins with Ted and Waxy Jack on the cliffs overlooking the deserted denes and North Beach. Saga V features the barges of the North Sea trade roads, and begins in the creeks of Oare and Faversham marshes and then in the sea village of Whitstable. The last barge trip ranges from Poole to the Humber River. There are sea roads that link the fishing ports of the east to the deepwater ports of Grimsby and Hull, and then north to Shetland and then to the Faroes and Iceland.

In the east, you can walk the north coast of Kent, and the marsh and river walls at Oare. Many old barges lie rotting in the mud. It was on this coast that the Viking raiders first over-wintered. It is possible to walk the whole of the Broomway on the Maplin Sands in the Thames estuary, from Wakering Stairs to Foulness isle. It is advisable to be accompanied or guided by local people on this 'most dangerous road in Britain.' Many are stranded by the tide, a familiar concern for pilgrims walking the flats to the Holy Isle of Lindisfarne hundreds of miles to the north. I walked the whole of the coast of East Anglia for my book, *This Luminous Coast*, and you will find maps and routes for the coast set out there.

For inland long-distance and pilgrim routes, you can seek out St Peter's Way, the Stour Valley Path, and Peddars' Way.

St Peter's Way in south Essex begins at the oldest wooden church in the world (so it is said) of St Andrews at Greenstead, and ends at St Peter's Chapel-On-The-Wall, built in 662CE by St Cedd from Lindisfarne, and then seen three hundred years later by Olaf and his raider fleet on route to the Battle of Mældune (Maldon). St Peter's Way passes Hanningfield Reservoir, now location for the first ravens in the east, and on the Dengie past the 1000 year old Mundon oaks.

The Stour Valley Path on the border of Essex and Suffolk forms part of the 80 mile St Edmund Way. It is where you can see dragons in the churches of Wiston and Wormingford, where you can visit the dragon's mere, and then see the dragon on the hills above Bures by the stone chapel where Edmund was crowned king of East Anglia on Christmas Day in 855CE. See my book, *The East Country*, for more on this territory.

The site of the beach village of Lowestoft can be walked from the museum beneath the lighthouse. The score alleys still wind ways from cliff top to sandy denes below.

Peddars Way is an important 70km pilgrim route that begins in Suffolk and follows a Roman road north to the coast at Holme-next-the-Sea. This is where the Woodhenge remains were found. The Fens are much reduced from the original vast wetlands. At their western edge, you can visit and walk the village of Crowland, called Croyland in the time of Saint Guthlac, and there are unique gold-leafed green men in the rafters of the Abbey. There were four other saints of Crowland: St Thurketyl, St Bettelin, St Cissa and St Etheldritha. The Trinity Bridge has three stairways meeting in the middle, but the river has long gone. For an insight into Neolithic and Bronze Age history, after the time of the Drowning of Doggerland, walk the Flag Fen archaeological site, causeway and surrounds.

The North Lands: Chapter 4 and Sagas VI and VII

The content of Chapter 4 and the two sagas takes place in the ports of Grimsby and Hull, in he Dales of North Yorkshire, and on the coast of Northumberland at Lindisfarne and the Farne Islands. At Hull, the fish docks have been filled with rubble, but you can visit the *Arctic Corsair* trawler and museum. Similarly, at Grimsby, the fish port is largely abandoned, with some surviving fish businesses and factories. The Fishing Heritage Centre contains fine historical displays and the opportunity to visit the *Ross Tiger* trawler.

There are many walking routes across north England, including the coast-to-coast pilgrimage route 300 km from Great Bees east to Whitby. There are important Abbeys on walks, including Whitby on the coast, and inland at Easby, Marrick and Jervaulx. The neighbouring church to Easby Abbey, St Agatha's, contains distinctive wall-paintings and was location of the famed Anglo-Saxon Easby Cross. Some of the rood screen remains from Jervaulx at in St Andrews Church by the walls of Aysgarth. The River Ure runs east then south eventually to join the Ouse, which flows through York (Jorvik), near the battle site of Stamford Bridge, and then to the Humber.

There are important walking and pilgrim routes to the Holy Isle of Lindisfarne, the location where Grim and his longship arrived in 792 CE. Try St Cuthbert's Way, 60 miles from Melrose and Jedburgh, east via Holburn to Lindisfarne. On route is St Cuthbert's cave in the Kyloe Hills, where monks carrying his coffin hid. The 100 mile St Oswald's Way begins at Heavensfield west of Newcastle and travels north to the coast at Warhurst, and then to Lindisfarne. St Hilda's Way is 40 miles from Hartlepool to Whitby, along the coast. It is possible to walk at low tide to and from the isle of Lindisfarne, but every year some cars are stranded on the causeway by the rising tide. A walking route takes you around the isle, from village to Abbey, to harbour and castle, and the square walled garden by Gertrude Jekyll, and north around the tall dunes and wet slacks. There are walks along the coast that take in the castles of Bamburgh and Dunstanburgh, and sea tips to the Farne Isles from Seahouses. On the Farnes is the chapel marking the site of St Cuthbert's well and hut. On the outer Farnesis the Longstone Lighthouse where lived the Darling lighthouse keeper family.

The Atlantic Isles: Chapter 5 and Saga VII

The content of Chapter 5 centres on the isles of Shetland, Skye and St Kilda to the west, and the Faroes on route to complete the clockwise circle of the book to Iceland. The story of the saga *Gift of Light* takes place mainly in the South Atlantic and the isle and ports of South Georgia. The whale hunters were recruited from villages all across Shetland, and the last hunters still meet regularly. There are old whaling stations at Olna Firth, Collafirth and Ronas Voe in the north and west of Shetland. The Iron Age and later Norse village at Jarlshof is near Sumburgh Head and airfield, an excellent location for bird viewing. St Ninian's isle is across a unique sand tombolo on the west coast north of Scousburgh. At the town of Lerwick is a very fine museum on the port side

St Kilda lies one hundred leagues west of the Scotland mainland, beyond the Western Isles of Harris and Lewis. The boat trip takes four hours each way, and you can walk freely on the isle of Hirta. It is also possible to stay for several days, but you do need to bring your own tent and all food supplies.

The Faroe isles offer many opportunities for walkers, along sounds (fjords), over mountains, through fishing villages and settlements. You can take a variety of sea journeys, including the post boat from Hvannasund (east by road and tunnel from Klaksvik), and then travel out to Fugloy and Svinoy. Many of the isles are now linked by new seabed tunnels. There are many walks along dramatic coasts, such as from Eiði church along the North West coast to Gjogv. The farmhouse museum at Saksun is located at the start of a fine walk to a black sand beach via the lake of Pollurin.

Iceland: Chapter 6

The content of Chapter 6 takes place in the south and east of Iceland. The famed *Njál's Saga* (*Saga of Burnt Njál*) is located across the west of Iceland, and then centres on his family farm at Bergthorshvol in sight of sea. You can visit the locations in this saga, the moors, paths and waterways, and little has changed in one thousand years. You can drive the coastal ring road No. 1 around the south of Iceland, and stop or stay at Vik with its famed back sand beach and silver sea. Further east lies Kirkjubærjarklaustur, where the fire mass was preached, and then across the vast landscape of glacial washes stop at the Skaftfell glacier. There are many walks in the national park, and you will sense the effect of the glaciers on the local weather and ecology.

Some of this chapter is set in and around Borgafjördur Eystri and the deserted villages and rugged mountains of the hinterland. You can divert off the No 1 road to Sænautavatn to visit an original wooden and turf-roofed farm (the model for Magnus and An abode in the saga 'Settlement'), and continue via the Krafla fire landscape, the deafening falls at Dettifoss, Mývatn lake and it million midges, and then onward to the town of Akureyri.

BIBLIOGRAPHY

Sagas and Epic Poems

Addis S and Lombardo S (trans.). 1993. *Lao-Tzu: Tao Te-Ching*. Hackett, Indianapolis/Cambridge

Aesop (trans. Temple O and Temple R). 1998. *The Complete Fables*. Penguin Classics, London

Apollonius of Rhodes (trans. Poochigan A). 2014. *Jason and the Argonauts*. Penguin Classics, London

Barraclough E R. 2016. *Beyond the Northlands*. Oxford University Press, Oxford

Bashō M. (trans. Yuasa N). 1968. *The Narrow Road to the Deep North and Other Travel Sketches*. Penguin, London

Bashō M. (trans. Reichhold J). 2008. *Bashō. The Complete Haiku*. Kodansha International, Tokyo

Basso K. 1996. *Wisdom Sits in Places*. University of New Mexico Press, Albuquerque

Blamires H. 1969. *Word Unheard: A Guide through Eliot's Four Quartets*. Methuen, London

Book of Chuang Tzu (trans. Palmer M). 1996 [2006]. Penguin Classics, London

Bringhurst R. 1999 [2011]. *A Story as Sharp as a Knife: The Classical Haida Mythtellers and their World*. Douglas & McIntyre, Madeira Park

Calvino I. 1980 [2002]. *Italian Folktales*. Penguin, London

Campbell J. 1949 [2008]. *The Hero with a Thousand Faces*. New World Library, Novato, CA

Campbell J. 2003. *Myths of Light*. New World Library, Novato

Campbell J. 2004. *Pathways to Bliss*. New World Library, Novato

Clunies Ross M. 2010. *The Old Norse-Icelandic Saga*. Cambridge University Press, Cambridge

Crossley-Holland K. 1980. *The Penguin Book of Norse Myths*. Penguin, London

Crossley-Holland K. 1999. *The Anglo-Saxon World: An Anthology*. Oxford World's Classics. Oxford University Press, Oxford

Elder Edda (trans. Orchard A). 2011. Penguin, London

Dalley S. (trans.), 1989. *Myths of Mesopotamia: Creation, The Flood, Gilgamesh and Others*. Oxford World's Classics. Oxford

Ellis Davidson H R. 1964. *Gods and Myths of Northern Europe*. Penguin, London

Epic of Gilgamesh (trans. George A). 1998. Penguin Classics, London

Erdoes R and Ortiz A. 1984. *American Indian Myths and Legends*. Pantheon Books, New York

Erdoes R and Ortiz A. 1998. *American Indian Trickster Tales*. Penguin, London

Fidler R and Gíslason K. 2017. *Saga Land*. ABC Books, Sydney

First Poems in English (trans. Alexander M). 1966 [2008]. Penguin Classics, London

Fischer N. 2008. *Sailing Home*. North Atlantic Books, Berkeley, CA

Gaiman N. 2017. *Norse Mythology*. Bloomsbury, London

Geoffrey of Monmouth (trans. Thorpe L). 1966. *The History of the Kings of Britain*. Penguin Classics, London

Gilligan S and Dilts R. 2009. *The Hero's Journey*. Crown House Publishing, Carmarthen

Gisli Sursson's Saga (trans. Regal M S). 1997. Penguin Classics, London

Heaney S. 1999. *Beowulf*. Faber and Faber, London

Heaney S. 2002. *Finders Keepers*. Faber and Faber, London

Homer (trans. Rieu E V). 1950. *The Iliad*. Penguin Classics, London

Homer (trans. Rieu E V and Rieu D C H). 1946 [2003]. *The Odyssey*. Penguin Classics, London

Hyde L. 1998. *Trickster Makes This World*. Canongate Books, Edinburgh

Hynes W J and Doty W G. 1993. *Mythical Trickster Figures*. University of Alabama Press, Tuscaloosa

Ibn Fadlān (trans. Lunde P and Stone C). 2016. *Ibn Fadlān and the Land of Darkness*. Penguin Classics, London

Ingram J (trans.). 1823 [2009]. *The Anglo-Saxon Chronicle*. Red and Black, St. Petersburg, FL

John Fire Lame Deer and Erdoes R. 1972. *Lame Deer: Sioux Medicine Man*. Davis-Poynter, London

Krakauer J and Roberts D. 1990. *Iceland: Land of the Sagas*. Villard, New York

Lindahl C, McNamara J and Lindow J. 2002. *Medieval Folklore*. Oxford University Press, Oxford

Luo Guanzhong (trans. Palmer M). 2018. *The Romance of the Three Kingdoms*. Penguin Classics, London

Mahābhārata (trans. Smith J D). 2009. Penguin Classics, London

McCarthy C. 2009. *Out of the Marvellous*. RTÉ Television, Dublin

Miller M. 2018. *Circe*. Bloomsbury, London

Njál's Saga (trans. Cook R). 1997. Penguin Classics, London

North R, Allard J and Gillies P. 2011. *Longman Anthology of Old English, Old Icelandic and Anglo-Norman Literature*. Longman, London

O'Driscoll D. 2009. *Stepping Stones: Interviews with Seamus Heaney*. Faber and Faber, London

Orkneyinga Saga (trans. Palsson H and Edwards P). 1978. Penguin Classics, London

Plotkin B. 2003. *Soulcraft*. New World Library, Novato, CA

Robertson R. 2018. *The Long Take*. Picador, London

Ross M C. 2010. *The Cambridge Introduction to the Old Norse-Icelandic Saga*. Cambridge University Press, Cambridge

Rumi (trans. Banks L). 1995. *Selected Poems*. Penguin Classics, London

Saga of King Hrolf Kraki (trans. Byock J L). 1998. Penguin Classics, London

Saga of the Volsungs (trans. Byock J). 1990. Penguin Classics, London

Sagas of the Warrior Poets (trans. Eiriksson L). 1997 [2002]. Penguin Classics, London

Sawyer R. 1942 [1962]. *The Way of the Storyteller*. Bodley Head, London

Smiley J. 2000. *The Sagas of the Icelanders*. Penguin Classics, London

Smith M. 2018. *Sir Gawain and the Green Knight*. Unbound, London

Snyder G. 1979 [2007]. *He Who Hunted Birds in his Father's Village: The Dimensions of a Haida Myth*. Counterpoint, Berkeley, CA

Stone B. 1959. *Sir Gawain and the Green Knight*. Penguin, London

Sturlusson S (trans. Magnusson M and Pálsson K). *King Harald's Saga*. 1966 [2002]. Penguin Classics, London

Sturlusson S (trans. Byock J). 2005. *The Prose Edda*. Penguin Classics, London

Tale of the Heike (trans. Tyler R). 2012. Penguin Classics, London

Tales of the Ise (trans. MacMillan P). 2016. Penguin Classics, London

Tarrant J. 1998. *The Light inside the Dark*. Harper Collins, London

Tolkein J R R. 1964. *Tree and Leaf*. George Allen & Unwin, London

Virgil (trans. Knight W F J). 1956. *The Aeneid*. Penguin Classics, London

Wissler C and Duval D C. 1908 [2007]. *Mythology of the Blackfoot Indians*. University of Nebraska Press, Lincoln

Yolen J. 1986. *Favourite Folktales from Around the World*. Pantheon Books, New York

Iceland

Baring-Gould S. 1863 [2007]. *Iceland: Its Scenes and Sagas*. Signal Books, Oxford

Baring-Gould S. 1880 [1998]. *Mehalah*. Praxis, London

Bates R, Erlendsson E, Eddudóttir S D, Möckel S C, Tinganelli L and Gísladóttir G. 2022. *Landnám*, land use and landscape change at Kagaðarhóll in Northwest Iceland. *Environmental Archaeology*, 27(2), 211–27

Byock J. 2001. *Viking Age Iceland*. Penguin, London

Collingwood W G and Stefánson J. 1899. *A Pilgrimage to the Saga-Steads of Iceland*. Reprinted by Viking Society for Northern Research (ed. Edgeler M, 2015), Raubling, Germany

Ehrlich G. 2001. *This Cold Heaven*. Harper Collins, London

Einarsson N. 2009. From good to eat to good to watch: whale watching, adaptation and change in Icelandic fishing communities. *Polar Research*, 28(1), 129–38

Einarsson N. 2011. Fisheries governance and social discourse in post-crisis Iceland: responses to the UN Human Rights Committee's views in case 1306/2004. *The Yearbook of Polar Law Online, 3*, 479–515

Einarsson N. 2011. *Culture, Conflict and Crises in Icelandic Fisheries*. Uppsala Studies in Cultural Anthropology 48, Uppsala University, Sweden

Fidler R and Gíslason K. 2017. *Saga Land*. ABC Books, Sydney

Hancox E. 2013. *Iceland Defrosted*. SilverWood, Bristol

Krakauer J and Roberts D. 1990. *Iceland: Land of the Sagas*. Villard, New York

Kreuger M. 2020. *Iceland: A Literary Guide*. Tauris Parke, London

Laxness H. 1968 [1972]. *Under the Glacier*. Vintage, New York

Laxness H. 1957 [2001]. *The Fish Can Sing*. Harvill Press, London

Leach T. 2018. *Smile of the Wolf*. Head of Zeus, London

Magnason A S. 2020. *On Time and Water*. Serpent's Tail, London

Magnússon S G. 2010. *Wasteland with Words: A Social History of Iceland*. Reaktion, London

McPhee J. 1989. *The Control of Nature*. Farrar, Straus and Giroux, New York

O'Connor R. 2002. *Icelandic Histories and Romances*. History Press, Stroud

Ogilvie E. 2017. *Out of Ice*. Black Dog, London

Ommanney F D. 1939. *North Cape*. Longmans, Green & Co, London

Oslund K. 2011. *Iceland Imagined*. University of Washington Press, Seattle

Piri P. 1996. *The Call of the Sagas: To Iceland in an Open Boat*. Pirius, Helsinki

Smiley J. 2000. *The Sagas of the Icelanders*. Penguin Classics, London

Smith L C. 2010. *The New North*. Profile, London

Sjón. 2008 [2004]. *The Blue Fox*. Telegram, London

Sjón. 2011 [2008]. *From the Mouth of the Whale*. Telegram, London

Snædal I. 2008. Icelandic landscape (in *Í fjarveru trjáa (*The Absence of Trees)). Bjartur, Reykjavik

Snorrason A, Jónsson Þ H and Eggertsson Ó. 2019. Aboveground woody biomass of natural birch woodland in Iceland: Comparison of two inventories 1987-1988 and 2005-2011. *Icelandic Agricultural Sciences 32*, 2–9

Stefánsson J K. 2007. *Heaven and Hell*. MacLehose Press, London

Sveinsson O. 2003 (2011). *Doom in the Deep*. Lyons Press, New Haven, CT

Sveinsson O. 2009. *Við Látrabjarg*. Utkall, Reykjavik, Iceland

Tallack M. 2015. *Sixty Degrees North*. Polygon, Edinburgh

Tisdall E, Barclay R, Nichol A, McCulloch R, Simpson I, Smith H and Vésteinsson O. 2018. Palaeoenvironmental evidence for woodland conservation in Northern Iceland from settlement to the twentieth century. *Environmental Archaeology*, 23(3), 205–16

Tómasdóttir K S. 2018. *Stormwarning*. Phoneme Media, Los Angeles

Wade R. 2009. Iceland as Icarus. *Challenge*, 52(3), 5–33

Wheeler S. 2010. *The Magnetic North*. Vintage, London

Witze A and Kanipe J. 2014. *Island on Fire*. Profile Books, London.

Denmark, Norway and Finland

Age of Bede (trans. Webb J F). 1965 [2004]. Penguin Classics, London

Andersen L and Björkman T. 2017. *The Nordic Secret*. Fri Tanke, Stockholm,

Artress L. 1995. *Walking a Sacred Path*. Riverland Books, New York

Bede. 1994 [2008]. *The Ecclesiastical History of the English People*. Oxford World's Classics. Oxford University Press, Oxford

Brits L T. 2016. *The Book of Hygge*. Penguin, London

Brownsworth L. 2014. *The Sea Wolves: A History of the Vikings*. Crux Publishing, London

Brownsworth L. 2014. *The Normans: From Raiders to Kings*. Crux Publishing, London

Byock J. 2001. *Viking Age Iceland*. Penguin, London

Campbell J. 1982 [1991]. *The Anglo-Saxon*s. Penguin, London

Cook R. 1974. *The Tree of Life*. Thames & Hudson, London

Crossley-Holland. 1982 [1999]. *The Anglo-Saxon World: An Anthology*. Oxford World's Classics. Oxford University Press, Oxford

Crumlin-Pedersen O and Jensen H. 2018. *Viking and Iron Age Expanded Boats*. The Viking Ship Museum, Roskilde

Ellis Davidson H R. 1964. *Gods and Myths of Northern Europe*. Penguin, London

Ellis Davidson H R. 1969. *Scandinavian Mythology*. Newnes Books, Middlesex

Gaiman N. 2017. *Norse Mythology*. Bloomsbury, London
Graham-Campbell J. 2013. *The Viking World*. Frances Lincoln, London
Haywood J. 2015. *North Men*. Head of Zeus, London
Heaney S. 1999. *Beowulf*. Faber and Faber, London
Jensen C. 2006. *We, the Drowned*. Random House, London
Jesch J. 1991. *Women in the Viking Age*. Boydell Press, Woodbridge
Jespersen K J. 2004 [2019]. *A History of Denmark*. Red Globe Press, London
Kaage E. 2017. *Silence in the Age of Noise*. Penguin, London
Kruger K (ed. Tolman R). 2012. *Monasteries and Monastic Orders*. H F Ullmann, Potsdam
Lichtenstein J. 2020. *The Berlin Shadow*. Simon & Schuster, London
Parker P. 2014. *The Northmen's Fury: A History of the Viking World*. Vintage, London
Piri P. 1996. *The Call of the Sagas: To Iceland in an Open Boat*. Pirius, Helsinki
Poe E A. 1838 (1974). *The Narrative of Arthur Gordon Pym of Nantucket and Related Tales*. Oxford World Classics, Oxford
Skeie T. 2018 (2021). *The Wolf Age*. Pushkin Press, London
Saxo Grammaticus (trans. Elton O.). 2020. *The Danish History*. Forgotten Books, London
Wiking M. 2016. *The Little Book of Hygge*. Penguin, London
Wiking M. 2017. *The Key to Happiness*. Penguin, London
Yilek J A. 2018. *History of Norway*. Wasteland Press, Shelbyville, KY

England East

Barratt H. 1967. *Early to Rise*. Faber and Faber, London
BBC. 2000. *Good Order! Songs from The Eel's Foot at Eastbridge*. CD, BBC, London
Bell A. 1930 [2000]. *Corduroy*. Penguin, London
Bell A. 1942 [2012]. *Apple Acre*. Little Toller Press, Dorset
Benham H. 1971. *Once upon a Tide*. Harrap, London
Benham H. 1979. *The Codbangers*. Essex County Newspapers, Colchester
Bennett A S. 1949. *Tide Time*. George Allen & Unwin, London
Bensusan S. L. 1949. *Salt of the Marshes*. Routledge & Kegan Paul, London
Bensusan S. L. 1954. *A Marshland Omnibus*. Duckworth, London
Beresford M W. 1954. *The Lost Villages of England*. Lutterworth Press, London
Blythe R. 1969. *Akenfield*. Penguin, London
Blythe R. 1979 [2005]. *The View in Winter*. Canterbury Press, Norwich
Blythe R. 1997. *Word from Wormingford*. Penguin, London
Blythe R. 2011. *At the Yeoman's House*. Enitharmon Press, London
Blythe R. 2013. *The Time by the Sea*. Faber and Faber, London
Butcher D. 1979. *The Driftermen*. Tops'l Books, Reading
Butcher D. 1980. *The Trawlermen*. Tops'l Books, Reading
Butcher D. 1982. *Living from the Sea*. Tops'l Books, Reading
Butcher D. 1987. *Following the Fishing*. Tops'l Books, Newton Abbot
Butcher D. 1995. *The Ocean's Gift: Fishing in Lowestoft during the Pre-industrial Era, 1550–1750*. Centre of East Anglian Studies, UEA Norwich
Butcher D. 2020. *The Last Haul*. Poppyland Publishing, Halesworth
Canton J. 2013. *Out of Essex: Re-imagining a History of Landscape*. Signal Books, Oxford
Collins J and Dodds J. 2009. *River Colne Shipbuilders*. Jardine Press, Wivenhoe
Cousineau P. 1998. *The Art of Pilgrimage*. Conari Press, Newburyport, MA
Davis R. 2019. *Lawrence Elkins: Consensus All American Twice*. Red Ant Press, Brownwood, TX
Dutt W. 1904. *Highways and Byways*. Macmillan, London
Emmett A and Emmett M. 1992. *Blackwater Men*. Seax Books, Bishop's Stortford
Ernle, Lord (Prothero R E).1912. *English Farming: Past and Present*. Longman Green, London

Evans G. E. 1955. *Ask the Fellows who Cut the Hay*. Faber and Faber, London

Evans G. E. 1960. *The Horse and the Furrow*. Faber and Faber, London

Evans G E. 1966. *The Pattern under the Plough*. Faber and Faber, London

Evans G E and Thomson D. 1972. *The Leaping Hare*. Faber and Faber, London

Finch R and Benham H. 1987. *Sailing Craft of East Anglia*. Terence Dalton, Lavenham

Glover M. 1998. *Whitstable*. Chalford, Stroud

Grieve H. 1959. *The Great Tide*. Essex County Council, Chelmsford

Griffiths M. 1932. *Magic of the Swatchways*. Conway Maritime Press, Whitstable

Griffiths M. 1999. *Swatchways and Little Ships*. Adlard Coles Nautical, London

Griffiths M. 1935 [1995]. *Little Ships and Shoal Waters*. Conway Maritime Press, London

Haggard L R. 1935 [1982]. *I Walked by Night: By the King of the Norfolk Poachers*. Oxford University Press, Oxford

Jefferies R. 1879 [2011]. *Wild Life in a Southern County*. Little Toller, Dorset

Leather J. 1971. *The Northseamen*. Terrence Dalton, Lavenham

Leather J. 1979. *The Salty Shore*. Terrence Dalton, Lavenham

Lee S. 2021. *The Nightingale*. Century, London

Lichtenstein J. 2020. *The Berlin Shadow*. Simon & Schuster, London

Lupton H. 2013. *Norfolk Folk Tales*. History Press, Stroud

Newhouse, M.L., 1966. Dogger Bank itch: Survey of trawlermen. *British Medical Journal*, 1(5496), 1142–5

Ogden D. 2013. *Dragons, Serpents and Slayers in the Classical and Early Christian Worlds*. Oxford University Press, Oxford

Orton J. and Worpole K. 2005. *350 Miles. An Essex Journey*. Essex Development and Regeneration Agency, Chelmsford

Owens S. 2020. *The Spirit of Place*. Thames & Hudson, London

Parkin D and Rose J. 1997 [2019]. *The Grit*. Corner Street, Halesworth

Patterson A. H. 1929 [1988]. *Wildfowlers and Poachers*. Ashford Press, Southampton

Pryor F. 2019. *The Fens*. Head of Zeus, London

Rob I. 2010. *Memories of the East Anglian Fishing Industry*. Countryside Books, Newbury

Roberts B. 1949 [2000]. *Coasting Bargemaster*. Seafarer Books, Woodbridge

Roberts B. 1960 [2001]. *The Last of the Sailormen*. Seafarer Books, Woodbridge

Rose J. 1981. *Jack Rose's Lowestoft*. Panda Books, Lowestoft

Roud, S., 2006. *The Penguin Guide to the Superstitions of Britain and Ireland*. Penguin, London

Roud, S., 2008. *The English Year*. Penguin, London

Schilling R S and Newhouse M L. 1966. Dogger Bank itch. *Proceedings of the Royal Society of Medicine*, 59(11), 1119

Schilling R S. 1966. Trawler fishing: An extreme occupation. *Proceedings of the Royal Society of Medicine*, 59(5), 405–10

Sebald W. G. 2002. *The Rings of Saturn*. Vintage, London

Sinclair I. 2002. *London Orbital*. Penguin, London

Smedley N. 1976. *Life and Tradition in Suffolk and NE Essex*. J M Dent & Sons, London

Smylie M. 2004 [2011]. *Herring*. History Press, Stroud

Street A G. 1932. *Farmer's Glory*. Faber and Faber, London

Temple C R. 1972. *East Coast Shipwrecks*. Wensum, Norwich

Tennyson J. 1939. *Suffolk Scene: A Book of Description and Adventure*. Blackie & Son, London

Thompson E P. 1977. *Of Whigs and Hunters*. Penguin, London

Thompson P. 2006. *Sea Change: Wivenhoe Remembered*. Tempus, Wivenhoe

Thompson P. 2010. *Upstreet, Downstreet, Rowhedge Recorded*. Rowhedge Heritage Trust, Rowhedge

Tripp H A. 1926 [1972]. *Suffolk Sea Borders*. Conway Maritime, Greenwich

Waller AJ. R. 1959. *The Suffolk Stour*. Norman Alard, Ipswich

Wentworth Day J. 1949. *Coastal Adventure*. Harrap, London

Westwood J and Simpson J. 2005. *The Lore of the Land*. Penguin, London

Wright P. 1999. *The River: The Thames in Our Time*. BBC, London

England North

Bartlett R. 2013. *Why Can the Dead Do Such Great Things?* Princeton University Press, Princeton

Blythe R. 1988. *Divine Landscapes*. Canterbury Press, Norwich

Butcher C A (trans.). 2018. *The Cloud of Unknowing*. Shambala, Boulder, CO

Cartwright R A and Cartwright D B. 1976. *The Holy Island of Lindisfarne and the Farne Islands*. David & Charles, Newton Abbot

Chapman P. 2002 [2012]. *Grimsby: The Story of the World's Greatest Fishing Port*. Breedon Books, Derby

Colegate. 2012. *A Pelican in the Wilderness*. Harper Collins, London

Courtenay T. 2000. *Dear Tom: Letters from Home*. Black Swan, London

Burrows M S and Sweeney J M. 2017. *Meister Eckhart's Book of Secrets*. Hampton Roads, Charlottesville

Davies O. 2003. *Popular Magic: Cunning-Folk in English History*. Hambledon, London

Greene J. 2012. *Rough Seas: The Life of a Deep-Sea Fisherman*. History Press, Stroud

Grace Darling Museum. 2020.www.bamburgh.org.uk/visiting-bamburgh/grace-darling/

Griffiths B. 2008. *Fishing and Folk: Life and Dialect on the North Sea Coast*. Northumbria University Press, Newcastle

Grimsby's Fish Merchants Association. 2011. *Memories of the Pontoon*. Grimsby

Hildergard of Bingen (trans.. Atherton M). 2001. *Selected Writings*. Penguin, London

Humphries S (Producer and Director). 2018. *Hull's Headscarf Heroes*. Testimony Films for BBC, London

Kruger K. 2008. *Monasteries and Monastic Orders*. H F Ullmann, Potsdam

Lavery B W. 2015. *The Headscarf Revolutionaries*. Barbican, London

Mitchell A and Tate A. 1991. *Fishermen: The Rise and Fall of Deep Water Trawling*. Hutton Press, Beverley

Mitchell M. 2014. *Hope Street*. TDM Books, Grimsby

Mortimer. 1987. *The Last of the Hunters*. Five Leaves, Nottingham

Morrison A. 1900. *Cunning Murrell*. Doubleday, Page & Co, New York

Nicholson. 2015 [2006]. *Rock Lighthouses of Britain*. Whittles Publishing, Caithness

Ommanney F D. 1939. *North Cape*. Longmans, Green & Co, London

Owens S. 2020. *Spirit of Place and the British Landscape*. Thames & Hudson, London

Peake M and Stockley V (Directors and Producers). 2018. *The Last Testament of Lillian Bilocca*. Northern Towns for BBC TV, London

Ramirez J. 2015. *The Private Lives of Saints*. WH Allen, London

Saint Teresa (trans. Cohen J M). 1957. *The Life of Saint Teresa of Avila by Herself*. Penguin Classics, London

Starkey D J, Reid C and Ashcroft N. 2000. *England's Sea Fisheries*. Chatham Publishing, London

Tallach M. 2016. *Undiscovered Islands*. Polygon, London

Triplow N, Bramhill T and James S. 2011. *Distant Water: Stories from Grimsby's Fishing Fleet*. North Wall, Grimsby

Triplow N, Bramhill T and Shepherd J. 2009. *The Women They Left Behind: Stories from Grimsby's Fishing Famliies*. Fathom Press, Grimsby

Tunstall J. 1962. *The Fishermen*. MacGibbon & Kee, London

Williams J. 2013. *Swinging the Lamp*. Riverhead, Hull

Atlantic Isles (Shetland, Orkney, Faroes)

Adomnán of Iona (trans. Sharpe R). 1995. *Life of St Colomba*. Penguin Classics, London

Beard T (Director and Producer). 2014. *Britain's Whale Hunters: The Untold Story*. Keo North for BBC Scotland.

Buchan J. 1936 [2018]. *The Island of Sheep*. Polygon, Edinburgh

Cook J. 1774. *Hunt for the Southern Continent*. Penguin, London

Cunningham M, Foxley M, Hunter J, and Wilson B. 2017. *On Scotland's Conscience: The Case for the Highlands and Islands*. Kessock Books, Brocksborn

Duarte J. 2020. *The Shetland Bus*. Cloud Press, Lexington, KY

Eacott T. 2020. *The Land of Maybe. A Faroe Islands Year*. Short Books, London

Fraser G. 2001. *Shetland's Whalers Remembered*. Nevisprint, Fort William

Gange D. 2019. *The Frayed Atlantic Edge*. William Collins, London

Gillies D J (ed. Randall J). 2010. *The Life and Death of St Kilda*. Origin, Edinburgh

Hadfield J. 2021. *The Stone Age*. Picador Poetry, London

Howarth D. 1951 (1998). *The Shetland Bus*. The Shetland Times, Lerwick

Hunter J. 1999. *The Last of the Free*. Mainstream, Edinburgh

Hunter, J. 2014. Rights-based land reform in Scotland: Making the case in the light of international experience. Community Land Scotland.

Hunter J. 2020. *Laek da laverik ida hömin: Identity and Development in the Highlands and Islands*. University of the Highlands and Islands, Oban

Jamie K. 2012. *Sightlines*. Sort Of Books, London

Johnson L. 2015. *Shetland's Whaling Tradition: From Willafjord to Enderby Land*. Shetland Ex-Whalers Association, Lerwick

Maclean A. 1984. *Night Falls on Ardnamurchan*. Penguin, London

Mackay Brown G. 1972. *Greenvoe*. Penguin, London

Mackay Brown G. 1973. *Magnus*. Polygon, London

Mackay Brown G. 1997. *For the Islands I Sing*. Polygon, London

Ommanney F D. 1938. *South Latitude*. Longmans, Green & Co, London

Poe E A. 1994. *The Narrative of Arthur Gordon Pym and Related Tales*. Oxford World Classics, Oxford University Press

Robertson R B. 1956. *Of Whales and Men*. Macmillan, London

Russell-Jeaffreson J. 1898. *The Faroë Islands*. Sampson Low and Marston, London

Steel T. 1975 [2011]. *The Life and Death of St Kilda*. Harper Press, London

Indigenous Worlds and Doggerland

Aruz J, Farkas A and Fino E V. 2006. *The Golden Deer of Eurasia: Perspectives on the Steppe Nomads of the Ancient World*. Metropolitan Museum of Art, New York.

Basso K. 1996. *Wisdom Sits in Places*. University of New Mexico Press, Albuquerque

Berkes, F. 1999. *Sacred Ecology*. Taylor & Francis, Philadelphia

Bird Rose D. 2000. *Dingo Makes Us Human*. Cambridge University Press, Cambridge

Blackburn J. 2019. *Time Song: Searching for Doggerland*. Jonathan Cape, London

Canton J. 2013. *Out of Essex: Re-Imagining a History of Landscape*. Signal Books, Oxford

Colegate I. 2002. *A Pelican in the Wilderness*. Harper Collins, London

Coles B J. 1998. Doggerland: a speculative survey. *Proceedings of the Prehistoric Society*, 64, 45–81

Coles B J. 2000. Doggerland: the cultural dynamics of a shifting coastline. *Geological Society*, 175, 393–401

Cummings V, Jordan P and Zvelebil M (eds). 2014. T*he Oxford Handbook of the Archaeology and Anthropology of Hunter-Gatherers*. Oxford University Press, Oxford

Cunliffe B. 2012. *Britain Begins*. Oxford University Press, Oxford

Europe's Lost Frontiers. 2018. Research 2016–18. University of Bradford (European Research Council), Bradford

Gaffney V L, Thomson K and Fitch S. (eds). 2007. *Mapping Doggerland: The Mesolithic Landscapes of the Southern North Sea*. Archaeopress, Oxford

Henriksen G. 2007. *I Dreamed the Animals*. Berghahn Books, New York and Oxford

Higham N. 2018. *King Arthur: The Making of a Legend*. Yale University Press, New Haven and London

Hoskins W G. 1955. *The Making of the English Landscape*. Penguin, London

Hutton R. 2013. *Pagan Britain*. Yale University Press, New Haven and London

Jackson J. 2016. *Black Elk: The Life of American Visionary*. Farrar, Straus and Giroux, New York

Kimmerer R W. 2013. *Braiding Sweetgrass*. Milkweed, Minneapolis

Lee R B. 1979. *The !Kung San*. Cambridge University Press, Cambridge

Lethbridge T C. 1950. *Herdsmen and Hermits*. Bowes & Bowes, Cambridge

Levin T (with Suzukei V). 2006. *Where Rivers and Mountains Sing*. Indiana University Press, Bloomington and Indianapolis

Lopez B. 1998. *About This Life*. Harvill, London

Monmouth G (trans. Thorpe L). 1966. *The History of the Kings of Britain*. Penguin Classics, London

Pretty J. 2014. *The Edge of Extinction*. Cornell University Press, Ithaca, NY

Reid A. 2002. *The Shaman's Coat: A Native History of Siberia*. Phoenix, London

Reid C. 1913 [2006]. *Submerged Forests*. Elibron Classics, online at: www.elibron.com

Smith O, Momber G, Bates R, Garwood P, Fitch S, Pallen M, Gaffney V and Allaby R G., 2015. Sedimentary DNA from a submerged site reveals wheat in the British Isles 8000 years ago. *Science*, 347, 998–1001

Stegner W. 1962. *Wolf Willow*. Penguin, London

Vainshtein S. 1980. *Nomads of South Siberia*. Cambridge University Press, Cambridge

Waddington C and Wicks K. 2017. Resilience or wipe out? Evaluating the convergent impacts of the 8.2 ka event and Storegga tsunami on the Mesolithic of northeast Britain. *Journal of Archaeological Science: Reports*, 14, 692–714

Waller M. 2016. *The Life of Merlin*. Amberley, Stroud

Weninger B. Schulting R, Bradtmöller M, Clare L, Collard M, Edinborough K, Hilpert J, Jöris O, Niekus M, Rohling E J and Wagner B. 2008. The catastrophic final flooding of Doggerland by the Storegga Slide tsunami. *Documenta Praehistorica*, 35, 1–24

White M J. 2006. Things to do in Doggerland when you're dead: Surviving OIS3 at the northwestern-most fringe of Middle Palaeolithic Europe. *World Archaeology*, 38, 547–575

The Sea

Allen O E. 1980. *The Pacific Navigators*. Time-Life, Alexandria, VA

Atlee J. 2017. *North Sea: A Visual Anthology*. Thames & Hudson, London

Baker J. A. 1967 [2005]. *The Peregrine*. New York Review Books, New York

Blass T. 2017. *The Naked Shore*. Bloomsbury, London

Bolster W J. 2012. *The Mortal Sea*. Harvard University Press, Cambridge, MA

Clare H. 2014. *Down to the Sea in Ships*. Chatto & Windus, London

Cocker M. and Mabey R. 2005. *Birds Britannica*. Chatto & Windus, London

Gange D. 2019. *The Frayed Atlantic Edge*. William Collins, London

Girling A. 2007. *Sea Change: Britain's Coastal Catastrophe*. Trans.world, London

Gooley T. 2010. *The Natural Navigator*. Virgin Books, London

Griffiths J. 2006. *Wild: An Elemental Journey*. Hamish Hamilton, London

Hamilton-Paterson J. 1992. *Seven-Tenths: The Sea and its Thresholds*. Vintage, London

Hanbury-Tenison R. 2006. *The Seventy Great Journeys*. Thames & Hudson, London

Hodgson W C. 1957. *The Herring and its Fishery*. Routledge & Kegan Paul, London

Kurlansky M. 1997. *Cod*. Vintage, London

Leslie E. E. 1988. *Desperate Journeys, Abandoned Souls*. Mariner, Boston

Lewis D. 1972. *We, the Navigators: The Ancient Art of Landfinding in the Pacific*. University of Hawaii Press, Honolulu

Mabey R. 1996. *Flora Britannica*. Sinclair Stevenson, London

Macfarlane R. 2007. *The Wild Places*. Granta, London

Macfarlane R. 2014. *Landmarks*. Hamish Hamilton, London

Masefield J. 2011. *Spunyarn: Sea Poetry and Prose*. Penguin, London

Neve C. 1990. *Unquiet Landscape*. Thames & Hudson, London

Pretty J. 2011. *This Luminous Coast*. Full Circle Editions, Saxmundham

Reason P. 2014. *Spindrift*. Vala, Bristol

Snyder G. 1990. *The Practice of the Wild*. Shoemaker Hoard, Washington, DC

Snyder G. 1995. *A Place in Space*. Counterpoint, New York

Consumption and the Climate Crisis

Andersen K. 2020. *Evil Geniuses*. Ebury Press, London

Berry T. 1999. *The Great Work*. Crown Publications, Camarthen

Boyle D and Simms A. 2009. *The New Economics: A Bigger Picture*. Earthscan, London

Bregman R. 2020. *Human Kind*. Bloomsbury, London

Couturier A. 2017. *The Abundance of Less*. North Atlantic Books, Berkeley, CA

Diamond J. 2005. *Collapse: How Societies Choose to Fail or Survive*. Penguin, London

Dorling D. 2020. *Slowdown*. Yale University Press, New Haven

Easterlin R A. 1974. Does economic growth improve the human lot? Some empirical evidence. In David P A and Reder M W (eds), *Nations and Households in Economic Growth*. Academic Press, London, pp. 89–125

Griffiths J. 2021. *Why Rebel*. Penguin, London

Hare B and Woods V. 2020. *Survival of the Friendliest*. One World, London

Hickel J. 2020. *Less is More*. William Heinemann, London

Jackson T. 2009. *Prosperity Without Growth*. Earthscan, London

Jackson T. 2021. *Post Growth*. Polity, Cambridge

Jahren H. 2020. *The Story of More*. Fleet, London

Hyde L. 1979 [2012]. *The Gift*. Canongate, Edinburgh

Kahneman, D. 2011. *Thinking, fast and slow*. Macmillan, Basingstoke

Kasser T. 2002. *The High Price of Materialism*. MIT Press, Cambridge, MA

Klein N. 2015. *This Changes Everything*. Penguin, London

Klein N. 2019. *On Fire*. Allen Lane, London

Kotler S and Wheal J. 2017. *Stealing Fire*. HarperCollins, London

Layard R. 2020. *Can We Be Happier*? Pelican, London

Levitin D. 2020. *The Changing Mind: A Neuroscientist's Guide to Ageing Well*. Penguin, London

Mason P. 2015. *Post-Capitalism*. Penguin, London

McKibben B. 2019. *Falter*. Headline, London

McPherson D (ed). 2017. *Spirituality and the Good Life*. Cambridge University Press, Cambridge

Meadows D, Randers J and Meadows D. 2004. *Limits to Growth: The 30-Year Update*. Chelsea Green Publishing, Hartford, VT

Mitchell B. 1976. Politics, fish and international resource management: The British–Icelandic cod war. *Geographical Review* 66, 127–38

Odell J. 2019. *How to Do Nothing*. Melville House, Brooklyn

Oreskes N and Conway E M. 2010. *Merchants of Doubt*. Bloomsbury, New York

Piketty T and Saez E. (2014). Inequality in the long run. *Science* , 344(6186), 838–43

Pretty J. 2007. *The Earth Only Endures*. Earthscan, London

Pretty J. 2014. *The Edge of Extinction*. Cornell University Press, Ithaca NY

Pretty J. 2023. *The Good Life: A Farewell to the Ills of Affluence*. Cornell University Press, Ithaca, NY

Putnam R. 1995. Bowling alone: America's declining social capital. *Journal of Democracy*, 6(1), 65–78

Pye M. 2014. *The Edge of the World*. Penguin, London

Raworth K. 2017. *Doughnut Economics: Seven Ways to Think like a 21st-Century Economist*. Chelsea Green Publishing, Hartford, VT

Ricard, M. 2015. *Happiness: A Guide to Developing Life's Most Important Skill*. Atlantic Books, London

Schumacher E F. 1973 [2011]. *Small is Beautiful*. Vintage, London

Sennett R. 2008. *The Craftsman*. Penguin, London

Sidelsky R and Sidelsky E. 2012. *How Much is Enough*? Penguin, London

Standing G. 2019. *Plunder of the Commons*. Penguin, London

Timms H and Heimans J. 2018. *#newpower*. Picador, London

Walker S. 2011. *The Spirit of Design*. Earthscan, London

WHR (eds Helliwell J F, Layard R, Sachs J D and De Neve J-E). 2020. *World Happiness Report 2020*. Sustainable Development Solutions Network

Wilkinson R and Pickett K. 2016. *The Inner Level*. Allen Lane, London

Wiking M. 2017. *The Key to Happiness*. Penguin, London

ABOUT THE AUTHOR

Jules Pretty OBE, PFHEA, FRSB, FRSA is Professor of Environment and Society at the University of Essex, and Director of the Centre for Public and Policy Engagement. He is Chair of the Essex Climate Action Commission.

He is a nature writer, scientist and storyteller. His sole-authored books before *Sea Sagas of the North* include *The East Country* (2017), *The Edge of Extinction* (2014), *This Luminous Coast* (2011, 2014), *The Earth Only Endures* (2007), *Agri-Culture* (2002) and *Regenerating Agriculture* (1995).

He is a Principal Fellow of the Higher Education Academy, Fellow of the Royal Society of Biology and the Royal Society of Arts, former Deputy-Chair of the UK government's Advisory Committee on Releases to the Environment, and has served on advisory committees for BBSRC and the Royal Society. Currently host of the podcast *Louder Than Words*, he was presenter of the 1999 BBC Radio 4 series *Ploughing Eden*, a contributor and writer for the 2001 BBC TV Correspondent programme *The Magic Bean*, and a panellist in 2007 for Radio 4's *The Moral Maze*. He received a 1997 award from the Indian Ecological Society, was appointed A D White Professor-at-Large by Cornell University from 2001, and is Chief & Founding Editor of the *International Journal of Agricultural Sustainability*. He received an OBE in 2006 for services to sustainable agriculture, an honorary degree from Ohio State University in 2009, and the British Science Association Presidential Medal (Agriculture and Food) in 2015. He was appointed President of Essex Wildlife Trust in 2019, and was a trustee for WWF-UK (2019–22).

Jules is a regular invited speaker at conferences and festivals, and to community and conservation groups. He has spoken at book festivals, on national and local radio. Festival appearances include the Hay Festival, Oundle Book Festival, Larne Folklore Society, Aye Write Festival (Glasgow), Chipping Camden festival, Dartington Festival of Words, Essex Book Festival, River Stour Festival, First Light Festival. Radio work for the BBC includes *Start the Week*, *The Moral Maze*, *BBC Five Live*, and regional BBC talk shows.

Invitation to share *Sea Sagas Of The North*

Dear Readers,

Hawthorn would be delighted if you would be kind enough to recommend *Sea Sagas* to friends! This will really help give support to this striking book and the intriguing stories it tells.

When I tell some of Jules Pretty's moving stories on walks with friends, such as the Icelandic cliff rescues of trawlermen, they get fired up. Some want to share book details, others suggest it for local bookshop talks, book festivals, for book clubs and even as a companion guide for planning journeys to the far North.

Sea Sagas of the North builds on our oral storytelling series, following on from *Storytelling for Nature Connection*, on the why, what and how of storytelling for change. I was profoundly moved by *Sea Sagas* as it re-connected me with old stories which my Yorkshire grandfather used to tell of Whitby, Lindisfarne and the Faroes. However, Jules Pretty poses many wonderful questions, but with a light touch: whereas an Icelandic author asked, 'How do we say goodbye to a glacier?' we will wonder if we need to say goodbye to some lowland parts of Eastern England? Are we adapting to rising seas, or are we just not 'looking up', disregarding the research? How is it that Denmark shrunk its empire successfully and now makes wellbeing central to all its people's lives? How did Iceland nearly destroy its fish commons, whereas Norway put its oil wealth into a sovereign wealth fund for the common good? Why do so few celebrate the charismatic Hull women who secured health and safety reform for fishermen in 1968? Recalling that Doggerland once sank beneath the waves, how are we welcoming refugees now?

Jules celebrates the launch of *Sea Sagas of the North* at the Lowestoft First Light Festival on 18th June 2022, at the Felixstowe and Essex Book Festivals on 26th June and Southwold Arts Festival on 30th June. He is open to giving talks for book festivals, local groups and bookshops. So please invite him or suggest invitations to event organisers. Book events are posted at www.hawthornpress.com and you can contact us via martin@hawthornpress.com with suggestions for sharing *Sea Sagas*.

Martin Large, Publisher, Hawthorn Press, May 2022

Other Books from Hawthorn Press

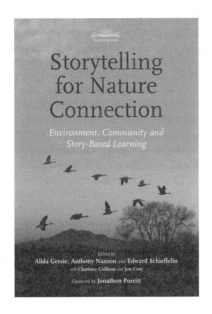

Storytelling for Nature Connection
Environment, community and story-based learning
Alida Gersie, Anthony Nanson
& Edward Schieffelin

A treasury of 43 stories, creative activities, techniques, tips and descriptions of inspiring practice to both empower newcomers and seasoned practitioners. This handbook offers 43 time-tested stories, creative activities and methods that environmental educators and storytellers can use to affect people's pro-environmental behaviour. It offers a range of distinctive but complementary approaches to the art of telling stories for environmental education in 21 chapters.

368pp; 234 x 156mm; paperback; ISBN: 978-1-907359-35-4

The Storyteller's Way
Sourcebook for inspired storytelling
Sue Hollingsworth & Ashley Ramsden

Whether you're just starting out or want to develop your storytelling expertise, *The Storyteller's Way* is an essential guide. Use it to tell stories for entertainment, teaching, coaching, healing or making meaning. It contains a wealth of stories, exercises, questions, tips and insights to guide your storytelling path, offering time-tested and trusted ways to improve your skills, overcome blocks and become a confident and inspirational storyteller.

256pp; 228 x 186mm; paperback; ISBN: 978-1-907359-19-4

The Natural Storyteller
Wildlife Tales for Telling
Georgiana Keable

Here is a handbook for the natural storyteller, with story maps, brain-teasing riddles, story skeletons and adventures to make a tale your own. Adventures between birds, animals and people. Fairytales from the forest and true tales of sea, earth and sky. Georgiana Keable shows through a range of techniques – sometimes the power of the story alone – how to interpret, re-tell and pass these stories on for the future. This diverse collection of stories will nurture active literacy skills and help form an essential bond with nature.

272pp; 228 x 186mm; paperback; ISBN: 978-1-907359-80-4

Creative Place-Based Environmental Education
Children and Schools as Ecopreneurs for Change
Jorunn Barane, Aksel Hugo, Morten Clemetsen

This book presents the why, what and how of creative place-based education. Design tools for developing place based educational curricula are made globally relevant, with case studies from Britain, Norway and Tanzania. Teachers from kindergarten to high school, teacher trainers, environmental educators and forest school educators will find this an invaluable resource.

172pp; 234 x 156mm; paperback; ISBN: 978-1-907359-73-6

World Tales for Family Storytelling
53 Traditional Stories for Children aged 4–6 years
Chris Smith

Young children are natural storytellers. They love both listening to parents telling stories and telling stories themselves. These 53 tales can be shared at bedtime, on journeys, at parties or around the camp-fire. Children will find them short, simple, and quick to learn. They draw on traditional tales, told in the voice of a storyteller. Parents can read or tell the stories, so children can soon tell the stories them-selves. Such oral storytelling builds children's confidence in their unique voices.

216pp; 228 x 186mm; paperback; ISBN: 978-1-912480-55-5

The Children's Forest
Stories & songs, wild food, crafts & celebrations all year round
Dawn Casey, Anna Richardson, Helen d'Ascoli

A rich and abundant treasury in celebration of the outdoors, this book encourages children's natural fascination with the forest and its inhabitants. An enchanting book where imagination, story and play bring alive the world of the forest. Full of games, facts, celebrations, craft activities, recipes, foraging, stories and Forest School skills, Ideal for ages 5-12 it will be enjoyed by all ages.

336pp; 250 x 200mm; paperback; ISBN: 978-1-907359-91-0

Small Steps to Less Waste
stories to inspire change
Claudi Williams

This book offers simple alternatives to mass-produced, shop-bought, highly packaged goods. It includes positive projects to help you to take back control of your waste and reduce our impact on the environment. An inspiring book that includes ten stories of personal enlightenment and the practical changes they made.

96pp; 256 x 189mm ; paperback; ISBN: 978-1-912480-29-6

Ordering Books

If you have difficulties ordering Hawthorn Press books from a bookshop,
you can order direct from our website www.hawthornpress.com, or from our UK distributor:
BookSource, 50 Cambuslang Road, Glasgow, G32 8NB
Tel: (0845) 370 0063   Email: orders@booksource.net.
Details of our overseas distributors can be found on our website.

Hawthorn Press

www.hawthornpress.com